Four Pillars of Destiny
Discover Your Code To Success

Lily Chung Ph.D. and Dr. Jin Peh

Edited by Charmaine Sam

ISBN:
ISBN-13: 978-1492334545

Foreword

This book has been a labor of love for me. I started the journey in the historic district of Rio de Janeiro and finished it overlooking the Arabian Gulf in Dubai. It truly has been a rewarding experience translating and co-authoring the English version of my teacher Lily Chung's book *Ren Ren Ba Zi* 人人八字, which translates as *Four Pillars For Everybody*. I ultimately decided not to go with that title as my friend the late Filipino Feng Shui master Victor Dy had already published a book by that title. So Lily and I decided on *Four Pillars Of Destiny: Discover Your Code To Success*.

Why Four Pillars rather than the more traditional name of Eight Characters or Ba Zi as is widely known amongst Chinese speakers? Well, the term Four Pillars of Destiny is already firmly entrenched in the minds of English speaking readers of Chinese Metaphysics due to previously published books. After all, Four Pillars and Eight Characters both refer to the chart that shows a person's Hour, Day, Month and Year of birth, which consists of eight Chinese characters lined up in four different pillars.

How did I commence my own journey in Four Pillars? Back in the Australian summer of 1999 when I was living in Perth, I attended a series of classes taught by a visiting Professor from China. They included units on basic Feng Shui, the Feng Shui Compass (Luo Pan) and the Four Pillars. It was the first time I was introduced to this system of Chinese Life Divination. Truth be told, it was too much information for me to digest over three days. It was hardly surprising that I could not remember what I had learnt without consulting my notes.

During my two year Feng Shui apprenticeship in Taiwan from 2000 to 2002, I sat in on my master's Four Pillars consults. However, the main focus for me at that time was on Feng Shui, with Four Pillars a side topic. My time with Four Pillars was yet to come.

During this time, I read both English and Chinese books on the Four Pillars. Most of the books I came across used the following method to interpret a chart:

Step 1: Ascertain whether a chart is Strong or Weak. This is determined by counting the number of elements in the chart. For example, if five characters belong to wood and the Day Master is wood, then it will be a Strong chart. If four Stems and Branches are metal and the chart is a Fire Day Master, then it will be a Weak chart.

Step 2: If a chart is Weak, Resources and Siblings are required.

Step 3: If a chart is Strong, Output, Wealth or Power are used.

Step 4: Look at the Luck Cycles that contain only one of the five elements. If it is a Power Luck Cycle, then the Strong charts will benefit and the Weak charts will suffer.

The only books that I read which did not use this method were written by an Indonesian master from Medan that my family knew. Unfortunately, I did not have the opportunity to study with him though I did translate into English for myself three of his four books. While he cited numerous examples from his clients and provided readers with a glimpse into his thought processes that were extremely different from others, he did not present it in a readily accessible format.

Armed with the knowledge that I had gained thus far, I started doing consults for clients when I moved to Dubai in 2004. Frankly, the consults were rather hit or miss. While I did get quite a few of them correct, some were way off the mark and I couldn't quite understand why. There were two female clients who stood out for me as they asked questions that I could not answer. One was adopted and wondered why I had not picked that up from her chart. Another had an accident involving her hand and wanted to know if I was able to tell her which year it happened. While I came up short on both occasions then, I am happy to say that following my time with Lily I am now able to identify charts of individuals who are adopted and also years in which there is a high likelihood of accidents for an individual.

And how did our paths cross? I suppose in Chinese Metaphysics as in life, we must have what the Chinese call yuan fen or destiny. In 2006 when I was living in Dubai, I had a friend tell me about a Four Pillars book that she had seen in a bookshop (which has since closed down) in the non-touristic part of Dubai. I drove over there almost immediately and picked up *Meng: The Path To Good Fortune* which I then read from cover to cover. However, in the pre-social networking days, I didn't know how to contact the author Lily Chung. And so I continued on with life in Dubai, knowing in the back of my mind that I would find a Four Pillars master the way I had found a Feng Shui master, someone who would literally put me on the right path.

The opportunity came three years later. In 2009, my friend Jerry King from Vancouver whom I had met while travelling in Yemen told me about his master Lily Chung who lived in San Francisco. I will always be indebted to Jerry for connecting us. Within a week following several long distance phone conversations with Lily in which we discussed my own Four Pillars chart, I flew over to the beautiful city by the bay to study with her.

On the first day of class, Lily and I met in a food court in the central business district. She handed me a piece of paper with the Four Pillars charts of Jacqueline Onassis, John F Kennedy Jr., Princes William and Harry and even Linda Evans to gauge my knowledge. I got all of them wrong. Not only was I unable to classify what types of charts they were, I also could not identify their useful elements. And so began two weeks of analyzing examples where I had to unlearn all the bad habits I had picked up over the years and reformat my thinking when it came to interpreting Four Pillars charts. While all classes started at nine sharp, we always arrived for lunch at one of San Francisco Chinatown's delicious dim sum restaurants just before 12. I always smile when I think of the discussions we had over steaming plates of dumplings or buns. After the first two weeks, I started making some progress towards grasping the subject.

There was no overnight eureka moment. Rather, as I returned to Lily each fall, my skills improved steadily. In between the yearly sessions, I continued with my consults and Lily made herself available when I came across some challenging charts. I also needed time for the techniques and thought processes to sink in. With each year, I noticed that I started to recognize with increasing confidence different types of charts. There is so much more to Four Pillars than just

Strong or Weak charts. For instance, there are charts that Follow, Competitive ones, Dominant charts and even some Special ones that defy classification. I suppose Four Pillars charts display how different we all are as individuals. After all, we cannot all fit into the same cookie cutter mold. After learning the method that Lily used to analyze Four Pillars charts, I will never return to Strong or Weak again.

But what makes our method different from the Strong/Weak model? The answer lies in the accuracy. By using the interactions between the Branches and the Stems and going with their flow, I am able to identify specific years in which good or bad events would have occurred to a person, something that the Strong/Weak model failed to do so. We have cited numerous examples in this book to illustrate the importance of the Stem and Branch interactions and going with the flow of the strongest element.

Due to my years of studying classical and tertiary level Chinese in National Taiwan University, Lily invited me to translate her Chinese book into English. I am extremely grateful to her for this opportunity. I hope that I have been able to capture the essence of her teaching and also bring to the book the analytical skills that I picked up from my university days in Australia.

Every project is a collaboration and this book is no different, so here is the list of people I have to thank:

First and foremost, my teacher Lily Chung, for showing me the right path to follow when it comes to Four Pillars.

Jerry King, my colleague and friend who has been extremely magnanimous in sharing his skills and knowledge with me and for introducing me to Lily.

My team of editors who worked with me tirelessly on refining the manuscript. Nadia Khan, thank you for getting the ball rolling. Charmaine Sam, thank you for the enthusiasm, dedication and passion that you brought to the project, the book will not be what it is without your contribution.

Tyler Rowe, thank you for your assistance in clarifying the Traditional Chinese Medicine concepts that are discussed in

Chapter Eight. I would also be nowhere without mon ami, the best fact checker in the world who wishes to remain anonymous. You know who you are and I miss your corner of the world.

Pankaj Shah, thank you for coming up with the cover design and making it reality with your exceptional photography skills.

Josephine and Hok Wong, thank you for working your magic on this book and making it accessible to all.

Juscelito Wainer, thank you for your generosity and kindness in helping me navigate through your beautiful city Rio. I miss your Lapa apartment.

Ken Wong, thank you for your friendship and support as I embarked on this project.

Bernadette King-Tuner, thank you Miz Daisy for sharing with me your lovely home where I finished the first draft.

Zola and K, thank you for making your home a haven for a writer like me.

Wendelin and Rita Niederberger, thank you for being with me from almost day one of my Four Pillars journey and for your support and trust over the years. I always look forward to my annual trip to Sarnen, Switzerland.

Michael Dvorak, thank you for inspiring me to sprint to the finish line.

Wolfgang and Angeline Bick, it was a pleasure to proof read the final draft of this book in your lovely home in Florsheim am Main. Thank you for always making me feel at home in Germany.

And finally, my father and mother, because without them, I would not be the person that I am today. I thank both of you every day with all my heart.

Table of Contents

List of Figures, Tables and Examples

Chapter Two Introduction to the Four Pillars

Figures
2.1 Five Elements and Associated Directions
2.2 The Sectors of the Four Pillars and What They Represent
2.3 February 2012 as shown in Ten Thousand Year Calendar

Tables
2.1 The Heavenly Stems
2.2 The Earthly Branches
2.3 The Six Xun or Divisions of Ten of the 60 Stem-Branch Pairs
2.4 What the Ten Stems Represent
2.5 Determining the Hour Stem from the Day Stem

Examples	Comments
2.1 David's Luck Cycles	Deriving the Luck Cycles for a Yang Male
2.2 Cristina's Luck Cycles	Deriving the Luck Cycles for a Yang Female

Chapter Three Basic Interpretation Techniques

Figures
3.1 The Five Heavenly Stem Combinations
3.2 The Six Harmony Branch Combinations
3.3 The Three Harmony Branch Combinations
3.4 The Directional Branch Combinations
3.5 Clash of the Branches

Tables
3.1 The Ten Gods
3.2 The 60 Stem-Branch Pairs

Examples	Comments
3.1 Ming Chengzu 明成祖	Relationship between Other Pillars and Day Master Follow the Resource chart
3.2 Steve Cohen	Combination between Day and Month Stems
3.3 Theodore Pickens Boone Jr.	Combination between Day and Month Stems
3.4 Donald Trump	Combination between Day

Chapter Four The Special Stars

Chapter Five Standard Charts

5.4 Ted Turner	Directional Wood Combination Partial Three Harmony Wood Combination Dominant Wood chart
5.5 Aristotle Onassis	Dominant Earth chart
5.6 Female	Competitive Water chart
5.7 Friedrich Nietzche	Competitive Earth chart
5.8 Alexandra Manley	Competitive Metal chart
5.9 Princess Margaret of England	Exercise
5.10 Clark Gable	Exercise
5.11 Chiang Kai Shek 蔣介石	Weak chart requiring Resources
5.12 Abraham Lincoln	Exercise
5.13 Female	Weak chart lacking Resources
5.14 John F Kennedy Jr.	Borderline chart to Follow or not to Follow
5.15 Cary Stayner	Borderline chart to Follow or not to Follow
5.16 Ruan Lingyu 阮玲玉	Borderline chart to Follow or not to Follow

Chapter Six Follow Charts, Transformation Charts

Tables
6.1 Butterfly Hu's Movie Output
6.2 Gary Cooper's Movie Output
6.3 Transformation charts and the Conditions Required

Examples	Comments
6.1 Bill Gates	Follow the Power (earth) chart
6.2 Chen Yi 陳毅	Follow the Power (water) chart
6.3 Oprah Winfrey	Follow the Power (metal) chart
6.4 Deng Xiaoping 鄧小平	Follow the Wealth (water) chart
6.5 Gordon Moore	Follow the Wealth (water) chart
6.6 Steve Ballmer	Follow the Wealth (wood) chart
6.7 John Templeton	Follow the Children (metal) chart
6.8 Sir Isaac Newton	Follow the Children (water) chart
6.9 Hu Die 蝴蝶 Buttefly Hu	Follow the Children (wood) chart
6.10 Adolf Hitler	Example
6.11 Soong Ching Ling 宋慶齡	Follow the Resource (water) chart
6.12 Qi Baishi 齊白石	Follow the Resource (water) chart
6.13 Gary Cooper	Follow the Resource (water) chart
6.14 District Governor	Earth Transformation chart

from ancient China	
6.15 Qing Taizong 清太宗	Water Transformation chart
6.16 Yongzheng 雍正	Wood Transformation chart
6.17 Guangxu 光緒	Wood Transformation chart

Chapter Seven Special Charts

Tables
7.1 Same Division Heaven-Earth Union Pairs
7.2 Talent Star as determined by the Day Branch
7.3 Day Master and Hour of Birth for Early Success in Life

Examples	Comments
7.1 Dr Albert Szent Gyorg	Same Division Heaven-Earth Union Involving Day and Month Pillars
7.2 Ali Abdullah Saleh	Same Division Heaven-Earth Union Involving Month and Year Pillars
7.3 Female	Same Division Heaven-Earth Union Involving Day and Month Pillars
7.4 Donald Trump	Different Division Heaven-Earth Union Involving Day and Month Pillars
7.5 Camilo Jose Cela	Different Division Heaven-Earth Union Involving Day and Month Pillars
7.6 Chiang Kai Shek 蔣介石	Mutual Exchange of the Sibling element between Day and Month Pillars and Day and Hour Pillars
7.7 Mao Zedong 毛澤東	Mutual Exchange of the Power element between Day and Month Pillars and Day and Hour Pillars
7.8 Lee Tsung-Dao 李政道	Mutual Exchange of the Resource element between the Day and Month Pillars Chart with Three of the Four Traveling Horse Branches
7.9 Michael Dell	Chart with Three of the Four Traveling Horse Branches
7.10 Edward Johnson the 3rd	Mutual Exchange of the Wealth element between the Day and Month Pillars
7.11 Bill Gates	Heavenly and Monthly Virtue Special Stars with the Wealth element
7.12 Richard Nixon	Nobleman Star with the Resource element
7.13 George Washington	Nobleman Star with the Resource element
7.14 Jacqueline Onassis	Nobleman Stars flanking the Day Master
7.15 Kangxi 康熙	Hidden Nobleman Star

7.16 Qing Taizong 清太宗	Year Stem in Hour Pillar
7.17 Mao Zedong 毛澤東	Resource reducing the Power element
7.18 Lily Chung	Resource reducing the Power element
7.19 Chinese Writer	Power element (Hurting Officer) with Resource in the same Pillar
7.20 Zhang Juzheng 張居正	Talent Star with the Resource element
7.21 Zhou Yushan 周玉山	Power element with the Monthly Virtue Star that combines with the Day Master
7.22 Stephen Chow 周星馳	Power element with the Monthly Virtue Star that combines with the Day Master
7.23 Lily Chung	Void Peach Blossom Star with the Nobleman Star

Chapter Eight Four Pillars and Health

Tables
8.1 Association between Five Elements and Body Organs and Parts

Examples	Comments
8.1 Steve Jobs	Pancreatic cancer when useful element wood under attack from metal Follow the Resource (wood) chart
8.2 Michael Milken	Prostate cancer when useful element wood under attack from metal Follow the Power (wood) chart
8.3 Ingrid Bergman	Breast cancer when useful element wood under attack from metal Dominant Water chart
8.4 Anita Mui 梅艷芳	Cervical cancer when useful element wood under attack from metal Strong chart using Wealth element metal
8.5 Robert Taylor	Lung cancer when useful element wood under attack from metal Follow the Resource (wood) chart
8.6 Gary Cooper	Lung cancer when useful element metal element under attack from fire Follow the Resource (water) chart
8.7 Susan Hayward	Brain tumor when useful element fire under attack from water Follow the Wealth (fire) chart
8.8 Rock Hudson	AIDS when useful element wood under attack from metal Weak self requiring Resources

8.9 Arthur Ashe	AIDS when useful elements earth and fire attacked by wood and water Dominant Earth chart
8.10 Isaac Asimov	Death related to AIDS when Competitors fought for Wealth element water Competitive Earth chart
8.11 Ted Kaczynski	Psychological issues when metal element present Weak wood self vulnerable to metal
8.12 Thomas Edison	Multiple illnesses during the metal Luck Cycles when useful element wood under attack Follow the Power (wood) chart
8.13 Franklin Roosevelt	Weakness in lower limbs due to excessive metal draining his Yin Earth Day Master
8.14 Ronald Reagan	Alzheimer's Disease when useful element wood under attack from metal Follow the Resource (wood) chart
8.15 Intellectually Challenged Male	Unable to Follow the Wealth element water due to presence of Competitors and the Resource element
8.16 Intellectually Challenged Female	Unable to Follow the Power element metal due to the presence of Competitors and Output element fire

Chapter Nine Identifying the Useful Element in a Four Pillars Chart

Figures
9.1 Pictorial Representation of Sir Frederic Banting's Four Pillars chart
9.2 Pictorial Representation of Bill Clinton's Four Pillars chart
9.3 Pictorial Representation of Leslie Cheung's Four Pillars chart
9.4 Pictorial Representation of Teresa Teng's Four Pillars chart
9.5 Pictorial Representation of Robert Kennedy's Four Pillars chart

Tables
9.1 Life Events of Sir Frederic Banting
9.2 Life Events of Bill Clinton
9.3 Life Events of Leslie Cheung
9.4 Life Events of Teresa Teng
9.5 Life Events of Robert Kennedy

Examples	Comments
9.1 Sir Frederic Banting	Dominant Wood chart
9.2 Bill Clinton	Follow the Resource (wood) chart
9.3 Leslie Cheung 張國榮	Competitive Water chart supported by Resources
9.4 Teresa Teng 鄧麗君	Multiple Classifications Follow the Resource (earth) Follow the Children (water) Commanding Pillars chart
9.4.1 Hwang Woo-Suk	Same Day, Month and Year as Teng Follow the Resource (earth) chart under attack from wood
9.4.2 Paulin Bordeleau	Same Day, Month and Year as Teng Follow the Resource (earth) chart transformed temporarily into Follow the Wealth (wood) chart
9.4.3 Lynne McGranger	Same Day, Month and Year as Teng Follow the Resource (earth) chart transformed into Follow the Children (water) chart
9.5 Robert Kennedy	Follow the Resource chart under attack from Competitors

Appendices

Tables
A1.1 Distribution of the Energy of the Five Elements in Each Month
A2.1 Different Aspects of the Eight Trigrams
A2.2 The Eight Trigrams and their Sectors on the Compass

Examples	Comments
A1.1	Theoretical Example born at the beginning of January 2012
A1.2	Theoretical Example born in the middle of January 2012
A1.3	Theoretical Example born at the beginning of February 2012
A3.1 Jerzy Szmajdinski	Metal-wood conflict seen in Rooster-Rabbit Clash
A3.2 Franciszek Gagor	Metal-wood conflict seen in Rooster-Rabbit Clash
A3.3 Przemyslaw Gosiewski	Metal-wood conflict seen in Rooster-Rabbit Clash
A3.4 Lech Kaczynski	Water-fire conflict seen in Rat-Horse Clash Metal Competitors fighting for Wealth element wood

A3.5 Slawomir Skrzypek	Follow the Resource (metal) chart Problems with Water Competitors
A3.6 Ryszard Kaczorowski	Follow the Children (wood) chart Yang Water Day Master caught in metal-wood conflict
A3.7 Anna Walentynowicz	Tiger-Monkey Clash Metal-wood conflict
A3.8 Captain Arkadiusz Protasiuk	Follow the Resource (fire) chart Luck Cycle contains all negative elements
A3.9 Major Robert Grzywna	Follow the Resource (fire) chart Negative metal Luck Cycle as useful element wood under attack
A4.1 Zine Al Abedine Ben Ali	Strong Earth self using Wealth element water Negative Luck Cycle (Power element wood)
A4.2 Hosni Mubarak	Follow the Wealth (earth) chart Negative Luck Cycle (Competitor element wood)
A4.3 Muammar al-Gaddafi	Follow the Power (fire) chart Negative Luck Cycle (Children element water)
A4.4 Bashar al-Assad	Follow the Children (metal) chart Negative Luck Cycle (Competitor element earth)
A4.5 Ali Abdullah Saleh	Fire Transformation chart Negative influence of the Resource element water
A5.1 Napoleon Hill	Follow the Children (water) chart
A5.2 Dale Carnegie	Follow the Power (wood) chart
A6.1 Larry Page	Dominant Metal chart with significant Wealth element wood
A6.2 Sergey Brin	Follow the Children (metal) chart
A6.3 Eric Schmidt	Dominant Earth chart
A6.4 Google	False Follow the Wealth (earth) chart
A7.1 Jeremy Lin 林書豪	Commanding Pillars chart

Chapter One - How The Book Came About

The Four Pillars of Destiny, also known as Zi Ping Ba Zi 子平八字 or Eight Characters of Birth, is believed to have originated in the Tang Dynasty and flourished throughout the Song, Yuan, Ming and Qing Dynasties. For several thousand years, the *Ten Thousand Year Calendar* (Wan Nian Li 萬年曆) has been used in China as an essential tool to calculate the Four Pillars of Destiny.

Since the founding of the Republic of China in 1911, the Four Pillars method of analyzing our destinies has spread throughout South East Asia through the work of Chinese Metaphysics masters. Since 1984, these masters from Hong Kong, Malaysia and Singapore have opened the doors of the Western world to this method of destiny analysis. For more than 20 years now, English books on the Four Pillars have been selling in the UK and North American markets. Despite the failure of these books to fully disclose the intricate methods required for thorough interpretation, the burgeoning sales of these books demonstrate that the subject has become extremely popular amongst English-speaking readers.

When I published *The Path to Good Fortune* in 1997, English-speaking readers were given one of the earliest opportunities to use the *Ten Thousand Year Calendar* to construct their own Four Pillars charts and Luck Cycles. As well as introducing the concept and structure of the Four Pillars, the book provided a calendar which utilized the alphabet to represent the Heavenly Stems and Earthly Branches. Readers were therefore able to determine which of the five elements were favorable for them. Using this information, they could identify their respective auspicious and inauspicious days, as well as their positive and negative Luck Cycles.

To follow up on the success of *The Path of Good Fortune*, my second book *Easy Ways to Harmony* (2000) introduced readers to the *I Ching* Method of life divination. In 2010, *The Truth of Ups and Downs* provided further guidance on identifying the useful element in an individual's Four Pillars chart.

Today, the Four Pillars has become a global phenomenon

through the proliferation of conferences, classes and training programs dedicated to it. Websites and Facebook groups devoted to Four Pillars and online programs that assist in calculating personalized Four Pillars charts are further testimony of its popularity. So, with the abundance of both English and Chinese materials on this subject, you may ask why do we need another book? Allow me to explain.

Understanding changes in energy

The Four Pillars method of Life Divination and the *Ten Thousand Year Calendar* are two of China's greatest discoveries. Yet, up till now, they have not really received the acclaim or acknowledgement they deserve for helping individuals determine their own direction in life.

For most of us, nothing is more important than living a full and meaningful life. We work day and night, study and make plans to achieve a better life, but after all these efforts, how do we really attain happiness and satisfaction and truly fulfill our potential? This is indeed one of life's greatest conundrums.

Before offering an answer, I would like to remind you that life is full of changes - both ups and downs. Do you really know anyone whose life always goes smoothly without any challenges? Why does life have its highs and lows? For instance, if we look at Thomas Edison, how did he progress from being a struggling student to a renowned inventor? More importantly, was it really a natural progression? Only the Chinese sages would recognize that this is the result of changes in universal energy, changes that influence our lives whether we are aware of it or not.

The *Ten Thousand Year Calendar* and the Four Pillars method are able to identify these changes of energy within the universe. Ironically, both have been erroneously labeled as superstition, especially by those who do not fully understand them. In this book, I will introduce the structure and practical usage of the *Ten Thousand Year Calendar* by engaging with historical and real life examples. From this, readers will be able to apply the concepts and derive their personal Four Pillars chart. In doing so, they can identify the positive elements in their chart and fully develop their own potential.

Interpreting Four Pillar Charts

Many Four Pillars books tend to focus on obscure poems and texts without providing any explanation about how this information can be applied or used on a personal basis. Readers are left with no choice but to guess the meanings encoded in the charts. At times, they may feel that they are trying to solve a riddle without any clear solution. Other more competent readers have spent a considerable amount of time reading the ancient texts but they may still lack the confidence to identify the useful element within a chart. This book serves to give readers the ability to interpret Four Pillars charts through the use of clear and concise case studies.

Popular Usage

The most popular method of Four Pillars chart analysis focuses on the Day Master and its relationship with the other Stems and Branches, such as the Ten Gods. Emphasis is placed on deciding whether a chart is strong or weak. This is then followed by balancing the elements in a chart. For instance, a Four Pillars chart is considered lacking if it does not have any water. By giving the individual a name that contains water, the imbalance can be addressed. Although this system is extremely popular and easily understood, in my humble opinion, it is inaccurate.

Everyone Is Unique

Life is full of change and those who are born at the same time, day, month and year will not have the same lives. When analyzing Four Pillars charts, we need to approach them on a case-by-case basis and not apply a single formula to everyone. From my years of research and analysis in Four Pillars, I have found that there are individuals (like Bill Gates and Ted Turner) who have achieved considerable success without having any balance of elements within their charts. Theories that subscribe to the Weak/Strong formula simply fail to take into account individual differences. There are many different types of charts such as those that change, those that go with the flow, those that follow the prevalent energy and those that are competitive. The insistence on applying a fixed formula means you will be unable to identify the prevalent energy in most Four Pillars charts.

From another perspective, although these differentiated charts (changing charts and those that follow) have always existed, authors have chosen not to publish their findings in an effort to keep their secret techniques from readers. These books only offer a straightforward formula in order to make it more accessible to readers and students. Charts of famous individuals that are extremely clear without any obstacles or contrasting flows are typically used to support the formula. Personally, I feel that while charts that change or follow are common, they are also at the same time more challenging to understand. People with these types of charts also require the most assistance in identifying the favorable elements and Luck Cycles. For these reasons, I will introduce readers to the correct method of interpreting Four Pillars charts, so that they are able to identify accurately the prevalent flows in their charts and lives.

Case Studies

To prevent readers from being confused, I will mostly mention case studies of well-known individuals that could be relevant to your own lives. But as this book was originally published in Chinese, I have also used examples from Chinese history that English readers may not be familiar with. In such cases, I have tried to identify the period in which these individuals are from (e.g. the Ming Dynasty). Through these examples, I hope readers will be able to understand and apply the theoretical principles with ease.

Useful Elements

The most important step in Four Pillars chart analysis is to identify the useful element and then verify it through reviewing events in the person's life. After classifying a chart according to its prevalent energy or flow, we can then identify the favorable and unfavorable elements. This information can be used to advise on the most appropriate careers, interests, business partners or spouses. The ultimate aim of learning about the Four Pillars method is to fully develop our potential.

Chapter Structure

Chapter Two introduces the structure of the *Ten Thousand Year Calendar* and its usage. I also highlight its overall contribution in measuring the energy present in the universe at any specific time. There is a brief introduction on the theoretical basis of the Four Pillars of Destiny. The Ten Heavenly Stems and 12 Earthly Branches are described. Steps on how to construct a Four Pillars chart and its Luck Cycles will be discussed.

Chapter Three discusses the relationships between the various Branches and Stems, which you will need to be familiar with when interpreting charts.

Chapter Four looks at Special Stars and their influence on our lives. These Stars are easily identifiable and provide reliable information about a person's Four Pillars chart. As these Stars are used as a shortcut by many untrained individuals to read Four Pillars charts, readers should avoid simply relying on them to understand their charts without grasping the main principles of Four Pillars.

Chapters Five, Six and Seven introduce different types of Four Pillars charts, as well as the theory behind their classification. In these chapters, I have combined various traditional theories present in the classics with my many years of experience in reading charts. I have done my best to present the findings in a practical, easy to follow and relevant manner.

There are three main types of charts: Standard charts, Follow charts and Transformation charts. In addition, these charts can also possess special qualities. Each type of chart has real life examples which illustrate the points that I have made.

When it comes to identifying favorable Luck Cycles and elements, I always consider the overall picture of each chart and tailor it to the individual being assessed. This is opposed to the common practice of trying to force a universal formula onto all charts.

Readers will need to be familiar with the interactions between the five elements as that is key in understanding the influences of various Luck Cycles and years. These elemental interactions can also be used in assessing the Feng Shui of an individual's environment and life. Readers may also consider collecting and analyzing the Four Pillars charts of family members, friends or acquaintances in order to hone their analytical skills and gain confidence in interpreting charts.

Chapter Eight analyzes the relationship between the five elements and illness. The elemental composition of a person's Four Pillars chart is of particular interest to practitioners of Traditional Chinese Medicine. If a negative element is present in a person's life, various illnesses, injuries and incidents may occur with varying degrees of harm. Whether these negative consequences are the results of his or her actions, the environment or just timing, this book will examine practical cases to help readers understand the theory behind these malignant influences. As such, they can try to seek ways in avoiding or reducing the negative consequences. After all, the lines that separate metaphysics, philosophy and medicine are unclear. When it comes to health issues, I hope that readers can approach them from various angles in order to fully appreciate the situation.

Chapter Nine considers the detailed steps in identifying the useful element in a Four Pillars chart. I have included five different examples of both Chinese and Western celebrities. There are also clear illustrations to show the favorable and unfavorable elements of each chart. Events from the individual's life history have been used to verify the positive and negative elements that I have identified.

Chapter Ten has my concluding remarks, by which time I hope readers would have gained a deeper insight into the wisdom of Four Pillars and appreciate the influence of Heaven, Man and Earth on our lives.

The appendices at the end of the book include further information about the nature of the five elements at different times of the year, the relationship between the Eight Trigrams and more case studies.

Chapter Two - Introduction To The Four Pillars

In Chinese books, the Four Pillars of Destiny method of Chinese Astrology often appears by other names, such as Ba Zi 八字 (the Eight Characters of Birth) and the Zi Ping 子平 method of Life Divination. It is named after Xu Zi Ping 徐子平, a man who lived in the period between the Tang and Sung Dynasties. While his birth details are not known, it is believed that he was a highly respected monk.

The astrology method that Xu Zi Ping devised achieved even greater popularity in the Ming and Qing Dynasties. During the Ming Dynasty, the classical texts *Di Tian Sui* 滴天髓 from Liu Bo Wen 劉伯溫 and *Bing Yao Lun* 病藥論 from Zhang Shen Feng 張神峰 contributed considerably to the knowledge of Four Pillars. As a result, the Four Pillars has maintained its place in Chinese Metaphysics for more than a millennium.

The theory of Four Pillars is derived from the principles of Yin and Yang and the Five Elements detailed in the *I Ching, the Book of Changes*. Its structure is derived from the Chinese Lunar Calendar, which was later developed into the *Wan Nian Li* 萬年曆 or the *Ten Thousand Year Calendar*. While there are other methods of divination such as the Five Stars, Qi Men 奇門 and Na Yin 納音, the Four Pillars has never lost its position as the foremost form of Chinese Astrology. The other major forms of Chinese Astrology that developed after the Sung Dynasty, such as Zi Wei Dou Shu 紫微斗數 (also known as Emperor Astrology or rather erroneously as Purple Star Astrology) and the He Luo Li Shu 河洛理數 (the He Tu Luo Shu method) still require the Four Pillars chart to be determined first before other calculations can be carried out.

As the *Ten Thousand Year Calendar* is the vital tool for calculating an individual's chart, Luck Cycles and auspicious dates, you will need to understand its structure and usage in order to gain a deeper insight into the Four Pillars.

Structure of the Ten Thousand Year Calendar

The origin of the Ten Thousand Year Calendar is attributed to Fu Xi 伏羲, a mythical Chinese sage who is believed to have discovered the universe and classified its energy into the five naturally occurring elements: metal, wood, water, fire and earth. Each of these elements occupy one of the four Cardinal Directions and the center as demonstrated in the figure below:

Figure 2.1 Five Elements and Associated Directions

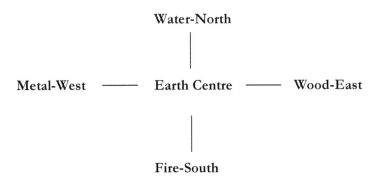

The qi or energy present in the five elements is further divided into Yin and Yang types, such as Yin Metal, Yang Metal, Yin Wood, Yang Wood and so on. These ten different types of energy are then represented by ten different Chinese characters and are collectively known as the Heavenly Stems. They are shown in Table 2.1. To fully study the Four Pillars, you will need to be familiar with the characters of the five Yang Stems and the five Yin Stems.

Table 2.1 The Heavenly Stems

Branch	甲 Jia Yang Wood	乙 Yi Yin Wood	丙 Bing Yang Fire	丁 Ding Yin Metal	戊 Wu Yang Earth	己 Ji Yin Earth	庚 Geng Yang Metal	辛 Xin Yin Metal	壬 Ren Yang Water	癸 Gui Yin Water
Yin/Yang	Yang	Yin	Yang	Yin	Yang	Yin	Yang	Yin	Yang	Yin
Element	Wood		Fire		Earth		Metal		Water	

The ten Heavenly Stems progress from the first Stem Yang Wood through to the last Stem Yin Water to denote the days, months and years. The Chinese also devised 12 characters to measure the changes in energy through time known as the Earthly Branches. They are seen in Table 2.2.

19

Table 2.2 The Earthly Branches

Branch	Hidden Stems	Yin/Yang	Element	Time	Lunar Month	Solar Marker	Animal
子 Zi Rat	癸 Yin Water	Yang	Water	23~1	11	Heavy Snow	Rat
丑 Chou Ox	己 Yin Earth / 癸 Yin Water / 辛 Yin Metal	Yin	Earth	1~3	12	Slight Cold	Ox
寅 Yin Tiger	甲 Yang Wood / 丙 Yang Fire / 戊 Yang Earth	Yang	Wood	3~5	1	Spring Begins	Tiger
卯 Mao Rabbit	乙 Yin Wood	Yin	Wood	5~7	2	Insects Awaken	Rabbit
辰 Chen Dragon	戊 Yang Earth / 乙 Yin Wood / 癸 Yin Water	Yang	Earth	7~9	3	Clear and Bright	Dragon
巳 Si Snake	丙 Yang Water / 戊 Yang Earth / 庚 Yang Metal	Yin	Fire	9~11	4	Summer Begins	Snake
午 Wu Horse	丁 Yin Fire / 己 Yin Earth	Yang	Fire	11~13	5	Grain Ear	Horse
未 Wei Sheep	己 Yin Earth / 丁 Yin Fire / 乙 Yin Wood	Yin	Earth	13~15	6	Slight Heat	Sheep
申 Shen Monkey	庚 Yang Metal / 壬 Yang Water / 戊 Yang Earth	Yang	Metal	15~17	7	Autumn Begins	Monkey
酉 You Rooster	辛 Yin Metal	Yin	Metal	17~19	8	White Dew	Rooster
戌 Xu Dog	戊 Yang Earth / 辛 Yin Metal / 丁 Yin Fire	Yang	Earth	19~21	9	Cold Dew	Dog
亥 Hai Pig	壬 Yang Water / 甲 Yang Wood	Yin	Water	21~23	10	Winter Begins	Pig

Note: The months noted in the table refer to the lunar months.

These 12 Earthly Branches represent the 12 months of the year. Although, these 12 Earthly Branches start with the character Zi 子 Rat, the character Yin 寅 Tiger represents the first month, with the next character Mao 卯 representing the 2nd month. Therefore, the Zi 子 Rat month is the 11th month of the lunar calendar. The 12 Earthly Branches also represent the 12 Shi Chen 時辰 or units of time in a day. One Shi Chen represents two hours.

The energies within the Earthly Branches tend to be more mixed than those of the Heavenly Stems. Most Branches contain two or three different types of energy as indicated in the table. The Rat branch is rather straightforward as it only contains Yin Water energy. However, the next branch Ox contains three different types of energy: Yin Water, Yin Earth and Yin Metal. As you can see from Table 2.2, the four earth Branches (Dragon Dog, Ox and Sheep) contain three different types of energy each.

The Sexagenary Cycle or 60 Stem Branch Pairs

When the Heavenly Stems are matched with the Earthly Branches, the 60 Stem-Branch Pairs are formed. The Stems always maintain a direct relationship with their Yin or Yang origins. For example, the Rat (a Yang animal) will always combine with Yang Wood, Yang Fire, Yang Earth, Yang Metal and Yang Water. Also known as the Sexagenary Cycle, the Heavenly Stems are repeated six times and the Earthly Branches five times. These 60 Pairs are then broken down further into six Xun 旬 or Divisions of Ten. Its significance will be discussed in Chapter Three.

Each Division starts with Yang Wood. As shown in Table 2.3, the first Division starts with Yang Wood Rat and ends with Yin Water Rooster. Although the cycle of Stems has been fully utilized, the cycle of Branches still has the 11th and 12th animal left (i.e. the Dog and Pig). So, the next Division will incorporate these two animals. It will then start with Yang Wood Dog and finish with Yin Water Sheep. Continuing with this pattern, the third Division will start with Yang Wood Monkey and concludes with Yin Water Snake and so on.

Prior to the introduction of the Western Calendar in 1911, the Chinese used the Xun or Division to calculate time. For example, the Yin Wood Ox day would be the second day of the Yang Wood Rat Xun or Division.

Table 2.3 The Six Xun or Divisions of Ten of the 60 Stem-Branch Pairs

甲 Yang Wood 子 Rat	甲 Yang Wood 戌 Dog	甲 Yang Wood 申 Monkey	甲 Yang Wood 午 Horse	甲 Yang Wood 辰 Dragon	甲 Yang Wood 寅 Tiger
乙 Yin Wood 丑 Ox	乙 Yin Wood 亥 Pig	乙 Yin Wood 酉 Rooster	乙 Yin Wood 未 Sheep	乙 Yin Wood 巳 Snake	乙 Yin Wood 卯 Rabbit
丙 Yang Fire 寅 Tiger	丙 Yang Fire 子 Rat	丙 Yang Fire 戌 Dog	丙 Yang Fire 申 Monkey	丙 Yang Fire 午 Horse	丙 Yang Fire 辰 Dragon
丁 Yin Fire 卯 Rabbit	丁 Yin Fire 丑 Ox	丁 Yin Fire 亥 Pig	丁 Yin Fire 酉 Rooster	丁 Yin Fire 未 Sheep	丁 Yin Fire 巳 Snake
戊 Yang Earth 辰 Dragon	戊 Yang Earth 寅 Tiger	戊 Yang Earth 子 Rat	戊 Yang Earth 戌 Dog	戊 Yang Earth 申 Monkey	戊 Yang Earth 午 Horse
己 Yin Earth 巳 Snake	己 Yin Earth 卯 Rabbit	己 Yin Earth 丑 Ox	己 Yin Earth 亥 Pig	己 Yin Earth 酉 Rooster	己 Yin Earth 未 Sheep
庚 Yang Metal 午 Horse	庚 Yang Metal 辰 Dragon	庚 Yang Metal 寅 Tiger	庚 Yang Metal 子 Rat	庚 Yang Metal 戌 Dog	庚 Yang Metal 申 Monkey
辛 Yin Metal 未 Sheep	辛 Yin Metal 巳 Snake	辛 Yin Metal 卯 Rabbit	辛 Yin Metal 丑 Ox	辛 Yin Metal 亥 Pig	辛 Yin Metal 酉 Rooster
壬 Yang Water 申 Monkey	壬 Yang Water 午 Horse	壬 Yang Water 辰 Dragon	壬 Yang Water 寅 Tiger	壬 Yang Water 子 Rat	壬 Yang Water 戌 Dog
癸 Yin Water 酉 Rooster	癸 Yin Water 未 Sheep	癸 Yin Water 巳 Snake	癸 Yin Water 卯 Rabbit	癸 Yin Water 丑 Ox	癸 Yin Water 亥 Pig

In the *Ten Thousand Year Calendar*, every day, month and year is represented by a Stem-Branch Pair indicating the prevalent energy of the universe at that point in time. For instance, on the Yang Wood Rat day, the water and wood energies are strong. On the Yang Fire Horse day, fire is strong. On the Metal Rooster day, metal is the prevalent energy. For the same Stem-Branch year and its associated energy to return, you will have to wait 60 years. For the same month to return, you will wait 60 months or 5 years. For the same day to return, the waiting time is 60 days or nearly two months.

In each year of the *Ten Thousand Year Calendar*, there are 24 special days. The 12 Jie 節 or Festivals mark the start of each solar month. The 12 Qi 氣 denote the midpoint of the solar month. These 24 Solar or Agricultural markers are used for planting and harvesting the crops.

The Four Pillars only uses the 12 Festivals or start of the solar month, so you will need to be familiar with the following terms: **the Start of Spring, Insects Awaken, Clear and Bright, the Start of Summer, Grain In Ear, Slight Heat, the Start of Autumn, White Dew, Cold Dew, and Slight Cold.**

Yin/Yang, 5 Elements and Metaphysics

The ancient Chinese classified the different types of energy or qi 氣 in the natural environment under each of the five elements. These five elements are used to measure the qi prevalent in the universe, land or living environment and time. Although Western scientists have discovered ways to measure atoms and molecules, the quantifying and measuring of qi that is present in the environment and how it influences humankind is still relatively unknown.

By looking at the *Ten Thousand Year Calendar*, you can see that energy present in the universe at a specific time is quantified and accounted for by one of the five elements. In the Han Dynasty, the sage Da Chung Xu 董仲舒 had already started his investigation into the effects of the five elements on life. Several centuries later during the Tang Dynasty, the sage Li Xu Zhong 李虛中 started analyzing the relationship between the five elements and life using the year of birth as the key instead of the day. At the end of the Tang Dynasty, Xu Zi Ping brought Li Xu Zhong's analysis a step further by using the Day Pillar as the key and created the Four Pillars of Destiny.

Analysis of the 5 Elements

This book uses real life examples of Four Pillars charts to demonstrate its efficacy. But before that, we must first introduce its structure. The Four Pillars uses the birth year, month, day and hour of a person to ascertain their life and destiny. This birth data constitute two major components in the chart: the Eight Characters and their Luck Cycles. The tools that you need for setting up the Four Pillars chart and the Luck Cycles are the *Ten Thousand Year Calendar* and the Day Stem-Hour of Birth table. Table 2.4 shows what the Ten Heavenly Stems represent.

Table 2.4 What the Ten Stems Represent

Stem	甲 Yang Wood	乙 Yin Wood	丙 Yang Fire	丁 Yin Fire	戊 Yang Earth	己 Yin Earth	庚 Yang Metal	辛 Yin Metal	壬 Yang Water	癸 Yin Water
Symbol	Tree	Plant Flower	Sun	Man Made i.e. Candle	Dry Earth	Wet Earth	Axe Knife	Scissors Jewelry	Ocean River	Rain Clouds Dew
Direction	East	East	South	South	Centre	Centre	West	West	North	North
Color	Green	Green	Red	Red	Brown	Beige	White	White	Blue	Black
Shape	Rectangle	Rectangle	Triangle	Triangle	Square	Square	Circle	Circle	Wavy Irregular	Wavy Irregular

Let us consider two examples. For instance, David and Cristina are both born on February 8, 2012 at 06:00 hours.

The Four Steps in deriving their Four Pillars Chart:

From the *Ten Thousand Year Calendar* as seen in Figure 2.3, we note down the Stem Branch Pair for 2012, which is 壬辰 Yang Water Dragon in this case.

From the Stem Branch Pair of the first month present at the top of the column, we note that 壬寅 Yang Water Tiger represents the month.

From the day February 8, written as 2-8, we note down the Stem Branch Pair 己亥 Yin Earth Pig.

From Table 2.5, we can then find out the Stem-Branch Pair for the hour of birth.

Figure 2.3 February 2012 as shown in *Ten Thousand Year Calendar*

月別	農曆正月大			
干支	壬寅			
節氣	立	春	雨	水
	十	18	廿	14
	三	時	八	時
	酉	22	未	18
	時	分	時	分
農曆	干	支	西	曆
			月	日
初一	癸	未	1	23
初二	甲	申	1	24
初三	乙	酉	1	25
初四	丙	戌	1	26
初五	丁	亥	1	27
初六	戊	子	1	28
初七	己	丑	1	29
初八	庚	寅	1	30
初九	辛	卯	1	31
初十	壬	辰	2	1
十一	癸	巳	2	2
十二	甲	午	2	3
十三	乙	未	2	4
十四	丙	申	2	5
十五	丁	酉	2	6
十六	戊	戌	2	7
十七	己	亥	2	8
十八	庚	子	2	9
十九	辛	丑	2	10
二十	壬	寅	2	11

公元二零一二年　歲次壬辰　生肖屬龍

We have now identified the Year, Month and Day Pillars. Even for those whom the hour of birth is unknown, we are still able to obtain significant information from the Three Pillars. Of course, much more information can be deduced if we do know the Hour Pillar. To identify the Stem of the Hour Pillar, we will need to identify the Branch for the time of birth. In this case, for those born at 06:00 hours, the Branch is 卯 Rabbit. So far, the chart looks like this:

Hour	Day	Month	Year
?	己 Yin Earth	壬 Yang Water	壬 Yang Water
卯 Rabbit	亥 Pig	寅 Tiger	辰 Dragon

To identify the missing Stem in the Hour Pillar, the steps are as follows:

1. Identify the Day Stem - 己 Yin Earth.

2. From the Hour of Birth column identify the branch 卯 Rabbit.

3. Find the Day Stem 己 Yin Earth at the top of the table. Now, travel down the far left hand column until you reach the 卯 Rabbit. Travel across the columns until the row and the column intersect. Where Yin Earth and Rabbit intersect, we can identify Yin Fire. This is therefore the Stem for the Hour Pillar. Below is the complete Four Pillars chart.

Hour	Day	Month	Year
丁 Yin Fire	己 Yin Earth	壬 Yang Water	壬 Yang Water
卯 Rabbit	亥 Pig	寅 Tiger	辰 Dragon

This method applies to everyone regardless of gender or birth year.

Table 2.5 Determining The Hour Stem from Day Stem

Day Stem →	甲 Yang Wood 己 Yin Earth	乙 Yin Wood 庚 Yang Metal	丙 Yang Fire 辛 Yin Metal	丁 Yin Fire 壬 Yang Water	戊 Yang Earth 癸 Yin Water
Hour ↓					
子 Rat 23:00-01:00	甲 Yang Wood	丙 Yang Fire	戊 Yang Earth	庚 Yang Metal	壬 Yang Water
丑 Ox 01:00-03:00	乙 Yin Wood	丁 Yin Fire	己 Yin Earth	辛 Yin Metal	癸 Yin Water
寅 Tiger 03:00-05:00	丙 Yang Fire	戊 Yang Earth	庚 Yang Metal	壬 Yang Water	甲 Yang Wood
卯 Rabbit 05:00-07:00	丁 Yin Fire	己 Yin Earth	辛 Yin Metal	癸 Yin Water	乙 Yin Wood
辰 Dragon 07:00-09:00	戊 Yang Earth	庚 Yang Metal	壬 Yang Water	甲 Yang Wood	丙 Yang Fire
巳 Snake 09:00-11:00	己 Yin Earth	辛 Yin Metal	癸 Yin Water	乙 Yin Wood	丁 Yin Fire
午 Horse 11:00-13:00	庚 Yang Metal	壬 Yang Water	甲 Yang Wood	丙 Yang Fire	戊 Yang Earth
未 Sheep 13:00-15:00	辛 Yin Metal	癸 Yin Water	乙 Yin Wood	丁 Yin Fire	己 Yin Earth
申 Monkey 15:00-17:00	壬 Yang Water	甲 Yang Wood	丙 Yang Fire	戊 Yang Earth	庚 Yang Metal
酉 Rooster 17:00-19:00	癸 Yin Water	乙 Yin Wood	丁 Yin Fire	己 Yin Earth	辛 Yin Metal
戌 Dog 19:00-21:00	甲 Yang Wood	丙 Yang Fire	戊 Yang Earth	庚 Yang Metal	壬 Yang Water
亥 Pig 21:00-23:00	乙 Yin Wood	丁 Yin Fire	己 Yin Earth	辛 Yin Metal	癸 Yin Water

The Day Master is the heart of the Four Pillars. The Zi Ping system classifies everyone into ten types of people. This is due to the fact that each of the five elements has two forms, Yin and Yang. The two examples have Yin Earth as their Day Master.

The Day Master in the Four Pillars chart indicates an individual's Yin/Yang nature and element. The remaining seven characters provide clues on whether the environment matches with the Day Master's needs. If they do, then the individual could expect a smooth life.

The composition of the Four Pillars represents the individual's ability, personality, appearance, family and marriage amongst other things.

Determining The Luck Cycle

We have now constructed the Four Pillars chart of an individual. The next step is to identify the Luck Cycles. This refers to the five year periods that govern various stages of our life. Its energy will influence the overall chart. It is important to note that there is a key difference in determining the Luck Cycles between men and women.

For men born in Yang years (with a Yang Heavenly Stem) or women born in Yin years (with a Yin Heavenly Stem), the Luck Cycles proceed forward in the order of ascending months. For women born in Yang years or men born in Yin years, the Luck Cycles travel backwards in the order of descending months. It is relatively straightforward as illustrated in Examples 2.1 and 2.2.

To calculate Luck Cycles for men born in a Yang year and women born in a Yin year, you must count forwards from the day of birth until the next solar marker. Once you have obtained this number, it is then divided by three.

For men born in a Yin year and women born in a Yang year, count from the day of birth backwards until the previous solar marker. Once you have obtained this number, it is then divided by three.

Example 2.1 David's Luck Cycles

We need to take gender into account in relation to the Yin/Yang nature of the Year Stem. For instance, David is a man born in a Yang Water year, so his Luck Cycle will move forwards.

To calculate the age at which the first Luck Cycle starts, you need to first count the number of days between the individual's birthday and the next Jie or Festival which marks the start of the next solar month. For David, it is Insects Awaken which falls on March 5. There are 26 days between David's birthday on February 8 and March 5. This is then divided by three, thereby providing us with a rounded number of 9.

David is born in the Yang Water Tiger month. In 2012 as seen on the *Ten Thousand Year Calendar*, the following month is represented by Yin Water Rabbit. For those without a Calendar at hand, refer to Table 2.3. As seen in the Table, the Yang Water Tiger Stem-Branch Pair is part of the Yang Wood Horse Division. The following Stem-Branch Pair is Yin Water Rabbit. This is therefore the Stem-Branch pair for David's first Luck Cycle.

Each Stem-Branch Pillar governs ten years and traditionally, you should at least write down the Luck Cycles up to the age of 70 or beyond. Note that the Stem governs the first five years and the Branch governs the next five years. However, there may be some overlap with no clear division.

The extra lunar months are not used, so the 4th lunar month Yin Wood Snake is only used once.

David's Luck Cycles are as follows:

Age	9	19	29	39	49	59	69	79
Stem	癸 Yin Water	甲 Yang Wood	乙 Yin Wood	丙 Yang Fire	丁 Yin Fire	戊 Yang Earth	己 Yin Earth	庚 Yang Metal
Branch	卯 Rabbit	辰 Dragon	巳 Snake	午 Horse	未 Sheep	申 Monkey	酉 Rooster	戌 Dog

Example 2.2 Cristina's Luck Cycles

David's Luck Cycles move forward. As mentioned previously, this is used for men born in a Yang year or women born in a Yin Year. But for Cristina, who is a woman born in

32

a Yang year, her Luck Cycles will move backwards.

As the Luck Cycles go backwards, we will need to use the first Jie (or first day of the solar month) before her birthday. In this case, it is the Start of Spring that falls on February 4. The number of days between February 8 and February 4 is four. When four is divided by three, it gives us slightly more than one. Thus, Cristina's Luck Cycles start at age one (rounded down).

As the Luck Cycles proceed backwards, the first Month Pillar before the month of birth is that of Yin Metal Ox, as seen from your copy of the calendar or Table 2.3. This means that the next in sequence would be Yang Metal Rat. Cristina's Luck Cycles are as follows:

Age	1	11	21	31	41	51	61	71
Stem	辛 Yin Metal	庚 Yang Metal	己 Yin Earth	戊 Yang Earth	丁 Yin Fire	丙 Yang Fire	乙 Yin Wood	甲 Yang Wood
Branch	丑 Ox	子 Rat	亥 Pig	戌 Dog	酉 Rooster	申 Monkey	未 Sheep	午 Horse

The same steps will apply to men who are born in a Yin year.

How To Analyze The Four Pillars

Each of the Year, Month, Day and Hour Pillar governs approximately 15 years of our lives. Each Branch also represents specific sectors of your life or members of your family as shown in Figure 2.2.

Figure 2.2 The Sectors of the Four Pillars and What They Represent

	Hour	Represents	Day	Represents	Month	Represents	Year	Represents
Heavenly Stem	丁 Yin Fire	Sons, Friends	己 Yin Earth	Self	壬 Yang Water	Father	壬 Yang Water	Father's Family
Earthly Branch	卯 Rabbit	Daughters	亥 Pig	Partner Health	寅 Tiger	Mother Career	辰 Dragon	Mother's Family
Age	45~60		31~45		16~30		0~15	

Luck Cycles

Age	9~13	19~23	29~33	39~43	49~53	59~63	69~73	79~83
Stem	癸 Yin Water	甲 Yang Wood	乙 Yin Wood	丙 Yang Fire	丁 Yin Fire	戊 Yang Earth	己 Yin Earth	庚 Yang Metal
Age	14~18	24~28	34~38	44~48	54~58	64~68	74~78	84~88
Branch	卯 Rabbit	辰 Dragon	已 Snake	午 Horse	未 Sheep	申 Monkey	酉 Rooster	戌 Dog

Note: With regard to the starting day of the Four Pillars within your chart, you need to take into account the starting day of your Luck Cycles. For instance, David's Luck Cycles will start at the age of 9, which means that the Year Pillar will exert its influence from the age of 9 to 23, while the Month Pillar exerts its effects from the age of 24 till 38. For Cristina, her Luck Cycles will start at age 1. This means that her Year Pillar represents her luck from the age of 1 to 15.

Chapter Three - Basic Interpretation Techniques

In comparison to other forms of Chinese astrology (i.e. Zi Wei Dou Shu), setting up the Four Pillars chart is relatively straightforward. But to really analyze a chart in detail and identify the useful element accurately, you will need to have a deeper insight into the underlying theoretical principles.

Looking At A Four Pillars Chart

Firstly, let us consider the family relationships as demonstrated in a Four Pillars Chart.

Example 3.1 Ming Chengzu 明成祖 (born July 17, 1402), Second Ming Emperor

Hour	Day	Month	Year
辛 Yin Metal	癸 Yin Water	辛 Yin Metal	庚 Yang Metal
酉 Rooster	酉 Rooster	巳 Snake	子 Rat

In the Four Pillars chart, the Heavenly Stems represent the influence of the male family members, while the Earthly Branches represent the female relatives.

Each Pillar represents different relationships

The Year Pillar signifies an individual's ancestors and grandparents, while the Month Pillar represents the parents. The Branch in the Day Pillar denotes the spouse or partner and the Hour Pillar the children and friends. It is important to note that the Earthly Branch in the Day Pillar is often referred to as the 'House of Spouse'. It represents the husband for female charts and the wife for male charts.

The 'Shi Shen' (十神) or Ten Gods

Each of the Stems and Branches contain one or more of the five elements with a clearly defined relationship to the Day Master such as Wealth, Power, Resource, Output (Talent, Expression) and Sibling/Rival. These are known as the 'Shi Shen' or Ten Gods. They are illustrated in Table 3.1 for easy reference.

For Emperor Chengzu, the Day Master of his Four Pillars chart is Yin Water born in the Snake month when metal is strong. Only two characters within the chart contain water, the others contain metal (the Rooster contains Yin Metal and the Snake contains Yang Metal). There are six metal characters which can produce the water Day Master.

The 'Mother' is the element that produces oneself and there are many Mothers that protect the only son in this chart. This chart is known as the chart of 'Many Mothers Protecting One Son'. As the six metal characters are present in the parents, spouse and children sectors, this person would receive support from all these family members.

In this case, the Year Pillar has a Rat that contains water. This may indicate another Rival or heir present in the family to compete for the title of 'Favored Son', i.e. the Son who will inherit the bulk of the family wealth. As no 'Mother' would want to support the wrong heir for fear of future retaliation, this means that the 'Mothers' can only witness the Rivalry between two Siblings without offering much assistance. As a result, the person may be prone to insecurity at times. It is therefore ideal to eliminate the Rival so as to become the only 'Favored Son' in order to enjoy the benefits of Multiple Resources or 'Many Mothers'.

The Rat present in the Year Pillar represents the mother's family. This signifies possible issues with the mother's male relatives. In reality, Emperor Chengzu had to battle with his family members in order to gain the throne in 1402. He was then able to move the capital of China from Nanjing to Beijing in 1421.

These events occurred in his youth as represented by the Year Pillar (remember that we allocate the Year Pillar to the first 15 years of a person's life). We can see from the chart why the Emperor was able to win this battle.

The Day Master is Yin Water. It sits above a Partial Three Harmony Metal Combination formed by his metal Day and Month Branches Snake and Rooster. The Rat is left in the periphery (Year Pillar), sitting alone and unable to offer much resistance.

When we look at the Ten Gods present in a chart, we need to consider the Day Master first. In this case, it is Yin Water. Next we look at the other Stems present in Emperor Chengzu's chart - Yang Metal and Yin Metal (this includes the Yang and Yin Metal that are hidden underneath the Earthly Branches). Here we see an abundance of the Resource element metal, which produces the Day Master. The Resource represents assistance, mentors and advisers. So the Resource element (metal) is the useful element for this chart.

When we turn to look at the Rat Branch in the Year Pillar, it reveals a Yin Water hidden underneath the Rat. This represents a Competitor or Rival to his authority.

Rivalry

If a Yang Wood Day Master encounters another wood in the chart, it would be like meeting another brother or sister with the same parents. They will compete with you for your parents' care, attention and finances. If a Yang Wood encounters another Yang Wood, it is known as encountering a 'Sibling' or 'Rival'. But if a Yang Wood encounters a Yin Wood, it is known as 'Rob Wealth'.

Within the Four Pillars, there are several differences between the Yang and Yin polarities of elements. If there are many similar elements like the Day Master (i.e. Siblings) within a chart, then it is known as a Sibling Rivalry or Competitive chart.

Output/Children

The elements produced by the Day Master are known as the Output or Children elements. These are traditionally named in Chinese as the 'Eating God' or 'Injury Officer' elements. As Yang Wood produces fire, Yang Fire is the Eating God (sharing the same polarity as the Day Master). Yin Fire is the Injury Officer (having the opposite polarity).

Wealth

The elements conquered or overwhelmed by the Day Master are known as the Wealth elements. For example, Yang Wood conquers Earth - Yang Earth is the 'Indirect Wealth' (same polarity). Yin Earth is its 'Direct Wealth' (opposite polarity). This may seem paradoxical but it is meaningful in the interplay of Yin and Yang elements with the polarity of the Day Master.

Power

Metal will attack or control wood (the Day Master) and it is the Power element. Yang Metal is the 'Seven Killings' (same polarity). Yin Metal is the 'Direct Officer '(opposite polarity).

Resource

Water gives birth to Wood (the Day Master). It is the Mother or Resource element. Yang Water is the 'Indirect Resource' (same polarity) and Yin Water is the 'Direct Resource' (opposite polarity).

For some readers, the chart of the Ten Gods may appear complex, but it is important to be familiar with the interactions between the five elements as shown in Table 3.1.

The Ten Gods are as follows:

- Sibling (or Rival)
- Rob Wealth
- Eating God
- Injury Officer
- Indirect Wealth
- Direct Wealth
- Seven Killings
- Direct Officer
- Indirect Resource
- Direct Resource

Table 3.1 The Ten Gods

Ten Gods

Stem Day Master →	甲 Yang Wood	乙 Yin Wood	丙 Yang Fire	丁 Yin Fire	戊 Yang Earth	己 Yin Earth	庚 Yang Metal	辛 Yin Metal	壬 Yang Water	癸 Yin Water
甲 Yang Wood	Sibling	Rob Wealth	Eating God	Hurting Officer	Indirect Wealth	Direct Wealth	Seven Killings	Direct Officer	Indirect Resource	Direct Resource
乙 Yin Wood	Rob Wealth	Sibling	Hurting Officer	Eating God	Direct Wealth	Indirect Wealth	Direct Officer	Seven Killings	Direct Resource	Indirect Resource
丙 Yang Fire	Indirect Resource	Direct Resource	Sibling	Rob Wealth	Eating God	Hurting Officer	Indirect Wealth	Direct Wealth	Seven Killings	Direct Officer
丁 Yin Fire	Direct Resource	Indirect Resource	Rob Wealth	Sibling	Hurting Officer	Eating God	Direct Wealth	Indirect Wealth	Direct Officer	Seven Killings
戊 Yang Earth	Seven Killings	Direct Officer	Indirect Resource	Direct Resource	Sibling	Rob Wealth	Eating God	Hurting Officer	Indirect Wealth	Direct Wealth
己 Yin Earth	Direct Officer	Seven Killings	Direct Resource	Indirect Resource	Rob Wealth	Sibling	Hurting Officer	Eating God	Direct Wealth	Indirect Wealth
庚 Yang Metal	Indirect Wealth	Direct Wealth	Seven Killings	Direct Officer	Indirect Resource	Direct Resource	Sibling	Rob Wealth	Eating God	Hurting Officer
辛 Yin Metal	Direct Wealth	Indirect Wealth	Direct Officer	Seven Killings	Direct Resource	Indirect Resource	Rob Wealth	Sibling	Hurting Officer	Eating God
壬 Yang Water	Eating God	Hurting Officer	Indirect Wealth	Direct Wealth	Seven Killings	Direct Officer	Indirect Resource	Direct Resource	Sibling	Rob Wealth
癸 Yin Water	Hurting Officer	Eating God	Direct Wealth	Indirect Wealth	Direct Officer	Seven Killings	Direct Resource	Indirect Resource	Rob Wealth	Sibling

To read Table 3.1, find your Day Master in the first row and then read down the table to find which element corresponds to the Hurting Officer, Direct Resource and so on.

To help you get a better understanding of the elemental relationships between the Ten Gods and the Day Master, we can look at it in a different way.

Traditionally, the Day Master is referred to I or me and the other relationships revolve around 'me'.

The element that gives rise to or supports the Day Master is the **Resource**. A Resource of the opposite polarity is known as the **Direct Resource**, whilst that of the same polarity is known as the **Indirect Resource**.

The element that *I produce* is known as the **Output or Children** element. The Children element of the opposite polarity is known as the **Hurting Officer**, while that of the same polarity is known as the **Eating God**.

The element that is the *same as* the Day Master is known as the **Sibling or Rival**. The element of the same polarity is the **Sibling**, while that of the opposite polarity is termed **Rob Wealth**.

The element that *controls m*e is the **Power** Element. The element of the opposite polarity is the **Direct Officer**, while that of the same polarity is the **Seven Killings**.

The element that *I control* is the **Wealth** Element. The element of the opposite polarity is the **Direct Wealth,** while that of the same polarity is the **Indirect Wealth**.

Interactions: Clashes and Combinations of the Five Elements

The Clashes and Combinations within a Four Pillars chart directly influence our life. We start by looking at Combinations. In Chinese Metaphysics, Combinations represent auspicious influences (such as harmony, cooperation, help from mentors) which are essentially the indicators of success. They can also represent special affinities with others.

A) The Five Heavenly Stem Combinations

Figure 3.1 The Five Heavenly Stem Combinations

Yang Wood 甲	Yang Fire 丙	Yang Earth 戊	Yang Metal 庚	Yang Water 壬
↕	↕	↕	↕	↕
Yin Earth 己	Yin Metal 辛	Yin Water 癸	Yin Wood 乙	Yin Fire 丁

The Ten Stems are divided into Five Combinations or Pairs. Each Pair consists of one Yin Stem and one Yang Stem. It indicates the unique growth that comes from the union of Yin and Yang. This type of Combination can be very auspicious. The Yang Stem is pairing up with its Wealth element while the Yin Stem is combining with its Power element.

Let us consider the charts of two people - one has a Yang Wood Day Master that combines with the other person's Yin Earth Day Master. This signifies a special harmony between these two individuals - whether between friends, husband and wife, parent and child or boss and employee. For example, a Yang Wood parent who combines with a Yin Earth child will have a devoted and obedient child.

In fact, if there are any harmonic pairs involving the Day Master in a Four Pillars chart, the individual is considered to be a 'people's person' and will interact sociably with others.

Elemental relationships also need to be taken into consideration. For instance, a Yang Wood Day Master encountering Yin Earth represents the prospect of wealth. This means that the individual will be able to accumulate wealth when the Combination exists in his or her Four Pillars chart or is present through a Luck Cycle or year.

For the other Day Masters, the Wealth relationships are as follows (Day Master first).

- Yang Water with Yin Fire
- Yang Fire with Yin Metal
- Yang Earth with Yin Water
- Yang Metal with Yin Wood

Example 3.2 Steve Cohen (born May 24, 1949), Congressman for Tennessee

Hour	Day	Month	Year
?	甲 Yang Wood	己 Yin Earth	己 Yin Earth
?	寅 Tiger	巳 Snake	丑 Ox

The Direct Wealth Yin Earth in the Month Pillar combines with the Yang Wood Day Master. This brings Cohen wealth.

Example 3.3 Theodore Pickens Boone Jr. (born May 22, 1928), American financier

Hour	Day	Month	Year
?	壬 Yang Water	丁 Yin Fire	戊 Yang Earth
?	戌 Dog	巳 Snake	辰 Dragon

The Yang Water Day Stem combines with the Yin Fire Month Stem, which represents its Wealth.

A1) Power Stem Combination

When a Yin Earth Day Master combines with Yang Wood, the Power element (Direct Officer) combines with the Day Master. This results in professional recognition.

Example 3.4 Donald Trump (born June 14, 1946)

Hour	Day	Month	Year
?	己 Yin Earth	甲 Yang Wood	丙 Yang Fire
?	未 Sheep	午 Horse	戌 Dog

Trump is a Yin Earth Day Master with a Yang Wood Stem in the Month Pillar (indicating the father). This shows that Trump was born to a privileged and successful family and went on to enjoy a highly successful career.

We need to bear in mind that the Day Master Combination is only part of the picture. For a better interpretation, we will have to analyze the rest of the chart as well.

B) Earthly Branches Six Harmony Combination (Liu He 六合)

These are the Six Harmony Combinations which involve the 12 Earthly Branches and the resultant element.

1) Rat and Ox (forms Earth)
2) Tiger and Pig (forms Wood)
3) Dog and Rabbit (forms Fire)
4) Snake and Monkey (forms Water)
5) Horse and Sheep (forms Fire)
6) Dragon and Rooster (forms Metal)

It is only in special circumstances that the combination between the Six Harmony Pairs can produce the resultant element, e.g. Rat and Ox combining to form Earth.

Figure 3.2 The Six Harmony Branch Combinations

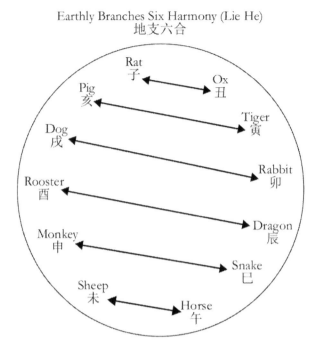

Earthly Branches Six Harmony (Lie He)
地支六合

The Six Harmony Combinations between the Branches are considered favorable as they combine the people skills of the Day Branch with the good fortune of receiving assistance from mentors. If the Month and Day Branches combine, this indicates a strong marriage. If the Month and Year Branches combine, the person will enjoy good relationships with parents and grandparents.

If there is no Six Harmony Branch Combination within a person's chart, then having a Six Harmony Combination with the Branch in the Luck Cycle or year means a mentor may appear to assist the person during these auspicious times.

C) Earthly Branches Three Harmony Combinations (San He 三合)

The Three Harmony or San He Combinations consist of four groups of Three Branches with a unique quality of chi.

1) Monkey, Water and Dragon (Water)
2) Tiger, Horse and Dog (Fire)
3) Pig, Rabbit and Sheep (Wood)
4) Snake, Rooster and Ox (Metal)

If all three branches of the Three Harmony Combination are present in a Four Pillars chart, then the resultant element will be formed immediately. For instance, the Monkey, Rat and Dragon combine to form water. Any two members of each San He or Three Harmony Trio can combine to form a Partial Three Harmony Combination and the resultant element. If the missing member of the Three Harmony Trio is found in the Luck Cycle or year, then the Three Harmony Combination is complete. The resultant element becomes prevalent.

Figure 3.3 The Three Harmony Branch Combinations

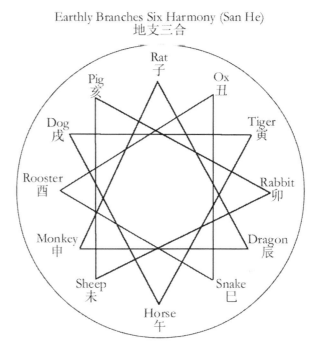

The strength of the element produced by the Three Harmony Combination surpasses that of the Six Harmony Combinations and is also considered more auspicious. When the House of Spouse (the Branch that sits below the Day Master) is involved in a Three Harmony Combination, the likelihood of marriage will be higher. The Three Harmony element is considered the useful element in a chart and brings much benefit.

Example 3.5 Zeng Guofan 曾國藩 (born November 26, 1811, died March 12, 1872), Qing Dynasty official and Confucian scholar

Hour	Day	Month	Year
己	丙	己	丙
Yin Earth	Yang Fire	Yin Earth	Yang Fire
亥	辰	亥	未
Pig	Dragon	Pig	Sheep

Example 3.6 Li Hongzhang 李鴻章 (born February 15, 1823, died November 7, 1901), Qing Dynasty statesman

Hour	Day	Month	Year
己	乙	甲	癸
Yin Earth	Yin Wood	Yang Wood	Yin Water
卯	亥	寅	未
Rabbit	Pig	Tiger	Sheep

In both charts, wood is the useful element.

Zeng's chart is considered a Follow the Resource chart. He did in fact become prominent during his wood Luck Cycles that strengthened the Partial Three Harmony Wood Combination present in his chart.

Li's chart is considered a Dominant Wood chart as it contains the Full Three Harmony Wood Combination. As a result, Li enjoyed a good reputation and attained much success in his lifetime.

Example 3.7 Ingrid Bergman (born August 29, 1915, 03:30 hours), Swedish Actress

Hour	Day	Month	Year
壬	壬	甲	乙
Yang Water	Yang Water	Yang Wood	Yin Wood
寅	辰	申	卯
Tiger	Dragon	Monkey	Rabbit

The Yang Water Day Master is born in autumn (Monkey month) and is intelligent and attractive. The Monkey and Dragon form a Partial Three Harmony Water Combination and makes it a Dominant Water chart. Bergman reached the peak of her career during the Rat Luck Cycle, which started when she was 39. The Rat completed the Three Harmony Water Combination of Monkey, Rat and Dragon.

When Bergman was 35 years old during the Yang Earth Luck Cycle, she had an extramarital affair with Italian director Roberto Rossellini while filming in Europe. Her husband and daughter remained behind in the United States. As a result, she became box office poison during this period and only returned to Hollywood for the production of 'Anastasia'.

The film was released in 1956 when she was 41 during the Rat Luck Cycle. Bergman won her second Academy Award for Best Actress for this role. She also separated from Rossellini during this period and married for the third time. The completion of the Three Harmony Water Combination saw Bergman enjoy professional recognition and the longest and happiest marriage of her life.

D) Earthly Branches Directional Combination (San Fang 三方)

The Earthly Branches combine in another fashion by virtue of their position or direction; this is known as Directional Combination or San Fang.

1) Pig, Rat and Ox, North, Water
2) Tiger, Rabbit and Dragon, East, Wood
3) Snake, Horse and Sheep, South, Fire
4) Monkey, Rooster and Dog, West, Metal

Figure 3.4 The Directional Branch Combinations

Earthly Branches Directional Combinations
地支方合

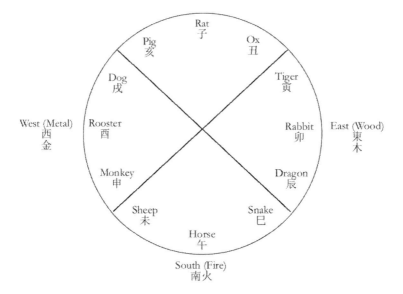

The strength of the element produced by the Directional Combination is stronger than that which is produced by the Three Harmony Combination. However, all three Branches must be present for the Directional Combination to occur. There is no Partial Combination as seen with the Three Harmony Combinations.

If there are only two Branches of the Directional Combination present in a chart and an additional Branch comes in the Luck Cycle or year, it can complete the Directional Combination.

For instance, if a Four Pillars chart only has the Pig and Rat, then in the Ox year, the Directional Water Combination can be formed. It can bring benefit and good fortune to the individual only if water is the useful element. If water is the negative element, then there will be misfortune.

When the resultant element of the Directional Combination is a positive element, the appearance of the missing Branch in the Luck Cycle will see the individual enjoying significant success. For instance, if the two Branches of the Directional Combination are present in the Month and Year Pillars and the missing Branch appears in the Luck Cycle or year, there will be success in competitions and awards.

Example 3.8 Ron Brown (born March 31, 1961), 1984 Olympics 100m Relay Gold Medalist

Hour	Day	Month	Year
?	癸 Yin Water	辛 Yin Metal	辛 Yin Metal
?	亥 Pig	卯 Rabbit	丑 Ox

1984 was the Year of the Yang Wood Rat. The Four Pillars chart of Ron Brown has the Pig and Ox of the Directional Water Combination. He achieved success in the Year of the Rat when the missing member of the Directional Combination appeared. This transformed Brown into a Dominant chart and allowed him to win a gold medal in the 1984 Olympics.

Regardless of whether one is an athlete or not, every person needs to triumph over their rivals and this can be achieved through the presence of a good year that completes the missing component of any Combination in their Four Pillars chart.

Examples can also be drawn from actors and singers in the entertainment industry as they tend to have more dramatic lives. The sudden appearance of the missing Branch in a Combination - whether Six Harmony, Three Harmony or Directional – can result in a sudden upswing in their career.

Example 3.9 Paula Abdul (born June 19, 1962, 14:32 hours)

Hour	Day	Month	Year
己	戊	丙	壬
Yin Earth	Yang Earth	Yang Fire	Yang Water
未	子	午	寅
Sheep	Rat	Horse	Tiger

4	14	24	34	44	54	64	74
乙	甲	癸	壬	辛	庚	己	戊
Yin Wood	Yang Wood	Yin Water	Yang Water	Yin Metal	Yang Metal	Yin Earth	Yang Earth
巳	辰	卯	寅	丑	子	亥	戌
Snake	Dragon	Rabbit	Tiger	Ox	Rat	Pig	Dog

Abdul is a Yang Earth Day Master born in the summer when fire is strong. Together with the Yang Fire in the Month Pillar and the earth present in the Hour Pillar, the main energy in her chart is that of fire and earth. Abdul's chart can be considered as a shaky Dominant Earth chart because the water in the Day Branch tries to control and dilute the earth.

Before the age of 40, Abdul had already been married twice, with both marriages only lasting for two years. Even if Abdul's chart is interpreted as a Follow the Resource (fire) chart, the presence of water in the Day Pillar does not bode well for her marriage. With the mixed energies present in her chart, she is especially vulnerable to changes of elements in the Luck Cycles and years.

Abdul became famous in 1989 (Yin Earth Snake year) at the age of 27 during the Yin Water Luck Cycle. The Snake in the Year completed the Fire Directional Combination in her chart (which contained the Horse and Sheep). This meant her chart became a Follow the Resource or Many Mothers, One Child chart. Her good fortune continued until 1990 (Yang Metal Horse year) when her debut album continued to sell strongly.

By 1994 (Yang Wood Dog year), Abdul was experiencing marital and health issues. It was only in 2002 (Yang Water Horse year) in the favorable Tiger Luck Cycle that she made a return to the public eye as a judge on the popular television show 'American Idol'.

E) Six Clashes of Earthly Branches (Liu Chong 六沖)

There are six potential Clashes between the Earthly Branches.

1) Rat with Horse
2) Ox with Sheep
3) Tiger with Monkey
4) Rabbit with Rooster
5) Dragon with Dog
6) Snake with Pig

Figure 3.5 Clash of the Branches

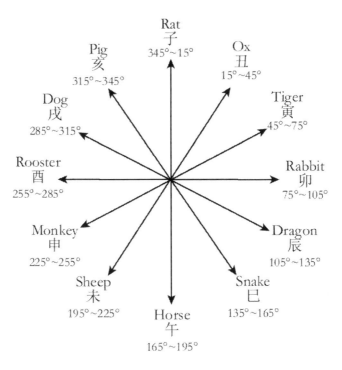

The Earthly Branch clashes with the one that is located directly opposite itself. In 2012, the year of the Yang Water Dragon, the Dog clashed with the Dragon. This situation is known as the Clash with the Tai Sui or Grand Duke of the year. The Clash represents conflict, accidents and mishaps, financial loss or health issues.

However, if a person born in the Dog Year has a Rat or Monkey in the chart, the effects of the Clash from a Dragon will be diminished. These animals will combine with the Dragon. Similarly, if the chart has the Tiger or Horse together with the Dog, the effects of the Clash will be reduced as these animals hold the Dog in place and shield it from the Dragon's attack. There are some who disagree with this theory, so readers will need to collate examples to support or disprove this theory.

When an individual's Birth Year Branch clashes with the current Year Branch, the consequences will need to be considered on a case-by-case basis. This does not mean that everyone experiencing a Clash will have a bad year as the other Branches within one's Four Pillars may alleviate the situation.

When there is a Clash of Branches within an individual's chart, there will be many changes in that person's life. If the Clash is between the Year and Month, the person will have difficult relationships with his or her parents and may move out of home early. If the Clash is between the Month and Day, husband and wife may spend time apart due to their work. If the Clash is between the Day and Hour, then the person will spend time apart from his or her children later on in life.

Even if there is no Clash involving the Branches within a person's Four Pillars chart, a Clash present in the Luck Cycle or year will result in negative developments regardless of whether the Clash involves the Year, Month, Day or Hour Branch.

We will now look at the chart of the airplane crash in Russia that killed 96 people, including the Polish president, his wife and other high-ranking officials.

Example 3.10 Polish Plane Crash (April 10, 2010, 10:44 hours)

Hour	Day	Month	Year
辛	庚	己	庚
Yin Metal	Yang Metal	Yin Earth	Yang Metal
巳	寅	卯	寅
Snake	Tiger	Rabbit	Tiger

On this day, two Yang Metals competed for one Rabbit with much conflict between the metal and wood present. For those with the Rooster in their chart, the Rabbit-Rooster Clash would have further exacerbated the competition between the two Yang Metals. Having the Rabbit present in the chart would also bring out the Competitor as there was an additional Wealth element to fight over. The charts of six of the seven main Polish politicians who perished in the clash contained the Rabbit-Rooster Clash.

Let us consider the crash victims individually. The charts of the victims are discussed in further detail in Appendix 3.

The former Defense Minister Jerzy Szmajdinski (born April 9, 1952) was born on a Rooster day and was going through the Rooster Luck Cycle.

The Chief of Staff of the Polish Armed Forces Franciszek Gagor (born September 8, 1951) was born in a Rooster month and was going through a Rabbit Luck Cycle.

Former Deputy Prime Minister Przemyslaw Goslewski (born May 12, 1964) was born on a Rooster day and was in the Rooster Luck Cycle.

President of the National Bank of Poland Slawomir Skrzypek (born May 10, 1963) was born in a Rabbit year and was going through the Rat Luck Cycle.

Polish President Lech Kacynski (born June 18, 1949) was born on a Rabbit day. The Rat Luck Cycle he was going through at that time clashed with the Horse present in his Month Pillar.

The female co-founder of the 'Solidarity Trade Union' Anna Walentynowicz (born August 13, 1929) was born in a Monkey month that clashed with the two Tigers present in the day and year.

It is important to note that the Polish President had a twin brother who was not on the plane that day. This just goes to show that those who are born on the same day do not necessarily have the same fate or life.

The individual should not be overly concerned when the year clashes with an Earthly Branch in a chart, as there are months, days or hours which can reduce the intensity of the

Clash by combining with an Earthly Branch.

F) The Yin and Yang nature of the Four Pillars

The Four Pillars can be Yang or Yin in nature. If an individual's Four Pillars are only Yang in nature, that person will be benevolent, just, logical, principled and focused. However, there is a tendency to be extreme in terms of beliefs or actions.

Chinese revolutionary Huang Hsing's 黃興 Four Yang Pillars made him a martyr for the country. President Eisenhower's Four Yang Pillars saw him become a five star General prior to being the head of state. Sir Isaac Newton's Four Yang Pillars carried him all the way in his unyielding pursuit of the truth. The Last Emperor of China Puyi or Xuantong 宣統 was unable to yield or adapt. He eventually lived out an undistinguished life. Composer Beethoven's Four Pillars chart also contains only Yang Pillars.

When all Four Pillars are Yin in nature, then that individual tends to be extremely ambitious and have many secrets. This ambition may be tempered by suspicion and selfishness, so the person may find it difficult to enjoy the pleasures in life. Chinese army leader and First President of the Republic of China (1912-1916) Yuan Shikai 袁世凱 had only Yin Pillars in his chart. He made an ill-fated attempt to re-establish the monarchy in China and make himself the First Emperor of his self proclaimed Dynasty. On the other hand, Ming Emperor Shenzhong 神宗 ruled for more than 40 years in spite of a Four Pillars chart with all Yin Pillars. The key difference is that his chart contained Pillars from the same Division, which will be explained later in this chapter.

When the Year and Hour Pillars are Yang with the other pillars being Yin, the person has courage, pays attention to detail and is good at defending themselves. When the Yin Pillars are located outside and the Yang Pillars within, then the person has a tendency to be stubborn. In extreme cases, the person may create problems for others. If the Four Pillars alternate Yang and Yin or Yin and Yang, then the person's personality is balanced. He or she will not resort to any extremes in behavior, thought or action.

These are just some general examples for quick reference.

To really grasp an understanding, detailed analysis of each individual's Four Pillars chart is required. Readers are encouraged to verify these observations with more real life examples derived from their family, friends and public figures.

G) Messages From the Six Divisions

The 60 Stem-Branch Pairs are grouped into six special groups, defined as the **Six Divisions**. They are shown in Table 3.2.

Table 3.2 The 60 Stem-Branch Pairs

Stem → / Division ↓	甲 Yang Wood	乙 Yin Wood	丙 Yang Fire	丁 Yin Fire	戊 Yang Earth	己 Yin Earth	庚 Yang Metal	辛 Yin Metal	壬 Yang Water	癸 Yin Water	空亡 Empty
甲子 Yang Wood Rat	甲子 Yang Wood Rat	乙丑 Yin Wood Ox	丙寅 Yang Fire Tiger	丁卯 Yin Fire Rabbit	戊辰 Yang Earth Dragon	己巳 Yin Earth Snake	庚午 Yang Metal Fire	辛未 Yin Metal Sheep	壬申 Yang Water Monkey	癸酉 Yin Water Rooster	戌亥 Dog Pig
甲戌 Yang Wood Dog	甲戌 Yang Wood Dog	乙亥 Yin Wood Pig	丙子 Yang Fire Rat	丁丑 Yin Fire Ox	戊寅 Yang Earth Tiger	己卯 Yin Earth Rabbit	庚辰 Yang Metal Dragon	辛巳 Yin Metal Snake	壬午 Yang Water Horse	癸未 Yin Water Sheep	申酉 Monkey Rooster
甲申 Yang Wood Monkey	甲申 Yang Wood Monkey	乙酉 Yin Wood Rooster	丙戌 Yang Fire Dog	丁亥 Yin Fire Pig	戊子 Yang Earth Rat	己丑 Yin Earth Ox	庚寅 Yang Metal Tiger	辛卯 Yin Metal Rabbit	壬辰 Yang Water Dragon	癸巳 Yin Water Snake	午未 Horse Sheep
甲午 Yang Wood Horse	甲午 Yang Wood Horse	乙未 Yin Wood Sheep	丙申 Yang Fire Monkey	丁酉 Yin Fire Rooster	戊戌 Yang Earth Dog	己亥 Yin Earth Pig	庚子 Yang Metal Rat	辛丑 Yin Metal Ox	壬寅 Yang Water Tiger	癸卯 Yin Water Rabbit	辰巳 Dragon Snake
甲辰 Yang Wood Dragon	甲辰 Yang Wood Dragon	乙巳 Yin Wood Snake	丙午 Yang Fire Horse	丁未 Yin Fire Sheep	戊申 Yang Earth Monkey	己酉 Yin Earth Rooster	庚戌 Yang Metal Dog	辛亥 Yin Metal Pig	壬子 Yang Water Rat	癸丑 Yin Water Ox	寅卯 Tiger Rabbit
甲寅 Yang Wood Tiger	甲寅 Yang Wood Tiger	乙卯 Yin Wood Rabbit	丙辰 Yang Fire Dragon	丁巳 Yin Fire Snake	戊午 Yang Earth Horse	己未 Yin Earth Sheep	庚申 Yang Metal Monkey	辛酉 Yin Metal Rooster	壬戌 Yang Water Dog	癸亥 Yin Water Pig	子丑 Rat Ox

58

As you can see from Table 3.2, there are ten Stem-Branch Pairs within each Division. If a Four Pillars chart has three or four Pairs from the same Division, the person will be blessed with wealth and power. This can be seen in the charts of successful individual. Examples:

1) Li Hongzhang 李鴻章 (born February 15, 1823), Qing Dynasty statesman
2) Princess Diana (born July 1, 1961)
3) Soong Tzu-wen 宋子文 (born December 4, 1891), Finance Minister of China

Example 3.11 Soong Tzu-wen 宋子文 (born December 4, 1891), Finance Minister of China

Hour	Day	Month	Year
己	庚	乙	甲
Yin Earth	Yang Metal	Yin Wood	Yang Wood
卯	辰	亥	午
Rabbit	Dragon	Pig	Horse

Within Soong's chart, the Pillars Yin Earth Rabbit, Yang Metal Dragon and Yin Wood Pig are part of the Yang Wood Dog Division. This means that he has three Pillars from the same Division.

Alternatively, having one Pillar from different Divisions indicates an individual who attains success through his own efforts and can be seen in the charts of leaders or scholars. Examples:

1) Zhou Enlai 周恩來 (born March 5, 1898), First Premier of the People's Republic of China
2) George Washington (born February 22, 1732)
3) Sir Isaac Newton (born December 25, 1642)
4) Shao Yung 邵雍 (born 1011), Soong Dynasty scholar
5) Mao Zedong 毛澤東 (born December 26, 1893, 07:30 hours)

Example 3.12 Mao Zedong 毛澤東 (born December 26, 1893, 07:30 hours)

Hour	Day	Month	Year
甲 Yang Wood	丁 Yin Fire	甲 Yang Wood	癸 Yin Water
辰 Dragon	酉 Rooster	子 Rat	巳 Snake
(甲辰) Yang Wood Dragon	(甲午) Yang Wood Horse	(甲子) Yang Wood Rat	(甲申) Yang Wood Monkey

The chart of Chairman Mao has one Pillar from a different Division.

Another favorable configuration would be to have the Year and Hour Pillars correspond to being the first and last Stem-Branch Combination of the same Division. A theoretical example of Yang Wood Rat in the Year Pillar and Yin Water Rooster in the Hour Pillar is shown below.

Hour	Day	Month	Year
癸 Yin Water	?	?	甲 Yang Wood
酉 Rooster	?	?	子 Rat

H) The Significance of Empty Stars

Within each Division, the last two Branches that are not part of the group are considered as two Empty (Void) Stars as shown in Table 3.2. Every individual has two Void Stars based on their Day Pillar. For example, the Yang Wood Dragon Division (the 5th Division from the top as seen in Table 3.2) contains 10 Stem-Branch Pairs, starting with the Yang Wood Dragon Pair and ending with the Yin Water Ox Pair. This means that the Tiger and Rabbit will be the Void Stars. For the Yang Wood Horse Division (4th Division from the top), the Empty or Void Stars will be the Dragon and Snake and so on.

These Void Branches have to be present within a Four Pillars chart to be significant. If they are present in the Luck Cycle or year, there will be no effects.

The Empty (or Void Star) nullifies the Branch it is on. This indicates loss and is inauspicious. When the Empty Branch is present in the Year Pillar, the individual's parentage is not clear. They may have been orphaned or their parents or grandparents were unable to offer much assistance. If it is seen in the Month Pillar, then the individual may experience multiple career changes.

President Eisenhower (born October 14, 1890) was born on a Yang Earth Dragon day with an Empty Branch present in the Month Pillar. He had to move around numerous battlefields in many locations before becoming a five-star general and eventually the President. Those individuals with Void signs in the Hour Pillar tend not to have male heirs or may find it difficult to spend time with their children.

When the Wealth and Power elements are Empty or Void, an individual may experience problems with money and career. However, when the Void is involved in a Three Harmony or Six Harmony Combination, it is possible to reduce or deflect the effects of the Void. We can therefore identify the times when the Empty Star is combined and use these times to alleviate any problems. On the other hand, if the negative element is sitting on a Void, then any possible harm to the individual is minimized. We will need to first identify correctly the positive and negative elements.

When a Four Pillars chart has three Empty Stars, then it becomes highly favorable. Being almost empty means that all obstacles would have been removed. This configuration is known as 'Prospering Within The Void'.

Example 3.13 Shao Yung 邵雍 (born 1011), Soong Dynasty scholar

Hour	Day	Month	Year
甲	甲	辛	辛
Yang Wood	Yang Wood	Yin Metal	Yin Metal
戌	子	丑	亥
Dog	Rat	Ox	Pig

The Empty Branches of the Yang Wood Rat division are the Dog and Pig. Both the Dog and Pig are present in his chart in the Hour and Year Pillars respectively. Apart from the Void Branches, the hidden elements within them can also result in Void Stems. For the Pig, Yang Wood and Yang Water are hidden within. There are two Yang Wood Stems present in Shao Yung's chart. This means that with the Void Branches Dog and Pig, there is a total of four Void Stems and Branches in Shao's chart. This makes it a **Prospering Within the Void** configuration.

This is also a Follow the Resource (water) chart due to the Water Directional Combination that is present (in this case, Pig, Water and Ox). When the Dog and Pig are present in a Four Pillars chart, it suggests a strong interest in metaphysics, religion and spiritual matters. With such a chart, it is no wonder that Shao Yung's success in metaphysics was unparalleled.

Chapter Four - The Special Stars

In the original Four Pillars system, the Special Stars did not play a major role. However, the recent proliferation of books on this subject has given much attention to the Special Stars. Most of the Special Stars are derived from Zi Wei Dou Shu (Emperor Astrology). Note that the basis of Zi Wei Dou Shu is derived from the Four Pillars and if there were no Four Pillars, then Zi Wei Dou Shu would not exist.

Different methods of Chinese Astrology share common ground and in reality, there is no one method of Life Divination that will simply provide the entire picture. Life is way too complicated for that. Just like different religions, they allow us to view and understand the world in different ways.

So what are the Special Stars in Four Pillars Astrology? The origins of Chinese Metaphysics are obscure as are the origins of the Special Stars. In theory, the Special Stars relate to the Stems and Branches. They provide further depth to Four Pillars analysis. The Chinese metaphysicians noted down the influences, collated them and left us with their findings. As to the exact years of their discoveries, we are still waiting for Chinese classical historians to determine them.

So what is the role of Special Stars? The Special Stars provide further details about the charts. We should not simply rely on them to provide conclusions with regard to an individual's personality or destiny. Using the Special Stars is undeniably convenient and the information they provide is clear and definite, but how reliable are they?

I have to emphasize once again that the theories of Chinese Metaphysics and Life Divination have never been universally acknowledged and given the accord and respect they deserve by society as a whole. There is an absence of an independent body which could verify the origins of Chinese Metaphysics. We are can only depend on the experiences and wisdom of ancient practitioners. From my own analysis, I feel that these Special Stars are worth investigating and understanding.

Are the Special Stars mere superstitions? I am sure we

have appealed to God whom we individually supplicate to in times of difficulty, especially when we felt that there was no other recourse. Regardless of whether we pray to the higher powers for help, we should not simply await the consequences in times of trouble without doing anything. We should progress from superstition to experimentation so as to ascertain any possible validity and reliability. The Hou or Encountering Hexagram (Strategy in Taking Risk) of the *I Ching* states: *We should not treat with fear events and opportunities that we harbor suspicion or uncertainty about. Rather we should strive to observe, test and ascertain them, so as not to miss out on any opportunities that may have presented themselves.*

We should examine their value and accuracy with open and enquiring minds. The Special Stars that I will discuss are collated from my many years of experience interpreting Four Pillars charts. In my opinion, they all contribute to the overall picture. Note that the Special Stars are not the entire story as they need to be considered in the context of the overall flow and useful elements of each chart. There are four major types of Special Stars.

A) Special Day Pillars

The first group of Special Stars focuses on the Stem-Branch Pairs. They can be broken into two sub-groups:

Those that apply only to the Day Pillar

Those that apply to the Day Pillar and the other Pillars (Year, Month and Hour)

The following three groups of Stem-Branch Pair Special Stars refer to the Day Pillar only.

Aa.1 Six Intellectual Pillars (Liu Xiu 六秀)
1) Yang Earth Rat 戊子
2) Yin Earth Ox 己丑
3) Yin Metal Snake 辛巳
4) Yin Fire Sheep 丁未
5) Yang Fire Horse 丙午
6) Yin Earth Sheep 己未

Those born on a day corresponding to one of the six pillars above will be highly intelligent, possess sharp minds and excel academically. Numerous scholars, professors and well-known individuals were born on such days.

Here are some examples:

<u>Yin Earth Sheep 己未</u>
- Abraham Lincoln (born February 12, 1809)
- Aristotle Onassis (born January 15, 1906)
- Donald Trump (born June 14, 1946)

<u>Yin Earth Ox 己丑</u>
- Sergey Brin (born August 21, 1973), Founder of Google

<u>Yang Fire Horse 丙午</u>
- Liang Qichao 梁啟超 (born February 23, 1873), Qing Dynasty scholar

<u>Yin Fire Sheep 丁未</u>
- Ronald Reagan (born February 6, 1911)
- Li Yuanhong 黎元洪 (born October 19,1864), the only man to be President of the Republic of China in Beijing twice, 1916-17 and 1922-23

Aa.2 Strategists (Duo Mei 多謀)
1) Yang Earth Rat 戊子
2) Yin Metal Snake 辛巳

These two groups of Day Pillars are highly intelligent individuals who make great strategists.

<u>Yin Metal Snake 辛巳</u>
- Ming Shizong 明神宗 (born September 16, 1507), the 11th Ming Emperor
- Zhang Tingyu 張延玉 (born October 29, 1672), Qing Dynasty official

<u>Yang Earth Rat 戊子</u>
- Deng Xiaoping 鄧小平 (born August 22, 1904), former Chinese Premier
- Lin Biao 林彪 (born December 5, 1907), Chinese

65

Communist Party military leader
- Sheng Xuanhuai 盛宣懷 (born November 4, 1844), Qing Dynasty Minister of Transportation

Aa.3 Smart Group of Ten (Shi Ling 十靈)
1) Yang Wood Dragon 甲辰
2) Yin Wood Pig 乙亥
3) Yang Fire Dragon 丙辰
4) Yin Fire Rooster 丁酉
5) Yang Earth Horse 戊午
6) Yang Metal Dog 庚戌
7) Yang Metal Tiger 庚寅
8) Yin Metal Pig 辛亥
9) Yang Water Tiger 壬寅
10) Yin Water Sheep 癸未

Those born on any of these ten days will be highly intelligent, extremely perceptive and adept.

The next three groups of Stem-Branch Pair Special Stars apply mainly to the Day Pillar, but they can also be applied to the Year, Month and Hour Pillars.

Ab.1 Red Light Pillars (Hong Yan 紅艷)
1) Yang Fire Tiger 丙寅
2) Yin Fire Sheep 丁未
3) Yin Water Sheep 癸未
4) Yin Metal Sheep 辛未
5) Yin Wood Sheep 乙未
6) Yang Wood Dog 甲戌
7) Yang Metal Dog 庚戌

These seven Red Light Pillars represent problematic romance, which in extreme cases, may cause harm to their own romantic relationships or marriages. It can even result in crimes of passion. Unlike the first group of Stem Branch pairs, these Red Light Pillars can also create problems when present in the Hour, Month or Year Pillars. However, their effect will be greatest when present in the Day Pillar.

If there is only one of these Red Light Pillars present in the Four Pillars chart, the harm is minimized. It would be of concern when the same Red Light Pillars is present in the chart of a person's partner or spouse. Jacqueline Kennedy Onassis (born July 28, 1929, 14:30 hours) had two Red Light Pillars in her chart. Her Yin Metal Sheep Pillar was also seen in the chart of President John F Kennedy (born May 29, 1917, 15:00 hours).

In 2002, the Red Light Pillar Yang Metal Dog was present in the Four Pillars charts of murder victim Laci Peterson (born May 4, 1975) and her killer - husband Scott Peterson (born October 24, 1972). For Laci, the Yang Metal Dog was her Day Pillar and for Scott, his Month Pillar.

Ab.2 Yin Yang Mismatch (Yin Cuo Yang Cha 陰錯陽差)

1) Yin Metal Rabbit 辛卯
2) Yang Water Dragon 壬辰
3) Yin Water Snake 癸巳
4) Yang Fire Horse 丙午
5) Yin Fire Sheep 丁未
6) Yang Earth Monkey 戊申
7) Yin Metal Rooster 辛酉
8) Yang Water Dog 壬戌
9) Yin Water Pig 癸亥
10) Yang Fire Rat 丙子
11) Yang Earth Tiger 戊寅
12) Yin Fire Ox 丁丑

Those born on these days will experience problematic relationships with their in-laws or spouses. The effects would be more pronounced if the Yin Yang Mismatch is the Day Pillar. If there is more than one Yin Yang Mismatch Pillar in a Four Pillars chart, it is better to maintain a diplomatic distance from the in-laws or have an arranged marriage so as to minimize conflicts.

Ab.3 Commanding or Bossy Pillars (Kui Gang 魁罡)

1) Yang Earth Dragon 戊辰
2) Yang Earth Dog 戊戌
3) Yang Metal Dragon 庚辰
4) Yang Metal Dog 庚戌
5) Yang Water Dragon 壬辰
6) Yang Water Dog 壬戌

Those born on these days are highly capable, extremely ambitious and highly motivated when it comes to achieving their goals. If there are three Commanding Pillars present in a chart (the Day Pillar must be included), then the individual will achieve much success and recognition. It is more auspicious when all three pillars are either the Dragon or Dog, as Commanding Pillars do not like to be clashed against, otherwise there may be health issues or mishaps.

Note that even if there is no Dragon Dog Clash within a chart that has Commanding Pillar(s), there will be Clash issues during the Dragon or Dog Luck Cycle, year, month, day or hour. Those with the Commanding Pillars in the Clash periods can take appropriate measures.

A person can attain success with two Commanding Pillars within the chart. With the onset of a third Commanding Pillar in the Luck Cycle or year, there will be even more success.

Professional basketball player Jeremy Lin 林書豪 (born August 23, 1988) has two Commanding Pillars in his chart (in the Day and Year Pillars). In 2012, the Yang Water Dragon year (another Commanding Pillar), he suddenly achieved recognition for his athletic prowess. Lin's chart is discussed in Appendix 7.

Unfortunately, the Commanding Pillars are more suited for men than women. Females born on a Commanding Pillar day insist on their point of view at all times and will not yield to others, especially their spouse. Women born on Commanding Pillar days can alleviate their situation by marrying late. Unusual illnesses may also occur in times of a Clash. Spirituality and religion are recommended for people with Clashes involving their Commanding Pillars.

B) Day Stem Special Stars

Table 4.1 shows the eight types of Special Stars that are determined by the Day Stem.

Table 4.1 Special Stars Based On Day Stem

Day Stems → / Stars	Yang Wood 甲	Yin Wood 乙	Yang Fire 丙	Yin Fire 丁	Yang Earth 戊	Yin Earth 己	Yang Metal 庚	Yin Metal 辛	Yang Water 壬	Yin Water 癸
Yang Nobleman Yang Gui 陽貴	Sheep 未	Monkey 申	Rooster 酉	Pig 亥	Ox 丑	Rat 子	Ox 丑	Tiger 寅	Rabbit 卯	Snake 巳
Yin Nobleman Yin Gui 陰貴	Ox 丑	Rat 子	Pig 亥	Rooster 酉	Sheep 未	Monkey 申	Sheep 未	Horse 午	Snake 巳	Rabbit 卯
Academic Wen Chang 文昌	Snake 巳	Horse 午	Monkey 申	Rooster 酉	Monkey 申	Rooster 酉	Pig 亥	Rat 子	Tiger 寅	Rabbit 卯
Study Hall Xue Tang 學堂	Pig 亥	Horse 午	Tiger 寅	Rooster 酉	Tiger 寅	Rooster 酉	Snake 巳	Rat 子	Monkey 申	Rabbit 卯
Red Light Hong Yan 紅艷	Horse 午	Horse 午	Tiger 寅	Sheep 未	Dragon 辰	Dragon 辰	Dog 戌	Rooster 酉	Rat 子	Monkey 申
Six Harmony Mentor Liu He Gui 六合貴	Yang Wood Rat 甲子 / Yang Wood Horse 甲午	Yin Wood 乙巳	Yang Fire Tiger 丙寅 / Yang Fire Dragon 丙辰	NA	Yang Earth 戊午		Yang Metal 庚午	Yin Metal 辛未	Yang Water Monkey 壬申	NA
Eating God Nobleman Gui Shi 貴食	Yang Fire Dragon 丙辰 / Yang Fire Tiger 丙寅 / Yin Fire Rooster 丁酉	Yin Fire Pig 丁亥 / Yin Fire Rat 丁子 / Yin Fire Rooster 丁酉	Yang Earth Rat 戊子 / Yang Earth Dragon 戊辰 / Yang Earth Horse 戊午	Yin Earth Snake 己巳 / Yin Earth Rat 己子 / Yin Earth Ox 己丑	Yang Metal Rat 庚子 / Yang Metal Rat 庚子 / Yin Earth 己丑	Yin Metal Snake 辛巳 / Yin Metal Pig 辛亥 / Yang Metal Monkey 庚申	Yang Water Rat 壬子 / Yang Water Dog 壬戌	Yin Water 癸亥 / Yin Water Snake 癸巳 / Yang Water 壬午	Yang Wood Monkey 甲申 / Yang Wood 甲子 / Yang Water Dog 壬戌	Yin Wood 乙丑 / Yin Wood Ox 乙丑 / Yin Wood Snake 乙巳
Harmony Nobleman Gui He 貴合	Yin Earth 己丑 / Ox 己丑 / Yin Earth Sheep 己未	Yang Metal Rat 庚子 / Yang Metal Monkey 庚申 / Yin Metal Pig 辛亥	Yin Metal Rooster 辛酉 / Pig 辛亥 / Yin Metal 辛亥	NA	Yang Water Rat 癸子 / Ox 癸丑 / Yang Water Sheep 癸未	Yang Wood Rat 甲子 / Z丑 / Yin Water Monkey 甲申			Yin Fire Snake 丁巳	NA

69

Using these Stars is relatively straightforward. For instance, those born on a Yang Wood day would have the Sheep as their Yang Nobleman Star, the Ox as their Yin Nobleman Star, the Snake as their Academic Star and so on.

The three Stars (1) Six Harmony Nobleman, (2) Eating God Nobleman and (3) Harmony Nobleman are present as Stem-Branch Pairs. For example, Yin Wood Day Masters have the Stem-Branch Pairs Yin Wood Snake and Yin Wood Ox as their Six Harmony Mentors.

Note that those born on the Yin Fire and Yin Water days lack a Special Star in two of the categories due to the lack of a Stem -Branch Pair that conforms to the required conditions of the pairing.

B1 Yang Nobleman and Yin Nobleman Stars (Yang Gui 陽貴, Yin Gui 陰貴)

These are based on your Day Stem. They are also known as Heavenly Nobleman Stars (Tian Yi Gui Ren 天乙貴人) and can be separated into the Yang and Yin Nobleman Stars. However, in real life, we do not deliberately differentiate our noblemen based on their gender. What is more important is to identify the days, months and years, as well as the position and direction pertaining to the Nobleman Stars. This will allow you to draw on the assistance of mentors. Cast your mind back to those who have extended a helping hand to you in the past. Check if they were born in the years, months, days or hours pertaining to the Nobleman Stars as determined by your Day Stem. Think about how these individuals have assisted you.

In challenging times, we can seek the advice or assistance of mentors or helpful individuals. While it may not be possible to find them in real life, we can always choose the Nobleman days from the *Ten Thousand Year Calendar*.

For instance, those born on a Yin Water day will have the Rabbit as their Nobleman Stars. The Rabbit day will be a Nobleman day, the Rabbit hour the Nobleman time and the East (75-105 degrees) represents the Nobleman direction or location. To seek out the Nobleman Stars, they can then pray towards the Nobleman direction or look out for those born in the year of the Rabbit. In terms of personal or home decoration, they can wear the Rabbit as a talisman or use decorations depicting the Rabbit.

So what is the actual impact of the Nobleman Stars on the individual and what is its accuracy? For those who have the Nobleman Stars present in their chart, it is not a guarantee of immediate success. Rather, it indicates accomplishment over their lifetime. Some charts that have obstacles or contrasting flows can still achieve success through the Nobleman Stars. Charts that have a clearly delineated flow may fail to achieve much in the absence of the Nobleman Stars. Princess Diana (born July 1, 1961, 15:45 hours) did not have the assistance of any Nobleman Stars and her good fortune and life were tragically short-lived.

Chinese politician Yuan Shikai 袁世凱 (born September 16, 1859) had a Follow the Resource chart. However, without the help of the Nobleman Stars, his attempts to start a new Empire were doomed. How did Jacqueline Kennedy Onassis (born July 28, 1929, 14:30 hours) manage to marry two highly influential and successful men? She had an auspicious chart with two Nobleman Stars flanking her Day Master in the Month and Hour Branches.

Chairman Mao Zedong 毛澤東 (born December 26, 1893,07:30 hours) had a Yin Fire Rooster Day Pillar. This means that he was sitting on both the Nobleman and the Academic Stars. Physicist Lee Tsung-Dao 李政道 (born November 24, 1926) has the Nobleman Stars present in the Month Pillar. Chairman Mao became the leader of China after fighting with his military opponents, while Lee Tsung-Dao overcame the struggle of having to abandon his academic studies and became one of youngest ever Nobel Prize Winners in history. President John F Kennedy (born May 29, 1917, 15:00 hours) had a Follow The Resource chart and attained success at a young age. Nevertheless, without the Nobleman Star, his success was short-lived.

The Nobleman Star is most vulnerable to Clashes as can be seen in the case of Senator Robert Kennedy (born November 20, 1925, 15:10 hours). He is a Yang Earth Day Master and the Ox and Sheep are his Nobleman Stars. There is an Ox present in his Year Pillar. He was assassinated on a Sheep day in the Sheep Luck Cycle, a time when his Ox Nobleman Star was clashed twice. Robert Kennedy's chart together with the flow of energy present at the time of his death is discussed in Chapter Nine.

B.2 Academic and Study Hall Stars (Wen Chang 文昌, Xue Tang 學堂)

Both the Academic and Study Hall Stars suggest success in examinations, writing and learning. The Study Hall Star indicates success and opportunities in study or the production of highly respected work. For those who have the Academic or Study Hall Stars in their chart, they will be good students. Even if the person is not too academic, he or she will still appear learned.

Like the Nobleman Stars, we can also identify and activate the Academic sectors and days to enhance our academic opportunities. For instance, we can work or study in the Academic sectors of our room or house. We can also place the animal corresponding to our Academic Star in the room where we work or study.

For example, a person born on a Yin Metal day will have the Rat as the Academic Star. The Rat sector and direction is the North, so the Northern sector of the home or business can be activated to improve academic success.

If there are no Academic or Study Hall Stars in a person's Four Pillars chart, their appearance in the Luck Cycle will bring forth success. Lee Tsung-Dao 李政道 won the Nobel Prize in 1957, the Yin Fire Rooster year, when both the Academic and Nobleman Stars were present in the Year Branch. It was hardly surprising that Lee achieved this level of success and recognition that year.

When the Academic or Study Hall Star contains an individual's Wealth element, he or she is likely to become wealthy through his or her talent. The Yang Earth Monkey 戊申 day is a good example. Some renowned individuals born on this day include

1) Zhang Zhidong 張之洞 (born September 4, 1847), Qing Dynasty politician
2) Mark Zuckerberg (born May 14, 1984)
3) Michael Dell (born February 23, 1965)

4) Samuel Tang 丁肇光 (born January 27, 1936), 1976 Nobel Prize Winner in Physics

5) Gordon Moore (born January 3, 1929), Founder of Intel

For these individuals, the Monkey is also located in the House of Spouse. This suggests that they will marry individuals who are not only talented but will also assist them in their lives.

B4 Red Light Star (Hong Yan 紅艷)

This Red Light Star refers to a Branch that is determined by the Day Stem. While it shares the effects of the Red Light Stem-Branch Pair discussed earlier, the difference is that the Red Light Pairs are not dependent on the Day Stem.

For example, if a person is born on a Yang Wood Day and has a Horse within their Four Pillars chart, he or she will have the Red Light Star and the associated problematic romances. They will also be highly charismatic and attractive, not necessarily a bad thing. It can create popular singers, movie stars, writers and even great leaders. The person will have to be careful with regard to matters of the heart in order to prevent any issues. Keep in mind that those with the Red Light Star have to work hard when it comes to their marriage, as romance can become stale easily.

B5 Six Harmony Nobleman Star (Liu He Gui 六合貴)

The Six Harmony Nobleman Star refers to a Stem-Branch Pair where the Stem sits on top of a Branch that combines with the Stem's Nobleman. Here are the steps:

Those born on a Yang Wood day would have the Ox and Sheep as their Nobleman Stars.

The Rat combines with the Ox and the Horse combines with the Sheep.

The Rat and Horse are the Six Harmony Combination Branches of the Yang Wood Day Stem.

Those born on the Yang Wood Rat and the Yang Wood Horse days are born on Six Harmony Mentor days.

The benefits of having the Six Harmony Nobleman Stem-Branch Pair will be greater than having the Nobleman in the Four Pillars chart. This is especially so in terms of wealth and good fortune during a person's middle age. The Six Harmony Nobleman Star has to be present in the Day Pillar to exert its positive influence. There are no effects if it is present in the other Pillars.

Table 4.1 illustrates the Six Harmony Mentor Stem-Branch Pairs for the Ten Stems. Note that the Nobleman for Yin Fire is the Rooster. The Dragon combines with the Rooster but the Dragon cannot combine with Yin Fire due to opposing polarities. Similarly, the Mentor for Yin Water is the Rabbit. It combines with the Dog. As Yin Water and the Dog are of opposite polarities they cannot combine together to form a Stem-Branch Pair. This means that there are no Six Harmony Nobleman Stem-Branch Pairs for those born on the Yin Fire or Yin Water days.

Those born on Six Harmony Nobleman days include:

1) Qi Jiguang 戚繼光 Yin Earth Snake 己巳, (born November 12, 1548), Ming Dynasty military general
2) Qing Taizong 清太宗 Yin Metal Pig 辛亥, (born November 28, 1592), 2nd Emperor of the Qing Dynasty
3) Zeng Guofan 曾國藩 Yang Fire Dragon 丙辰, (born November 21, 1811), Qing Dynasty scholar
4) Steve Jobs Yang Fire Dragon 丙辰, (born February 24, 1955)
5) Bill Clinton Yin Wood Ox 乙丑, (born August 19, 1946)
6) John F Kennedy Yin Metal Sheep 辛未, (born May 29, 1917)

B6 Eating God Nobleman Star (Gui Shi 貴食)

To derive the Eating God Nobleman Stem-Branch Pair, the steps are as follows:

Identify the Eating God of the Day Stem. For a Yang Wood Day Stem, the Eating God or Output element of the same polarity is Yang Fire.

The next step will be to identify the Nobleman Stars for the Eating God Yang Fire They are the Rooster and Pig.

These Nobleman Stars are of a different polarity with Yang Fire, so an additional step is required.

We then consider the Six Harmony Branches for the Rooster and Pig, which are the Dragon and the Tiger.

The Eating God Nobleman Stem-Branch Pairs for Yang Wood are Yang Fire Tiger and Yang Fire Dragon.

We will now consider the Eating God Nobleman Stem-Branch Pair for a Yin Metal Day Stem:

The Eating God (Output element of the same polarity) for a Yin Metal Day Stem is Yin Water.

The Nobleman Stars for Yin Water are Rabbit and Snake.

The Eating God Nobleman Stem-Branch Pairs for Yin Metal are Yin Water Rabbit and Yin Water Snake.

When the Eating God Nobleman Star is present in an individual's Four Pillars chart, he or she will have a good income over their entire lifetime. The ideal position for the Eating God Nobleman Stem-Branch Pair is the Month Pillar. When the Eating God Nobleman Stem-Branch Pairs are present in the Luck Cycle or year, there will be opportunities to generate wealth or seek a salary increase.

B7 Harmony Nobleman Star (Gui He 貴合)

To derive the Harmony Nobleman Stem-Branch Pair, the steps are as follows:

For a Yang Wood Day Stem, we first identify the Stem that it combines with, which is Yin Earth.

The Nobleman Stars for Yin Earth are the Ox and Sheep.

The Harmony Nobleman Stem-Branch Pair for a Yang Wood Day Stem would be Yin Earth Ox and Yin Earth Sheep.

The Harmony Nobleman Stem-Branch Pair influences a person's career and position. If the Harmony Nobleman Stem-Branch Pair is present in a Four Pillars chart, then the individual will have professional satisfaction and recognition throughout his or her life.

When the Harmony Nobleman Stem-Branch Pairs are present in the Luck Cycle or year, then the person would be able to obtain a job promotion or find a better position.

C) Month Branch Special Stars

Table 4.2 shows the Special Stars that are determined by the Month Branch.

Table 4.2 Special Stars Based on Month Branch

Stars / Month Branch →	Rat 子	Ox 丑	Tiger 寅	Rabbit 卯	Dragon 辰	Snake 巳	Horse 午	Sheep 未	Monkey 申	Rooster 酉	Dog 戌	Pig 亥
Heavenly Relief Tian Shu 天赦	Yang Wood Rat 甲子	Yang Wood Rat 甲子	Yang Earth Tiger 戊寅	Yang Earth Tiger 戊寅	Yang Earth Tiger 戊寅	Yang Wood Horse 甲午	Yang Wood Horse 甲午	Yang Wood Horse 甲午	Yang Earth Monkey 戊申	Yang Earth Monkey 戊申	Yang Earth Monkey 戊申	Yang Wood Rat 甲子
Heavenly Happiness Tian Xi 天喜	Sheep 未	Sheep 未	Dog 戌	Dog 戌	Dog 戌	Ox 丑	Ox 丑	Ox 丑	Dragon 辰	Dragon 辰	Dragon 辰	Sheep 未
Heavenly Virtue Tian De 天德	Snake 巳	Yang Metal 庚	Yin Fire 丁	Monkey 申	Yang Water 壬	Yin Metal 辛	Pig 亥	Yang Wood 甲	Yin Water 癸	Tiger 寅	Yang Fire 丙	Yin Wood 乙
Monthly Virtue Yue De 月德	Yang Water 壬	Yang Metal 庚	Yang Fire 丙	Yang Wood 甲	Yang Water 壬	Yang Metal 庚	Yang Fire 丙	Yang Wood 甲	Yang Water 壬	Yang Metal 庚	Yang Fire 丙	Yang Wood 甲

Example 4.1 Lily Chung (born July 3, 1937, between 11:00 and 13:00 hours)

Hour	Day	Month	Year
甲	辛	丙	丁
Yang Wood	Yin Metal	Yang Fire	Yin Fire
午	卯	午	丑
Horse	Rabbit	Horse	Ox

Chung is born in the Horse month. She has a Heavenly Relief Star Yang Wood Horse in the Hour Pillar, a Heavenly Happiness Star (Ox) in the Year Branch, and a Monthly Virtue Star Yang Fire in the Month Stem. She does not have the Heavenly Virtue Star in her chart, but she can expect to enjoy the benefit of one when it shows up in her Luck Cycle or during the year, month, day or hour. She can also look out for individuals who are born with a Pig in their chart as these individuals will protect her.

The benefits of the stars are as follows.

C1 Heavenly Relief Star (Tian Shu 天恕)

This Star confers a high degree of protection. If the Heavenly Relief Star is present in a person's chart, even if he or she had committed a criminal offense, they will receive a light sentence or may even be found not guilty of the crime. When the Heavenly Relief Star is present in the hour or day, it is useful for legal matters. So if you have a legal case, it would be beneficial to use the Heavenly Relief day. The Heavenly Relief Star can also be seen in the Hour, Month or Year Pillars.

C2 Heavenly Happiness Star (Tian Xi 天喜)

The Heavenly Happiness Star makes the person optimistic, highly satisfied with their life and generous to a fault. The person will not be involved with petty victories or details. When faced with challenges and obstacles, he or she will also work hard to resolve these issues. He or she will shoulder the responsibility and will not apportion blame onto others for any predicament. There are relatively few charts that contain either the Heavenly Relief or Heavenly Happiness Stars. When a chart contains both of these Stars, then the person will be blessed.

C3 Heavenly Virtue, Monthly Virtue (Tian De 天德, Yue De 月德)

These two Stars exert the same effect. The Heavenly Virtue Star represents the Yang type of protection that is stronger and more reliable. The Monthly Virtue Star is more Yin in nature and offers a gentler form of protection. Regardless of their polarity, both Stars can alleviate any negative influences. If you have these Stars present in your Four Pillars chart, then you will be kind, benevolent, generous and will receive assistance from the universe.

Successful and hardworking individuals tend to have one or both of these Stars. They include:

1) Chairman Mao Zedong 毛澤東 (born December 26, 1893)
2) Zhou Enlai 周恩來 (born March 5, 1898), the first Premier of the People's Republic of China
3) Yue Fei 岳飛 (born March 24, 1103), Southern Song Dynasty military general
4) Dwight D. Eisenhower (born October 14, 1890)
5) Napoleon Bonaparte (born August 15, 1769)

In more recent times, some of the Silicon Valley movers and shakers have either the Heavenly or Monthly Virtue Stars in their charts:

1) Bill Gates (born October 28, 1955)
2) Larry Ellison (born August 17, 1944)
3) Larry Page (born March 26, 1973)
4) Steve Jobs (born February 24, 1955)
5) Jeff Bezos (born January 12, 1964)

If the Virtue Stars are not present in your chart, you can still use them when they appear in the Luck Cycle or year. Keep in mind the ways in which the benefits manifest will be different for all of us, so we need to observe what happens to us when the Virtue Stars appear and note down the effects.

In the chart of Bill Gates, his Wealth element contains the Virtue Stars, so it is hardly surprising that he is known for his philanthropy. If the Power element is a positive element for the individual and contains the Virtue Stars, there will be professional recognition and awards. If the Resource element contains the Virtue Stars, the benefits will be magnified. For instance, Ming Emperor Ming Chengzu 明成祖 had the Wealth element present in his three Heavenly/Monthly Virtue Stars. His chart was discussed in Chapter Three, Example 3.1.

D) Year Branch Special Stars

The Special Stars derived from the Year Branch are seen in Table 4.3. Note that the Traveling Horse and Peach Blossom Stars can also be derived from the Day Branch.

Table 4.3 Special Stars Based on Year Branch

Year Branch / Stars	Rat 子	Ox 丑	Tiger 寅	Rabbit 卯	Dragon 辰	Snake 巳	Horse 午	Sheep 未	Monkey 申	Rooster 酉	Dog 戌	Pig 亥
Traveling Horse Yi Ma 驛馬	Tiger 寅	Pig 亥	Monkey 申	Snake 巳	Tiger 寅	Pig 亥	Monkey 申	Snake 巳	Tiger 寅	Pig 亥	Monkey 申	Snake 巳
Peach Blossom Tao Hua 桃花	Rooster 酉	Horse 午	Rabbit 卯	Rat 子	Rooster 酉	Horse 午	Rabbit 卯	Rat 子	Rooster 酉	Horse 午	Rabbit 卯	Rat 子
Isolation Gu Chen 孤辰	Tiger 寅	Tiger 寅	Snake 巳	Snake 巳	Snake 巳	Monkey 申	Monkey 申	Monkey 申	Pig 亥	Pig 亥	Pig 亥	Tiger 寅
Widow Gua Suo 寡宿	Dog 戌	Dog 戌	Ox 丑	Ox 丑	Ox 丑	Dragon 辰	Dragon 辰	Dragon 辰	Sheep 未	Sheep 未	Sheep 未	Dog 戌
Loss Sang Men 喪門	Tiger 寅	Rabbit 卯	Dragon 辰	Snake 巳	Horse 午	Sheep 未	Monkey 申	Rooster 酉	Dog 戌	Pig 亥	Rat 子	Ox 丑
Condolence Diao Ke 弔客	Dog 戌	Pig 亥	Rat 子	Ox 丑	Tiger 寅	Rabbit 卯	Dragon 辰	Snake 巳	Horse 午	Sheep 未	Monkey 申	Rooster 酉
Anxiety 元辰	Sheep 未	Monkey 申	Rooster 酉	Dog 戌	Pig 亥	Rat 子	Ox 丑	Tiger 寅	Rabbit 卯	Dragon 辰	Snake 巳	Horse 午
*Yin Male/ Yang Female	Snake 巳	Horse 午	Sheep 未	Monkey 申	Rooster 酉	Dog 戌	Pig 亥	Rat 子	Ox 丑	Tiger 寅	Rabbit 卯	Dragon 辰
*Yang Male/ Yin Female	Sheep 未	Monkey 申	Rooster 酉	Dog 戌	Pig 亥	Rat 子	Ox 丑	Tiger 寅	Rabbit 卯	Dragon 辰	Snake 巳	Horse 午

Example 4.2 Lily Chung (born July 3, 1937, between 11:00 and 13:00 hours)

Hour	Day	Month	Year
甲 Yang Wood	辛 Yin Metal	丙 Yang Fire	丁 Yin Fire
午 Horse	卯 Rabbit	午 Horse	丑 Ox

Based on the Year Branch Ox, Chung has a Peach Blossom Star (Horse) and the Loss Star (Rabbit). Based on the Day Branch Rabbit, the Yin Metal Day Master also has the Rat as a Peach Blossom Star. While there is no Rat present in the chart, the Rat can appear in the Luck Cycle, year or month. Of course, the effects of the Peach Blossom Star in these instances will be weaker. In the Snake or Pig Luck Cycles or years, Chung will travel more as they are her Travelling Horse Stars.

We will now consider the Stars mentioned in Table 4.3.

D1 Traveling Horse Star (Yi Ma 驛馬)

The Traveling Horse Star signifies movement such as shifting from one place to another, migration, changing jobs, traveling or other changes in lifestyle. When the Traveling Horse Star represents a positive element, the person will be intelligent and adaptable and will be proactive in his actions. When the Traveling Horse Star represents a negative element, the person may make the wrong move or lack perseverance. If a person's chart has the Traveling Horse Star, there will be always be activity and change in his or her life.

Consider the case of Nobel Prize winning molecular biologist Sidney Altman (born May 7, 1939). Born in a Rabbit year, his Traveling Horse Star (Snake) is present in his Month Pillar.

In 1960, Altman graduated from the Massachusetts Institute of Technology (MIT). In the following year 1961, he started graduate studies in Columbia University before leaving to study and work in Colorado in 1962. After receiving his Ph.D., Altman then embarked on research fellowships in Harvard University and Cambridge University in England before becoming an assistant professor at Yale University in 1971. In slightly more than a decade, he moved five times. In 1989 (the Yin Earth Snake year), another Traveling Horse year, Altman flew to Sweden to receive his Nobel Prize.

The effect of the Traveling Horse Star varies from chart to chart. When the Traveling Horse Star is positive, it brings with it job promotions, good news and opportunities. If the Traveling Horse Star is located together with the favorable Wealth element, there is the possibility of generating wealth quickly. If it is associated with the favorable Power element, there will be unexpected career opportunities. If the Traveling Horse Star belongs to a negative element, there will be hard work for little gain or benefit. When the Traveling Horse Star is located with the Isolation and Condolence Stars, there is the possibility of leaving home for little benefit.

We need to consider our two Traveling Horse Stars when they appear in the year and month. Note that the Traveling Horse Star may be paired with a different Stem. This means that the effects may be different each time. For Altman, the Traveling Horse Star was clearly positive.

Another point to consider: if we desire good fortune, we should always go with the flow of things. When the Traveling Horse Star approaches, even if there were no opportunities for moving, travel or a new job, we should still take advantage of this opportunity to renovate and redecorate our home, exercise more or take up a new sport or hobby. If we do nothing, the possibility of accidents or injury is increased. This may compel us to stay in a hospital, which is also a different environment from the one where we normally live.

D2 Peach Blossom Star (Tao Hua 桃花)

Traditional Chinese culture tends to take a conservative view on romantic relationships, which has given the Peach Blossom Star a negative image. This is especially so with regard to women, as it is associated with infidelity and bad marriages. For men, it suggests multiple extra-marital affairs. Do these stereotypes have any basis?

In modern times, a Peach Blossom Star is associated with good interpersonal skills and charisma. Individuals with a Peach Blossom Star are likely to be intelligent, generous,

83

sensitive, considerate of others and charismatic. These are qualities that are highly appreciated.

Many celebrities (actors, singers and authors) have the Peach Blossom Star:

1) Leslie Cheung 張國榮 (born September 12, 1956), Hong Kong singer and actor

2) Anita Mui 梅艷芳 (born October 10, 1963), Hong Kong singer and actress

3) Teresa Teng 鄧麗君 (born January 29,1953),Taiwanese singer

Peach Blossom Stars are popular among successful politicians, military men or intellectuals including:

1) Zhou Enlai 周恩來 (born March 5, 1898)

2) Xi Jiping 習近平 (born June 15, 1953), President of the People's Republic of China

3) Cai Yuanpei 蔡元培 (born January 11, 1868), Chinese educator

4) George Washington (born February 22, 1722)

5) Nikita Khruschev (born April 15, 1894)

6) Yu Youren 于右任 (born April 11, 1879), Republic of China politician

7) Liang Qichao 梁啟超 (born February 23, 1873)

8) Yue Fei 岳飛 (born March 24, 1103), Song Dynasty military general

9) Hai Rui 海瑞 (born January 23, 1514), Ming Dynasty official

10) Kangxi 康熙 (born May 4, 1564), Qing Dynasty Emperor

11) Yongzheng 雍正 (born December 13, 1678), Qing Dynasty Emperor

The Peach Blossom Star is most affected by Combinations, Punishment or Clash. These may result in relationship issues. To prevent any problems, we should note the years or months when this occurs and exercise self-control and restraint during these periods.

When the Peach Blossom Star is in the same Branch as the Nobleman Star and in the same Pillar as the Heavenly and

Monthly Virtue Stars, an auspicious configuration is formed. It signifies success and recognition. When the Peach Blossom and Academic Stars happen to be in the same branch, the person is likely to publish a bestseller.

D3 Isolation and Widow Stars (Gu Chen Gua Suo 孤辰寡宿)

These two Stars have similar qualities, so we can discuss them together. They both represent solitude, isolation from family members or being single throughout one's life. It also signifies contemplation and several Nobel Prize winners have one of these Stars. Men of the cloth tend to have the Widow Star. Do not be too concerned if you have one of these Stars in your chart as it may also represent academic success. However, if you have two or more of these Stars, the likelihood of isolating yourself is higher.

If these Stars are not present in your chart, but in the Luck Cycle or year, there is a likelihood of separation, divorce, migration and travel. When the Luck Cycle or year passes, the person's life will return to normal.

D4 Loss and Condolence Stars (Sang Men Diao Ke 喪門弔客)

These two Stars have similar effects and are discussed together. These Stars represent worry, stress, hardship and emotion. They also suggest the loss of someone close. If a person has two or more of these Stars in his or her chart, there is a tendency to suffer from melancholia and depression. If these Stars are present in a Luck Cycle or year, the likelihood of loss or stress is increased.

D5 Great Anxiety Star (Yuan Chen 元辰)

The Great Anxiety Star is associated with difficulties and obstacles that create fear or anxiety. When present in the Month and Day Pillars, the person will be constantly troubled by his or her partner or spouse. But when the Great Anxiety Star is paired up to form a Full or Partial Three Harmony Combination, it becomes highly auspicious. For example, for a man who has the Dragon as his Great Anxiety Star, he will enjoy good luck during the Monkey Luck Cycle, as the Dragon and Monkey pair up to form a Partial Three Harmony

Water Combination. This process applies to the external cosmic flows (year, month, day and hour) at any time.

When a person sits on the Great Anxiety Star in the Day Pillar, he or she can use the *Ten Thousand Year Calendar* to verify what happens in the years, months or days when there is a Combination. For instance, for those born on a Dragon day when the Dragon happens to be the Great Anxiety Star, note what happens on the Monkey, Rat and Rooster years, months and days. You can also use representations or images of the Combination animals in your home to stimulate the positive effects of the Great Anxiety Star.

Conclusion

In our study of Four Pillars Astrology, understanding these Special Stars is one of the more straightforward steps. By understanding their effects, we can apply them in Date Selection to enhance our chances of success.

Chapter Five - Standard Charts

One of the standard procedures of science is to classify objects into specific categories. This also applies to metaphysics when the complex lives of individuals are being analyzed according to a multitude of categories.

There are two main energy flows:
1. Those who are able to stand on their own.
2. Those who rely on others.

The first type of energy flow is found in Standard Charts and will be discussed in this chapter. There are also four subgroups of charts within Standard Charts. For example, there are Dominant charts and Strong charts which possess the ability to achieve success in life. There are also charts that have mixed energies. For these individuals, success will be more challenging and they will have to work harder to achieve their aims. At times, hard work does not necessarily translate into payoffs.

The second type of energy flow is found in Follow and Transformational charts. Support from other sources is required as they are regarded as feeble or extremely feeble. When these individuals receive assistance from others, they will obtain the rewards. We can characterize these charts as being like young children who need supervision and help from stronger sources. When assistance is provided, these charts are considered to be of medium to high quality. When the energy present in the chart is mixed, i.e. like that of teenagers, they can only rebel against their elders and are unable to achieve much themselves. These charts are therefore considered low quality.

The flow of the chart and the presence of any obstacles are taken into account when classifying and characterizing charts. In addition, there are also charts that carry special qualities. They will be discussed in Chapter Seven.

The main source of strength for Standard Charts is from themselves. We will now look at the various categories that fall within the Standard Charts.

A) Dominant Charts

The Dominant Charts are the strongest of the Standard Charts, which is why they are usually capable and successful. These charts are often associated with heads of state and world leaders who are renowned for their courage, ambition, foresight, restraint, responsibility and generosity.

To qualify as a Dominant Chart, there must be a Three Harmony Combination (either Partial or Full) or a Directional Combination present in the Branches that is of the same element as the Day Master. The criterion for Dominant Earth Charts is different as there is no specific Three Harmony Earth Combination. This is discussed in Example 5.5.

The Dominant Chart describes a ruler towering over his subjects and demanding obedience with a firm hand. Below are several examples of Dominant Charts:

Example 5.1 Liang Qichao 梁啟超 (born February 23, 1873, between 11:00 and 13:00 hours), Chinese scholar and political reformist

Hour	Day	Month	Year
癸	丙	甲	癸
Yin Water	Yang Fire	Yang Wood	Yin Water
巳	午	寅	酉
Snake	Horse	Tiger	Rooster

A Partial Three Harmony Fire Combination of Tiger and Horse is present in Liang's Month and Day Pillars. This makes his Yang Fire Day Master Dominant.

Example 5.2 Larry Page (born March 26, 1973), founder of Google

Hour	Day	Month	Year
?	辛	乙	癸
	Yin Metal	Yin Wood	Yin Water
?	酉	卯	丑
	Rooster	Rabbit	Ox

The Yin Metal Day Master has a Partial Three Harmony Metal Combination of Rooster and Ox. They are able to combine in spite of the Rabbit present in the Month Pillar.

Example 5.3 Warren Buffett (born August 30, 1930, 15:00 hours)

Hour	Day	Month	Year
戊	壬	甲	庚
Yang Earth	Yang Water	Yang Wood	Yang Metal
申	子	申	午
Monkey	Rat	Monkey	Horse

The Yang Water Day Master has a Partial Three Harmony Water Combination of Monkey and Rat. In this case, there is one more Monkey to reinforce the Partial Combination. While this makes it more powerful, it is still not as powerful as a Full Three Harmony Combination. His Spouse Palace, the Rat, is caught between the two Monkeys. They compete to pair up with his Rat which disrupted his marriage.

Example 5.4 Ted Turner (born November 19, 1938, 08:50 hours)

Hour	Day	Month	Year
庚	乙	癸	戊
Yang Metal	Yin Wood	Yin Water	Yang Earth
辰	卯	亥	寅
Dragon	Rabbit	Pig	Tiger

The Yin Wood Day Master has the Directional Wood Combination of Tiger, Rabbit and Dragon. There is also a Partial Three Harmony Wood Combination of Rabbit and Pig. This is a clear Dominant Wood chart. Turner will also reap extra benefits from the presence of an additional Sheep (completes the Wood Three Harmony Combination) or Tiger (combines with the Pig to form a Six Harmony Combination, leaving the Full Directional Wood Combination intact). Turner's chart will be discussed in detail further on in this chapter.

Example 5.5 Aristotle Onassis (born January 20, 1906, 10:00 hours)

Hour	Day	Month	Year
己	己	己	乙
Yin Earth	Yin Earth	Yin Earth	Yin Wood
巳	未	丑	巳
Snake	Sheep	Ox	Snake

The Yin Earth Day Master has six other earth components or characters in the chart. Onassis's chart will also be discussed further on in this chapter.

The five Dominant charts mentioned above are chosen because each represents a Dominant flow of one of the five elements. Apart from Aristotle Onassis's Dominant Earth chart, the other Day Masters have a Combination involving their Self element within the Branches of their chart in the form of the Full or Partial Three Harmony Combination or the Directional Combination. The Six Harmony Combinations may also lead to a Dominant chart, but you will need to verify with the individual's life events.

Dominant Earth

To ascertain a Dominant Earth chart is more difficult, as ideally, it needs to have all four Earth Branches, i.e. Ox, Dragon, Sheep and Dog. This is extremely rare.

It is only from my experience of having done multiple readings that I can identify a Dominant Earth chart with confidence. I will then verify this by analyzing events from the individual's past. In the case of Aristotle Onassis, his Dominant Earth chart is fairly clear. He is born in the Ox month, a time when the earth energy is strong. The other earth components also work together. There is no wood Stem or Branch directly adjacent to the Day Master to weaken or challenge the earth. The earth in his chart has the support of the season and the flow. This explains why it is a Dominant Earth chart.

Looking at the life events of Aristotle Onassis, we can see that he suffered misfortune in the years when the energy of wood was strong. Onassis paid a heavy fine of several million dollars at the start of 1954 (Yang Wood Horse year). Onassis died in 1975 (Yin Wood Rabbit year) during a wood month. The worst enemy for a Dominant Earth chart is the Power element wood.

For Dominant charts, the useful element is the Self element. The next best element is the element that empowers the Self element, i.e. the Resource element. Example 5.1 Liang Qichao 梁啟超 has a Dominant Fire chart, so his useful element is fire. Wood produces fire, so Liang's next best element is the Resource element wood. His negative element is the Power element water as it destroys fire. Since fire is vulnerable to water, the Output or Children element earth is crucial in blocking the water in order to protect fire. Earth is also a favorable element.

For Example 5.2 Larry Page, his best elements are the Self or Sibling element metal and the Resource element earth. As Page has only two of the Three Harmony Metal Branches in his chart, he requires a Snake in the Luck Cycle or year to complete the Full Metal Three Harmony Combination of Snake, Rooster and Ox. Page's best animal is the Snake.

Example 5.3 Warren Buffett's best elements are the Self or Sibling element water and the Resource element metal. His worst element is the Power element earth. In 2012 (Yang Water Dragon year), the full Three Harmony Water Combination of Monkey, Rat and Dragon was formed. The Dragon is a highly favorable animal for him as it completes the Three Harmony Water Combination.

We will now analyze the chart of Ted Turner (born November 19, 1938, 08:50 hours) in detail, so as to understand the effects of positive and negative elements.

Example 5.4 Ted Turner (born November 19, 1938, 08:50 hours)

Hour	Day	Month	Year
庚	乙	癸	戊
Yang Metal	Yin Wood	Yin Water	Yang Earth
辰	卯	亥	寅
Dragon	Rabbit	Pig	Tiger

6	16	26	36	46	56	66	76
甲	乙	丙	丁	戊	己	庚	辛
Yang Wood	Yin Wood	Yang Fire	Yin Fire	Yang Earth	Yin Earth	Yang Metal	Yin Metal
子	丑	寅	卯	辰	己	午	未
Rat	Ox	Tiger	Rabbit	Dragon	Snake	Horse	Sheep

The Yin Wood Day Master is born in the Pig month when water and wood are strong. The Full Directional Wood Combination (Tiger, Rabbit and Dragon) is also present. There is a Yin Water Month Stem to water the plants and trees. There is also a Partial Three Harmony Wood Combination (Rabbit and Pig) which needs a Sheep to complete the Combination. In 1991 (Yin Metal Sheep year), Turner became Time Magazine's Man of the Year.

With regard to marriage, a Combination between the Branch of the Year and the Branch in the House of Spouse suggests a good opportunity for a strong relationship. In 1991, Tuner married actress Jane Fonda. It was his third marriage and lasted a decade. Apart from the Sheep, the other positive animals for him are the Rabbit and Pig. In 1980, when he was 42 years old in the second year of the Rabbit Luck Cycle, Tuner established CNN, which became the leading global cable news provider.

We will now consider the effects of the Power element metal, the element that controls wood. Turner's father shot himself when Turner was 24. This happened during the Ox cycle when metal was strong. Due to his father's sudden death, Turner had to take over the family business. He also left Brown University during this period and did not complete his degree. Towards the end of this Luck Cycle, Turner also ended his first marriage. Note that his marriage to Jane Fonda ended in 2001 (Yin Metal Snake year), another year when the negative metal element was strong.

Metal is not the only negative element. The Wealth element earth controls the Resource element water, interfering with the growth of wood. This makes it problematic. Turner's second marriage ended in 1988 (Yang Earth Dragon year), when thick earth prevented water from flowing. As a result, his wood was injured.

So how does a Dominant Wood person protect himself from metal? When the metal element is strong, there are two ways of reducing its strength:

1) Through water, which metal produces and
2) Through fire, which controls metal.

Water and fire clash with each other, so these two elements should not be used simultaneously. Symbols and colors associated with these elements can be used in furnishings or the person's wardrobe. At times when the metal energy is strong, the person should be low key and avoid making major decisions. Such is the importance of going with the flow of universal energy in order to minimize any damage to ourselves.

Not every Dominant Wood chart will have the same development when metal is encountered. Some may fall sick while others may suffer financial loss. Regardless, the results are negative.

For the other Dominant charts, the presence of the negative element will create problems. For Aristotle Onassis, his Dominant Earth chart is threatened by wood. Onassis fell sick in 1974 (Yang Wood Tiger year) and passed away in 1975 (Yin Wood Rabbit year).

Warren Buffett's Dominant Water chart is vulnerable to earth. When he went through the earth Luck Cycles, Buffett left Wharton University and transferred to the University of Nebraska, Lincoln. In another earth Luck Cycle, he separated from his wife. As can be seen, the negative effects during the bad years differ from person to person.

To alleviate the negative energy of problematic years, you can use Feng Shui in your home or office, exercise self-restraint and avoid high risk activities. The 2010 plane crash that killed the Polish President and other government officials occurred on a day that clashed with the charts of several of the passengers. The President's twin brother decided not to travel on that day and escaped the crash. On the Clash days, it is preferable not to travel.

Ted Turner's misfortune associated with metal is manifested in his marriages. Is there any way someone in a similar situation could avoid a divorce? The person could always separate from his or her partner in a difficult year and wait until the negative metal energy wanes before living together again. The individual can also use colors symbolizing the fire element such as red and avoid using colors that represent metal such as white, silver, grey and gold.

B) Strong Charts: Competitive/Sibling Rivalry Charts

Competitive or Sibling Rivalry charts fulfill the following conditions:

1. There are other components or elements similar to the Day Master within the chart. For example, if the Day Master is metal and there are two or three metal Stems and Branches. Or if the Day Master is wood and there are several wood Stems and Branches present in the chart.
2. Unlike the Dominant charts, there are no Combinations and similar Stems and Branches are scattered throughout the chart without any pattern.
3. If the Day Master is supported by the Month Branch, the competition is stronger.

These types of charts are characterized by the same element (Sibling or Rob Wealth) competing with the Day Master. Life will be challenging and full of obstacles.

To understand the Competitive chart, we will now consider the following two examples:

Example 5.6 Female (born August 25, 1954, 05:30 hours)

Hour	Day	Month	Year
乙	癸	壬	甲
Yin Wood	Yin Water	Yang Water	Yang Earth
卯	丑	申	午
Rabbit	Ox	Monkey	Horse

6	16	26	36	46	56	66	76
辛	庚	己	戊	丁	丙	乙	甲
Yin Metal	Yang Metal	Yin Earth	Yang Earth	Yin Fire	Yang Fire	Yin Wood	Yang Wood
未	午	巳	辰	卯	寅	丑	子
Sheep	Horse	Snake	Dragon	Rabbit	Tiger	Ox	Rat

She is a Yin Water Day Master born in the Monkey month when metal and water are strong. This person possesses the qualities of water: she is intelligent, good looking, courageous and has the drive to succeed. Unfortunately, her road to success is filled with obstacles as there are two Yang Water Stems in her chart (one hidden in the Monkey). They act as Rivals and Competitors for everything she seeks in her life, especially in wealth and romance. This is a Competitive or Sibling Rivalry Water chart.

The useful elements for this person will be those that weaken the Competitors. Wood (the Output element) drains water, so wood is a useful element. Earth (the Power element) controls the water Rivals and is another useful element. Metal (the Resource element) not only produces her Water Day Master but also strengthens her Competitors. It is therefore negative. The Wealth element fire is a focus of competition amongst the Rivals. It is also considered problematic. Water represents her Rivals and causes issues.

This individual obtained a degree in bio-technology and after saving for a few years, she acquired a gas station. However, the profits from her business went into supporting her three children who were young adults at that time. In 1992 (Yang Water Monkey year) when she was 38, this lady suffered considerable financial losses when a joint business venture with her husband collapsed. Fortunately, she was in the favorable Yang Earth Luck Cycle and was able to recover from this setback.

95

In her early 40s during the Dragon Luck Cycle, the Dragon combined with the Monkey in her chart to form a Partial Three Harmony Water Combination. This converted her into a Dominant Water Self. She managed to acquire another gas station and purchased a large home in a prestigious neighborhood.

However, in her late 40s during the Yin Fire Luck Cycle (when the Water Rivals competed with her Day Master for the Wealth element fire), she started having multiple health issues that did not respond to treatment. Her husband also commenced divorce proceedings and clamored for half of her assets in 2004 (Yang Wood Monkey year). There was an additional water Rival competing for her Wealth. Once again, she was left with financial losses and had to give up one of her gas stations.

We can see that issues arose for this person when Rivals represented by water appeared to compete for her Wealth. The best Luck Cycle of her life was when she became a Dominant Water Self as a result of the Three Harmony Water Combination.

Coping With The Unfavorable Periods

Competitive charts are in essence extremely strong charts. This suggests that the incidence of having unusual illnesses is high. The constant fighting between Rivals may manifest as mental illness, premature births and emotional breakdowns, especially on the days, months or years when the Competitor or the Wealth element is present.

Here are two strategies to consider for those with Competitive charts:

1) Use the *Ten Thousand Year Calendar* to identify auspicious and problematic days. For example, those with Competitive Metal charts should avoid metal and wood days. This refers to days when the Rooster, Yang Metal, Yin Metal, Yang Wood, Tiger, Rabbit, Sheep and Pig are present. During these times, exercise caution and self-restraint with regard to spending and exercise or study more. To maximize the positive days when one becomes Dominant, i.e. the Snake or Ox days, make important decisions on these days. You can also consider

wearing talismans of the Ox and Snake or use their images within your home.

2) Use the relationships between the five elements to reduce the energy of metal. Water weakens metal and fire controls metal. Note that as water and fire are in conflict, they cannot be used simultaneously. You can use water (blue, black) or fire colors (red, orange, purple, pink) in your furnishings and clothing. Avoid using white, gray, silver, gold or green.

Example 5.7 Friedrich Nietzsche (born October 15, 1844, died August 25, 1900), German Philosopher

Hour	Day	Month	Year
丁	戊	甲	甲
Yin Fire	Yang Earth	Yang Wood	Yang Wood
巳	辰	戌	辰
Snake	Dragon	Dog	Dragon

8	18	28	38	48
乙	丙	丁	戊	己
Yin Wood	Yang Fire	Yin Fire	Yang Earth	Yin Earth
亥	子	丑	寅	卯
Pig	Rat	Ox	Tiger	Rabbit

Friedrich Nietzsche was an extremely influential German philosopher. He remained single throughout his life and suffered from various illnesses and maladies. While his contribution to philosophy is universally recognized, he was plagued by mental illness during his life and finally succumbed to pneumonia. When Nietzche was stricken by ill health, he required his mother and sister to care for him.

The Yang Earth Day Master is born in the Dog month when earth is strong. There are four other earth Branches present in the chart which suggests a strong presence of earth. The presence of two Yang Wood Stems prevents it from becoming a Dominant Earth chart. The constant pressure of wood on the earth Branches categorizes it as a Competitive Earth chart.

The Yang Wood Stem is present in the position of the father. When Nietzsche was only five years old, his father died at the age of 30 with what was then referred to as softening of the brain. Nietzsche inherited his father's genes and also ended up with mental illness.

A Competitive Earth chart is most vulnerable to the presence of Competitors and the Resource element. This means that issues arise when earth and fire are present. The Wealth Luck Cycle is also problematic as it becomes a focus of conflict amongst the Rivals.

Problems started for Nietzsche in the Rat Luck Cycle between the ages of 23 and 27 as water represented the Wealth element for the Yang Earth Day Master. The Wealth element stimulated the other earth Rivals within his chart to fight for it. Competitive charts find it difficult to accumulate wealth due to the constant presence of Rivals.

The Rat Luck Cycle proved to be a time of misfortune for Nietzsche. In 1868 (Yang Earth Dragon year) at the age of 24, two other earth Rivals were introduced via the year, thereby bringing the total of earth influences in his chart to seven. As a result, he was injured in an accident. In 1870 (Yang Metal Horse year) at the age of 26, the fire and earth elements were also strong. Nietzsche had to leave his teaching position due to his illness and this resulted in a loss of income.

Nietzsche's best element is metal which reduces the strength of earth. Unfortunately, after the age of 28, only fire and earth Luck Cycles followed. In 1879 (Yin Earth Rabbit year) during the Ox Luck Cycle, Nietzsche retired from teaching at 35.

At 38, Nietzsche entered the Yang Earth Luck Cycle and his emotional state deteriorated further. In 1883 (Yin Water Sheep year) when he was 39, six Yang Earth components (five within his chart and one in the Luck Cycle) attempted to combine with the Yin Water Wealth element present in the year and a relationship ended. His Spouse element (Wealth) was taken away by his Rivals. On January 6, 1889, he had a nervous breakdown:

Hour	Day	Month	Year
?	壬 Yang Water	乙 Yin Wood	戊 Yang Earth
?	午 Horse	丑 Ox	子 Rat

On this day, there were three earth components (Competitors) fighting for the two water components (Wealth).

Nietzsche passed away as a result of pneumonia on August 25, 1900.

Hour	Day	Month	Year
?	庚 Yang Metal	甲 Yang Wood	庚 Yang Metal
?	午 Horse	申 Monkey	子 Rat

On this day, the Rat and Monkey combined with the two Dragons in his chart to produce water. This created significant amounts of Wealth in which the Yang Earth Rivals in his chart fought over. With the Yang Earth Rivals fighting in his chart, his Yang Earth Day Master was unable to fend off much of the competition. On the Yang Metal day (metal represents the lungs), the large amount of water entered his lungs, which contributed to the failure of his breathing organs.

These two examples of Competitive or Sibling Rivalry charts illustrates the conflicts within. It would be incorrect to assume that all Competitive charts have such challenging lives. In reality, many individuals with Competitive charts do well in life as they are more ambitious and have a tendency to stand by their beliefs and fight for them. Physically, they can also be more attractive.

If the Day Stem within a Competitive chart is stronger than the other Rivals, then he or she will be able to triumph over adversity and achieve a degree of success. As those with Competitive charts are subjected to many challenges and battles throughout their lives, they are especially vulnerable to illnesses in general, including depression.

Here is an example where the Day Master is stronger than the other Rivals within the chart:

Example 5.8 Alexandra Manley (born June 30, 1964), former wife of Prince Joachim of Denmark

Hour	Day	Month	Year
?	庚 Yang Metal	庚 Yang Metal	甲 Yang Wood
?	戌 Dog	午 Horse	辰 Dragon

Alexandra Manley is of English-Chinese parentage and was born in Hong Kong.

The Day Master is Yang Metal and there is another Yang Metal in the Month Pillar. This is considered a Competitive Metal chart. Fortunately, the Yang Metal Day Stem is on top of a Dog and receives support from the earth and metal present within it. The other Yang Metal is under attack from the fire within the Horse underneath it and is not able to offer much resistance. The Day Master can easily attain wealth and status in life.

In 1995 (Yin Wood Pig year), the Yin Wood that year combined away the Yang Metal Competitor in the Month Pillar. This was the year that she married Denmark's Prince Joachim.

After Manley's marriage ended in divorce in 2005 (Yin Wood Rooster year), she remarried in 2007 (Yin Fire Pig year).

Here are two more examples for readers to analyze:

Example 5.9 Princess Margaret of England (born August 21, 1930, 21:22 hours)

Hour	Day	Month	Year
癸 Yin Water	癸 Yin Water	甲 Yang Wood	庚 Yang Metal
亥 Pig	卯 Rabbit	申 Monkey	午 Horse

The Monkey Month Branch contains Yang Water, a Rival. Can you explain why she divorced in 1978 and passed away due to a stroke on February 9, 2002, 06:30 hours?

Example 5.10 Clark Gable (born February 1, 1901, 05:30 hours)

Hour	Day	Month	Year
庚	辛	己	庚
Yang Metal	Yin Metal	Yin Earth	Yang Metal
寅	亥	丑	子
Tiger	Pig	Ox	Rat

The Yin Metal Day Stem is sitting on the Wealth element. Gable was married five times. Is it due to the wood or metal within his chart? What is the reason for this?

C) Mixed Energies Charts: Strong Enough Not To Compete, Weak Enough To Require Resources

Charts in this category are not Dominant but are not too feeble either. The main characteristic is that the Resource element is offering a degree of protection and support. For instance, a Water Day Master will have metal within the chart, while a Wood Day Master will have water in the chart and so on. While these charts may contain obstacles and hurdles, they are still able to recover from any setbacks through the support of the Resource element. As there is an absence of Competitors, these individuals are determined, self-confident and secure.

Example 5.11 Chiang Kai Shek 蔣介石 (born October 31, 1887, 12:20 hours), former President of the Republic of China

Hour	Day	Month	Year
庚	己	庚	丁
Yang Metal	Yin Earth	Yang Metal	Yin Fire
午	巳	戌	亥
Horse	Snake	Dog	Pig

8	18	28	38	48	58	68	78
己	戊	丁	丙	乙	甲	癸	壬
Yin Earth	Yang Earth	Yin Fire	Yang Fire	Yin Wood	Yang Wood	Yin Water	Yang Water
酉	申	未	午	巳	辰	卯	寅
Rooster	Monkey	Sheep	Horse	Snake	Dragon	Rabbit	Tiger

The Yin Earth Day Master is born in the Dog month, a time when earth is strong. The Snake and Horse in the Day and Hour Pillars also contain earth. While it appears as though it is a Competitive Earth chart, the Combination between the Horse in the Hour Pillar and the Dog in the Month Pillar form fire which produces earth. The Horse and Dog, which were previously Competitors, are now converted into Resources. Chiang is highly intelligent and resourceful. He had the ability to convert his enemies into friends which allowed him to thrive in a hostile environment.

The Yin Fire present in the Year Stem also acts a Resource for the Yin Earth Day Master. The two Yang Metals present in the Month and Hour Pillars means that the Hurting Officer or Output element is prominent. This allowed Chiang to be a charismatic leader.

With the use of the Resource element fire, Chiang was able to battle against the Japanese and later the Communists for 8 years from 1937 to 1945. In the Snake Luck Cycle (from 1940 to 1945), the Resource element fire was still present to offer support even though the Snake Luck Cycle clashed with the Pig in the Year Pillar.

The Resource element was prominent in Chiang's youth and it allowed him to become a military leader early in life. When he was 62 in 1949 (Yin Earth Ox year), the Dragon Luck Cycle clashed with the Dog and his Resource element fire was destroyed. The chart became full of Competitors. Chiang lost control of the Chinese mainland to Mao Zedong.

Chiang's chart used the Resource element and issues arose when it was damaged.

Below is the chart of Abraham Lincoln for readers to analyze. He is also a chart that uses the Resource element. In the Dog Luck Cycle, Lincoln achieved success. Do you know why?

Example 5.12 Abraham Lincoln (born February 12, 1809, 06:54 hours, died April 15, 1865)

Hour	Day	Month	Year
丁	己	丙	己
Yin Fire	Yin Earth	Yang Fire	Yin Earth
卯	未	寅	巳
Rabbit	Sheep	Tiger	Snake

3	13	23	33	43	53
乙	甲	癸	壬	辛	庚
Yin Wood	Yang Wood	Yin Water	Yang Water	Yin Metal	Yang Metal
丑	子	亥	戌	酉	申
Ox	Rat	Pig	Dog	Rooster	Monkey

D) Mixed Energies Charts: Weak Charts Lacking Resources

Some Four Pillars charts have mixed energies and lack a clear useful element. Such individuals will lack confidence and ability. Regardless of their social status or financial situation, they may find it difficult to attain success. However, with favorable Luck Cycles they can enjoy more comfortable lives.

Example 5.13 Female (born December 17, 1960, 18:00 hours)

Hour	Day	Month	Year
癸	己	戊	庚
Yin Water	Yin Earth	Yang Earth	Yang Metal
酉	卯	子	子
Rooster	Rabbit	Rat	Rat

The Yin Earth Day Self is born in the Rat month in winter. There are three water and two metal components in this chart, with an absence of the Resource element fire. Earth is weakened by metal and overwhelmed with water. Yin Earth can be likened to mud and it is not able to stand up by itself. This means the individual needs to rely on others. This will allow it to be a Follow chart, which in this scenario is considered favorable.

Unfortunately, there is a Yang Earth Competitor adjacent to the Yin Earth Day Master. This prevents it from following the other elements in the chart. This chart becomes a Standard chart and is considered weak without much capability. In reality, this person is attractive but stubborn, lacks confidence and is unable to support herself financially. She requires the support of her husband and in-laws.

The Rabbit in the House of Spouse is under attack from the Rooster in the Hour Pillar. She has a difficult marriage, as her husband has an extra-marital relationship.

E) Mixed Energies Charts: At The Borderline of Being Able or Unable to Follow the Prevalent Element

Example 5.14 John F. Kennedy Jr. (born November 25, 1960, 00:20 hours)

Hour	Day	Month	Year
庚	丁	丁	庚
Yang Metal	Yin Fire	Yin Fire	Yang Metal
子	巳	亥	子
Rat	Snake	Pig	Rat

4	14	24	34	44
戊	己	庚	辛	壬
Yang Earth	Yin Earth	Yang Metal	Yin Metal	Yang Water
子	丑	寅	卯	辰
Rat	Ox	Tiger	Rabbit	Dragon

John F. Kennedy Jr. was a handsome and well-educated member of a highly prominent family. He had all the opportunities in life, so why was his life cut short? Why did he have little to show in his life even when he approached 40? His chart is a classic example of a second generation scion, whose good looks and sophistication distracted others from focusing on his lack of achievement and ability.

The Yin Fire Day Master is born in the Pig month in winter. Fire is extremely weak and cannot lead its life. To make matters worse, there are two water and two metal components in his chart. Metal empowers water and these two elements surround the Day Master, further enfeebling the fire. The Fire Day Master has to follow or surrender to the metal and water for protection and provision. This should make a good case for a comfortable life.

Unfortunately, another Yin Fire in the Month Pillar and a Fire hidden in the Snake (House of Spouse) threaten the Follow configuration. The wood in the Month Pillar (Pig) strengthens his Yin Fire Day Master and gives him a false sense of confidence. It allows Kennedy to believe in himself even though he lacked the actual skills and ability to carry out what he envisioned.

The conflict within the chart causes the individual to be in a predicament. The person lacks a clear direction in life, yet wishes for the best to come without effort. Individuals with contrasting elemental flows in their charts tend to be physically attractive, persuasive, slick and clever but not wise. As the Day Master is weak, the person will lack the ability to plan in detail and the patience to carry out plans to their conclusion. The bottom line is that metal and water are slightly ahead and they guide him in his life as useful elements. Wood, earth and fire are his negative elements.

Upon examining his life events, we can see how these elements worked together. Up till he was three years old, Kennedy enjoyed a good life and lived like a prince in the White House. The significant metal and water energies from the year flows suppressed the fire and wood elements in his chart. This created a Follow the Power element water chart.

On November 22 1963, Kennedy's father was assassinated. Let us consider the flow.

Hour	Day	Month	Year
庚 Yang Metal	己 Yin Earth	癸 Yin Water	癸 Yin Water
午 Horse	己 Snake	亥 Pig	卯 Rabbit

There was a Partial Three Harmony Wood Combination (from the Pig and Rabbit in the Month and Year Pillar) which was supported by the two Yin Water Stems. It was also an earth day and fire hour. All his negative elements were present at the time of this catastrophic event. At age 4, Kennedy entered the Yang Earth Luck Cycle which controlled the favorable element water.

In 1968 (Yang Earth Monkey year), the Monkey in the year joined the Rat in his Year Pillar to form a Partial Three Harmony Water Combination. Kennedy's mother Jacqueline married the Greek shipping magnate Aristotle Onassis. For the five years during the Rat Luck Cycle, he lived comfortably in Greece and enjoyed the benefits of the water flow.

In 1975 (Yin Wood Rabbit year), his stepfather Onassis died and once again the Rabbit year took away a father figure in his life. Then came the Yin Earth Luck Cycle, another difficult period as the favorable water element was controlled.

The Ox Luck Cycle from the age of 19 to 23 was possibly the happiest time of Kennedy's life. The Ox combined with the Pig and Rat present in his chart to form the Directional Water Combination. The Yang Wood hidden within the Pig was converted into water and the threat presented by wood was temporarily removed. Kennedy was able to become a Follow the Power (water) chart.

During this Luck Cycle, he graduated from Brown University and continued that momentum in the Yang Metal Luck Cycle that followed. With the positive metal flow, Kennedy worked in the New York City Office of Business Development from 1984 to 1986. However, he left his position in 1987 (Yin Fire Rabbit year). The Rabbit that year combined with the Pig in his Month Pillar to form wood. This was the third time that problems arose during a Rabbit year.

In 1999 (Yin Earth Rabbit year), at the age of 39, Kennedy entered the Rabbit Luck Cycle. At that time, the two Rabbits in the year and Luck Cycle combined with the Pig in his Month Pillar to form wood. He died on July 16, 1999, when the plane he was flying crashed.

Hour	Day	Month	Year
甲	己	辛	己
Yang Water	Yin Earth	Yin Metal	Yin Earth
戌	巳	未	卯
Dog	Snake	Sheep	Rabbit

On that day, the full Three Harmony Wood Combination was formed as the Sheep in the month combined with the Rabbit year and the Pig in his Month Pillar. There was a major conflict between the wood and fire flow in his chart and the favorable metal and water flow. His plane crashed into the sea and it took several days before his body was recovered from the ocean floor. While the Rabbit year accounted for much of the negative flow, the additional Yin Earth Year Stem did not help as it controlled his favorable element water. The Snake Branch of the day also clashed with the Pig in his chart. These negative influences manifested themselves in the fatal crash.

Kennedy's negative elements fire and wood are located in the parents' palace of his chart (in the Month Pillar) and it was difficult for him to enjoy a good relationship with them. He lost his father at age 3, followed his mother when he was 8 to a foreign country and lost his stepfather at 15. Kennedy's House of Spouse contained the element that was negative for him (fire). It signified that his spouse would not get along with his family members. If tabloid reports were to be believed, that could be true.

Kennedy's chart is contradictory. There was no doubt that his chart was feeble but why was he unable to follow? Being stuck at the border between being able and unable to follow a prevalent element was the main issue. In conclusion, whichever classification his chart belongs to is not important. What is more vital is to identify the periods when his chart was able to Follow the Prevalent element and make major decisions then. As for the difficult periods, it would have been advisable to maintain a low-key lifestyle and be more discreet during those times to avoid any issues.

Was Kennedy able to change his destiny if he had known about the negative influences? The Rabbit Luck Cycle (from age 39 to 43) was the most dangerous period in his life and the 15 years after that contained the positive water influence. He would have been able to build upon his career with his charisma and popularity. In the Rabbit Luck Cycle, he should have led a low-key life by avoiding the limelight and high risk activities like flying a plane in poor visibility. Helping others through public or private works would have also been beneficial in difficult periods. In addition, the application of Feng Shui principles in his home that eliminate wood and fire energy would have also been helpful.

Example 5.15 Cary Stayner (born August 13, 1961, 20:37 hours), Yosemite Killer

Hour	Day	Month	Year
壬	戊	丙	辛
Yang Water	Yang Earth	Yang Fire	Yin Metal
戌	寅	申	丑
Dog	Tiger	Monkey	Ox

2	12	22	32	42	52
乙	甲	癸	壬	辛	庚
Yin Wood	Yang Wood	Yin Water	Yang Water	Yin Metal	Yang Metal
未	午	已	辰	卯	寅
Sheep	Horse	Snake	Dragon	Rabbit	Tiger

Cary Stayner, also known as the Yosemite Killer, murdered four women between February and July 1999 in Yosemite Park in Southern California.

The Day Master is Yang Earth born in the Monkey month when metal is strong. As the strong metal drains the Earth Day Master, the person is weak, like a child who is unable to fully develop his ability to support himself. His only option to a good life is to Follow the Prevalent element metal for provision in the same way a child faithfully depends on his parents.

Unfortunately, the Yang Fire in the Month Pillar and another hidden fire in the Tiger Day Branch prevent him from surrendering to the metal. This makes him a rebellious child who is going nowhere. It becomes a False Follow chart that requires the support of external water, metal and wood. This is to ensure the earth child is able to faithfully obey the metal to fulfill the criteria for a Follow chart.

The Tiger in the House of Spouse not only has the negative fire and earth, it also clashes with the Monkey in the

Month Pillar (the Mother sector). This suggests difficult relationships between his mother and wife. The negative Yang Fire in the Month Pillar also indicates a problematic relationship with his father. The Academic Star (Monkey) and Nobleman Star (Ox) are present in the chart and they offer some relief.

Let us find out how the flows of the five elements changed his life. At the age of 7 in 1968 (Yang Earth Monkey year), Stayner was considered a child prodigy. The Yang Water present within the Monkey extinguished the negative element fire. This allowed him to follow the flow of metal. The two Academic stars (the Monkey of the year and in his Month Pillar) allowed Stayner to do well academically.

In junior high during the Yang Wood Luck Cycle, he was considered a talented cartoonist. The strong wood controlled the earth and allowed Stayner to go with the flow of metal. This was possibly his best Luck Cycle.

After graduating from high school in the Horse Luck Cycle (which had significant fire), Stayner bounced around taking menial casual jobs and depended on family support. The negative fire and earth plunged him into depression and negative thoughts. In 1990 (Yang Metal Horse year) when fire was strong, his uncle was murdered when Stayner was living with him. In 1991 (Yin Metal Sheep year), earth from the Sheep year drove him into depression and a suicide attempt.

In 1997 (Yin Fire Ox year), Stayner started a business that eventually failed. On February 15 and 16, 1999, days when the fire and earth elements were strong, he murdered three women in Yosemite Park.

Stayner was arrested on July 24 1999:

Hour	Day	Month	Year
?	丁 Yin Fire	辛 Yin Metal	己 Yin Earth
?	丑 Ox	未 Sheep	卯 Rabbit

The flow was basically wood with substantial metal. Stayner was under the control of both prevalent elements which made him docile like a child. He confessed to the

109

murders after being arrested.

In 2000 (Yang Metal Dragon year), the Dragon combined with the Monkey in his Month Pillar to form water. Stayner entered a plea of not guilty by reason of insanity. In 2002 (Yang Water Horse year), the strong fire and earth saw him being sentenced to death for murder, a decision that is currently under appeal.

Example 5.16 Ruan Lingyu 阮玲玉 (born April 26, 1910, between 19:00 and 21:00 hours), female Chinese movie icon from the 1930s

Hour	Day	Month	Year
甲	己	辛	庚
Yang Wood	Yin Earth	Yin Metal	Yang Metal
戌	亥	巳	戌
Dog	Pig	Snake	Dog

The Output elements are prevalent in this chart (Yang Metal and Yin Metal). This suggests a highly charismatic and talented individual who enjoyed a good reputation. This meets the conditions of being a movie star. However, she did not enjoy wealth or a happy marriage. Why is this so?

Charts that are on the borderline of being able to follow may belong to those born to a good family. They will still enjoy the comforts of life despite not having any success or achievement of their own. Those who are born into poverty without any means of surviving will have much more challenging lives. So how can the family help in these situations? Parents should observe the potential of their children from a young age and direct them to the appropriate field or career. By focusing on the right career, a person would be constantly working with the useful energy needed to ultimately become an achiever through his or her own hard work.

If the individual does not respect the flow of universal energy and switches frequently amongst unsuitable fields or careers, they would further deplete their limited positive energy or confuse it with more negative energies. Little would be achieved in this manner.

Chapter Six - Follow Charts, Transformation Charts

Follow Charts

As discussed in Chapter Five, the energy of Dominant charts is akin to that of a king commanding his loyal subjects. At the other extreme, there are charts with the energy of infants or children who are dependent on the parents for their survival. When charts follow the energy of a prevalent element, it is like receiving unconditional assistance from powerful providers. This is known as a Follow chart which is auspicious as it means that the person will receive assistance from a higher source and will not simply depend on himself.

Individuals with Follow charts will be warm-hearted, benevolent, sincere, sensitive, perceptive, intuitive and intelligent. Most of them tend to be physically attractive. The special characteristic of a Follow chart is that they do not antagonize others.

Many successful historical individuals as well as Nobel Prize winners belong to this group. Examples include Song Dynasty metaphysician Shao Yung 邵雍, Song Dynasty scholar Chu Xi 朱熙, Song Qing Ling 宋慶齡, Albert Einstein, Sir Winston Churchill and Steve Jobs, to name a few.

The natural order of the universe is the balance of Yin and Yang energies. When there is an absence of Yin energy with only Yang energy present, it is difficult to achieve much success. Follow charts are the exception to the rule as they receive assistance from the universe and go with the flow of the prevalent energy.

Differing Grades of Follow Charts

A Follow chart varies in grades or quality, just as the strength of children varies through different life stages.

An infant is the most helpless, eliciting total unconditional care and provision – this is the best life. A feeble self who has an energy system of an infant following a prevalent element will have the best life. Fame and wealth will be flowing along continuously.

At about 5 years old, they get conditional support as he or she can perform small tasks without help. When the self has the strength of a teenager, then there is the possibility of rebellion or disobedience. These would then be known as False Follow charts.

Ancient texts considered the False Follow charts similar to orphans who have the possibility of success one day with the help of mentors. These charts are a lot better than the Competitive Sibling Rivalry charts and the Mixed Energies charts mentioned in Chapter Five. They can enjoy occasional good fortune and sudden success upon the appearance of the positive elements.

The False Follow charts are often confronted by obstacles as they attempt to achieve their goals. They are typically apprehensive and meticulous. As they have something to cover up in their faulty system, they are anxious and concerned about their appearance and expression.

We will now discuss the four different types of Follow charts.

A) Follow The Power

The Power element is translated from traditional texts as the Direct Officer or Seven Killings, depending on the polarity with the Day Master. The Power element is the element that controls the Day Master. For those born on Yang Water or Yin Water days, the Power element would be earth. For those with metal Day Masters, the Power element would be the fire element and so on. There are common misconceptions that you should be aware of.

(1) The Power element is negative and
(2) Only the Seven Killings (Same polarity as the Day Master) rather than the Direct Officer (Opposite polarity as Day Master) should be used.

In reality, if there is a strong presence of the Power element in the chart, it is considered auspicious. Note there is also no differentiation made between the Seven Killings and the Direct Officer.

The Power element represents pressure and leadership. If the Day Master is weak and surrenders to the Power element, the person will obtain protection from the prevalent Power element. These types of charts are known as Follow the Power charts. The Resource element must not be prominent in the chart for it to comply with a Follow the Power classification.

In order to thrive under the Power element, the person will have to rely on his or her instincts and ability to provide the right answer at the right time to satisfy those who are in power. The person will also need to have good interpersonal and social skills to please the boss with intelligence, a sense of right and wrong and diplomacy. Follow the Power charts are considered the most intelligent of all the Follow charts. It is hardly surprising that many Nobel Prize winners have Follow the Power charts.

The success of Follow the Power charts depends on the strength of the Power element. The moment the Power is lost or threatened, the chart's configuration is broken. The chart resembles a naughty child who is being abandoned or punished by the boss. This will result in the immediate loss of assistance. Life will become more challenging as the Day Master must now depend on his or her own abilities. The quality of Follow charts is comparable to children who are unable to survive independently. This will be illustrated in the following examples.

Example 6.1 Bill Gates (born October 28, 1955)

Hour	Day	Month Monthly Virtue	Year
?	壬 Yang Water	丙 Yang Fire	乙 Yin Wood
?	戌 Dog	戌 Dog	未 Sheep
	Six Harmony Mentor Combination		

6	16	26	36	46
乙 Yin Wood	甲 Yang Wood	癸 Yin Water	壬 Yang Water	辛 Yin Metal
酉 Rooster	申 Monkey	未 Sheep	午 Horse	巳 Snake

56	66	76	86
庚 Yang Metal	己 Yin Earth	戊 Yang Earth	丁 Yin Fire
辰 Dragon	卯 Rabbit	寅 Tiger	丑 Ox

Bill Gates is a Yang Water Day Master born in the Dog month when earth is extremely strong. The first three pillars of his Four Pillars charts contain three earth and one fire component. There is no water present that competes with the Day Master. This Follow chart is very clear. Fire and earth are both prevalent and work in harmony as one produces the other.

The Dog Branches contain fire and earth. Both the fire and earth elements are in the same palace. Fire represents wealth and earth represents power. Gates' chart can be considered either as Follow the Wealth or Follow the Power. With fire and earth in the same location, both prevalent elements work in tandem to protect the Day Master. This indicates a chart that has both immense wealth and power.

As the Day Master follows the Power element, both earth and fire are the useful elements. The negative elements are water (the Original Self and Competitor) and wood (destroys the earth element). In the wood Luck Cycles in his early life, Gates did not perform well at school. At the age of 21 during the Monkey Luck Cycle (metal and water), the Day Master possessed the energy of a petulant ten year-old child and Gates dropped out of Harvard. With his parents' support, he spent his time in the basement concentrating on starting his own software programming company. He did not achieve success until he formed an alliance with Paul Allen.

The special trait of Follow charts is that they require the assistance of a mentor or helper to take the first step. This is considered borrowing the energy from someone else. Follow charts cannot really succeed on their own actions alone. In times of trouble, the Follow chart would benefit from seeking the assistance of others for the initial step.

At the age of 32 in 1987 (Yin Fire Rabbit year) in the Sheep Luck Cycle, the strong fire that year generated more earth and Gates became the world's youngest billionaire. In the Yang Water Luck Cycle, Gates worked hard to develop and perfect the Windows 95 operating system. In 1997 (Yin Fire Ox year) when Gates was in the second year of the Horse Luck Cycle (fire and earth), he became the richest man in the world.

Gates' worst element is water as it revives his Original Self or Day Master. The Resource element metal is also negative as it empowers the water self. From the age of 46 when he entered the Yin Metal Luck Cycle, Gates resigned as head of Microsoft to focus on the Bill Gates Foundation. His ambition was to improve the quality of countless lives in Africa and other developing countries.

Currently, Gates is in the Yang Metal Luck Cycle which he began at the age of 56. As it is the Resource Luck Cycle, Gates dropped a few positions in his ranking amongst the world's richest men but remained the world's richest philanthropist. So far, there have not been any scandals involving Gates. This indicates that keeping a low profile during negative Luck Cycles can steer us away from trouble.

There are other Silicon Valley billionaires who were born in 1955 such as Steve Jobs and Eric Schmidt (Executive Chairman of Google). While billionaires born in the Yin Wood Sheep Year are significant in number, there is not another who shares exactly the same birth date (year, month and day) as Gates. He has a very clear and distinct Follow chart. Even for those who may have a similar chart as Gates, the influence of Luck Cycles, genes, family background and personal principles are all variables that must be taken into account.

We will now consider a Follow chart that is more mixed in nature.

Example 6.2 Chen Yi 陳毅 (born August 26, 1901, 08:20 hours, died January 6, 1972), Chinese communist military commander and politician

Hour	Day	Month	Year
壬	丙	丙	辛
Yang Water	Yang Fire	Yang Fire	Yin Metal
辰	子	申	丑
Dragon	Rat	Monkey	Ox

6	16	26	36	46	56	66
乙	甲	癸	壬	辛	庚	己
Yin Wood	Yang Wood	Yin Water	Yang Water	Yin Metal	Yang Metal	Yin Earth
未	午	巳	辰	卯	寅	丑
Sheep	Horse	Snake	Dragon	Rabbit	Tiger	Ox

Chen Yi was a Chinese military commander who fought against the Japanese and later became the Mayor of Shanghai and the Foreign Minister of China.

There are different conditions for Follow charts compared to Dominant charts. For instance, the Earthly Branches in the Follow charts do not necessarily have to form a Partial or Full Three Harmony Combination unlike in Dominant charts. However, if a Partial or Full Combination is formed, then the Follow chart is considered superior, as the support from the prevalent element is much stronger. Chen Yi is a Yang Fire Day Master who is born in the Monkey month. There is a Full Three Harmony Water Combination involving the Monkey, Rat and Dragon. Chen definitely has a Follow chart that depends on his Power element water for support.

With water as his main useful element, metal comes next as it empowers water. Additional water in the Hour Stem and metal in the Year Stem are indeed reinforcing the Follow the Power Configuration. Are there any obstacles that disrupt the

116

Follow system? There is a Yang Fire Competitor in the Month Pillar that constitutes a slight obstacle to the flow. Fortunately, this Yang Fire combines with the Yin Metal in the Year Stem. As a result, it is neutralized. This is a very favorable chart as it indicates a person with great problem-solving skills who is able to triumph over his adversaries.

The main obstacle in this chart is the Ox in the Year Pillar. Readers will recall that the Ox represents wet earth that will threaten the flow of water. This creates frustration and insecurity for the individual. However, this threat gradually declined over Chen's adolescent years and kept the water clear throughout his adulthood.

Wood is another threat to the flow as it revives the original Fire Day Master. In 1955 (Yin Wood Sheep year), when Chen was 54 in the Rabbit Luck Cycle, he encountered a Partial Three Harmony Wood Combination. As a result, he was hospitalized for a tooth infection that developed into septicemia. Chen had to take further time off to recuperate from this potentially life threatening illness.

If an individual with this chart were born in times of peace, he would have enjoyed a stable life with ample opportunities in terms of wealth and career. But Chen was born in times of war and turmoil where he had to struggle to defend his country. Later in life, he fell victim to the Cultural Revolution and was unable to enjoy much peace. We cannot underestimate the influence of the environment on our lives.

Chen's best Luck Cycles were those of Yang Metal and Yin Metal. Metal not only produced water, it also served as a filter and channel for water to exert its influence. In the Yin Metal Luck Cycle, he was successful in leading the Communists to victory over the Kuomintang in 1947 and 1948. In 1949, Chen became the mayor of Shanghai. During the Yang Metal Luck Cycle in 1958, he became the Foreign Minister of China.

At the age of 66, Chen entered the Yin Earth Luck Cycle and the wet earth influence affected his health and judgment. His best element water was not able to offer much protection. Chen was persecuted during the Cultural Revolution and his powers were stripped from him prior to his death in 1972.

Regardless of gender, individuals with charts that Follow the Power element tend to be hardworking and highly intelligent. Women with these charts will marry a capable husband. However, there should not be another competitor in the chart. For instance, Oprah Winfrey has a Follow the Power chart and is a self-made billionaire. By definition, she should have married a highly successful man by now. In Winfrey's chart, there is an additional Yin Wood Competitor that competes with the Day Master for the husband or Power element. The following is her chart for readers to practice their skills:

Example 6.3 Oprah Winfrey (born January 29, 1954, 04:30 hours)

Hour	Day	Month	Year
戊	乙	乙	癸
Yang Earth	Yin Wood	Yin Wood	Yin Water
寅	酉	丑	巳
Tiger	Rooster	Ox	Snake

The Yin Wood Day Master is unable to control the Yin Wood Competitor in the Month Pillar. The Yin Wood Competitor is closer to the water source (Yin Water) and is therefore stronger than the Day Master. In the romance stakes, this other Yin Wood is ahead. Even though Winfrey is a self-made woman, she remains single. Charts that Follow the Power element find the Resource element negative. The Yin Wood Day Master here is harmed by the fire, water and wood elements.

B) Follow The Wealth

The Day Master is feeble as it is under the control of the prevalent Wealth element. Individuals with Follow the Wealth charts have good earning capacity and are discreet about their wealth (notably frugal). They are also industrious, talented and highly intuitive when it comes to finances and business. Men with Follow the Wealth charts are very respectful of women.

Example 6.4 Deng Xiaoping 鄧小平 (born August 22, 1904, 03:34 hours)

Hour	Day	Month	Year
甲	戊	壬	甲
Yang Water	Yang Earth	Yang Water	Yang Wood
寅	子	申	辰
Tiger	Rat	Monkey	Dragon

5	15	25	35	45
癸	甲	乙	丙	丁
Yin	Yang	Yin	Yang	Yin
Water	Wood	Wood	Fire	Fire
酉	戌	亥	子	丑
Rooster	Dog	Pig	Rat	Ox

55	65	75	85
戊	己	庚	辛
Yang	Yin	Yang	Yin
Earth	Earth	Metal	Metal
寅	卯	辰	巳
Tiger	Rabbit	Dragon	Snake

Deng Xiaoping is a Yang Earth Day Master born in the Monkey month when metal and water dominate. There is a Full Three Harmony Water Combination within his chart which involves the Monkey, Rat and Dragon. The feeble Yang Earth follows the lead of the prevalent water flow, which makes it a Follow the Wealth chart. The Yang Water present in the Month Pillar reinforces the case further. With such a large flow of water, wood is required to direct and prevent it from flowing aimlessly. There are two Yang Wood Stems present in the Year and Hour Pillars. Deng enjoyed a long and distinguished career as a politician and the Supreme leader of the People's Republic of China.

Deng lived in extremely turbulent times marked by the Second Sino-Japanese War, the Chinese Civil War and the Cultural Revolution. His good flow allowed him to glide over the obstacles in life.

Let us see how the different elemental flows affected his fortune. In 1969 (Yin Earth Rooster year), Deng was 65 at the beginning of the Yin Earth Luck Cycle. He was demoted to repairing farm tools after losing his position as a party leader during the Cultural Revolution. Deng bounced back to regain leadership of the party in the Rabbit Luck Cycle in 1974 (Yang Wood Tiger year). This was a period of significant wood energy that was further reinforced by the energy of the year. The strong wood energy was able to control the negative effects of earth.

His moment of glory finally arrived in 1976 (Yang Fire Dragon year) at the age of 80, the second year of his Rabbit Luck Cycle. He inherited Mao Zedong's position to become China's national leader. The Dragon in the year added more water to the Full Three Harmony Water Combination already present in Deng's chart. In the Yang Metal Luck Cycle that followed, Deng enjoyed another good period as metal gave birth to water, his best element.

Example 6.5 Gordon Moore (born January 3, 1929), Chairman of Intel

Gordon Moore is a Yang Earth Day Master that follows the water element as the Day, Month and Year Branches (Monkey, Rat and Dragon) form a Full Three Harmony Water Combination. As water represents Moore's wealth, he has a Follow the Wealth chart. Water and metal are his useful elements. Earth is his negative element.

Hour	Day	Month	Year
?	戊 Yang Earth	甲 Yang Wood	戊 Yang Earth
?	申 Monkey	子 Rat	辰 Dragon

1	11	21	31	41
乙 Yin Wood	丙 Yang Fire	丁 Yin Fire	戊 Yang Earth	己 Yin Earth
丑 Ox	寅 Tiger	卯 Rabbit	辰 Dragon	巳 Snake

51	61	71	81
庚 Yang Metal	辛 Yin Metal	壬 Yang Water	癸 Yin Water
午 Horse	未 Sheep	申 Monkey	酉 Rooster

Moore's chart is very similar to Deng Xiaoping's 鄧小平. Both are Yang Earth Day Masters that Follow the Wealth element water and have a Full Three Harmony Water Combination present in their charts.

Unlike Deng, Moore lived in a much more settled environment with social, cultural and political stability. Regardless of the Luck Cycles, Moore always had a happy, productive and smooth life. He was born in San Francisco to well-off parents and obtained a degree in Chemistry from the University of California, Berkeley. In 1966 (Yin Wood Snake year), at the age of 37 during the Dragon Luck Cycle, he published Moore's Law which states that the number of transistors on integrated circuits doubles every two years. In 1968 (Yang Earth Monkey year) in the same Luck Cycle, Moore established Intel, the multinational semi-conductor and microchip corporation.

In 1991 (Yin Metal Sheep year) when Moore was 62 in the Yin Metal Luck Cycle, he was honored by President George Bush as a great scientist. We can see how a Hurting Officer (Yin Metal) or Output element of the Yang Earth Day Master contributes to one's glamour and fame.

While Deng launched the economic reforms that saved his country from poverty, Moore brought benefits to countless individuals with his inventions and philanthropy. Both are leaders in their respective fields of politics and computing. In terms of lifestyle, career paths and life experience, the differences are vast.

The charts basically represent the opportunities that we have been given by the universe, as well as our inherent abilities and character traits. Our genetics, upbringing, living environment and personalities differ from one another and this accounts for the differences in the lives of people who are born at the same time in different parts of the world.

Apart from having a chart with favorable flow, Moore was also born in the USA, a country known for its prosperity and stability. This allowed him to enjoy a peaceful life. In contrast, Deng was born in China at a time of great political uncertainty and social upheaval. While his success and achievement is undeniable, Deng's life was not as peaceful as Moore's. In these cases, the influence of the environment definitely plays a critical role.

Another positive characteristic of Moore's chart is that the Yang Wood Stem sits in the Month Pillar, allowing the water present in his chart to be regulated. The Month Pillar affects us our entire life. The influence of the Year Pillar fades after one's youth. This is why Moore's chart is slightly superior to Deng's as it has a more definitive direction. From another point of view, Deng's contributions to the Chinese were done in the spirit of self-sacrifice and cannot be measured in monetary terms.

For readers who like to examine another Follow the Wealth chart, they can analyze the life of Rupert Murdoch's son, James Murdoch (born December 13, 1972). He is also a Yang Earth Day Master. The difference lies in the fact that water is not involved in a Combination.

Example 6.6 Steve Ballmer (born March 24, 1956), Microsoft CEO

Hour	Day	Month	Year
?	庚 Yang Metal	辛 Yin Metal	丙 Yang Fire
?	寅 Tiger	卯 Rabbit	申 Monkey

4	14	24	34
壬 Yang Water	癸 Yin Water	甲 Yang Wood	乙 Yin Wood
辰 Dragon	己 Snake	午 Horse	未 Sheep

44	54	64	74
丙 Yang Fire	丁 Yin Fire	戊 Yang Earth	己 Yin Earth
申 Monkey	酉 Rooster	戌 Dog	亥 Pig

Ballmer's chart represents a different kind of Follow the Wealth chart. He is a Yang Metal Day Master born in the Rabbit month (spring) when wood is extremely strong and earth and metal are extremely weak. The Wealth element has the support of the season and is being energized by water from the adjacent Monkey Year Branch. Ballmer's chart is that of Yang Metal that follows the Wealth element wood.

The challenge from the Yin Metal Competitor located in the Month Stem is combined away by the Yang Fire in the Year Stem. This is fortunate as apart from removing an obstacle to the Follow the Wealth chart, it also indicates an individual who is able to solve problems. This favorable configuration is similar to Chen Yi's 陳毅 chart where the obstacle is eliminated, thereby creating a highly capable individual. Ballmer's main useful element is wood with water as his next favorable element.

Ballmer was born into a well-off family and graduated from Harvard in Mathematics and Economics. Let us see how his favorable elements were able to bring him good fortune. In 1980 (Yang Metal Monkey year) in the Yang Wood (Wealth) Luck Cycle, Ballmer joined Microsoft and became its first business development manager. On January 13, 2000, when it was still the Yin Earth Rabbit year, he became the CEO of Microsoft after Bill Gates stepped down. The Rabbit in the year was able to contribute to the positive wood energy, which is also present in Ballmer's Rabbit Month Branch. In 2010 (Yang Metal Tiger year), the Tiger year brought in more wood (wealth) and Ballmer was ranked within the top 20 richest men in the world.

C) Follow The Children

In the Four Pillars system, the traditional terms Eating God or Hurting Officer are also referred to as the Day Master's Children. This is the element generated by the Day Master. When the Children become the chart's prevalent element, it controls the Day Master and this formation is known as the Follow the Children chart.

It has two distinctive features that set it apart from other Follow systems. First, unlike the other types of Follow Chart, the element that produces the useful element (in this case, the Children or Output element) is also the same as the Self, i.e. Siblings or Rivals. Having more Rivals or Competitors will be negative as it will break the Configuration of the Follow chart. So the presence of more Siblings will cause problems even though they produce the useful element.

Secondly, for the Day Master to continue enjoying good fortune, the Children have to give birth to Grandchildren. That is, a Water Self following wood (Children) would be more fortunate to have some fire (Grandchildren) in the chart or Luck Cycle. By the same token, a Fire self that follows earth should have some metal to interact with its system so as to generate more good fortune. What is behind the claim? Expansion is a natural process of any growth.

Those with Follow the Children charts have a relaxed and laid back approach to life. They are sophisticated in their tastes and are highly refined. Like others with a Follow system, they are physically attractive, mellow in temperament, of a pleasant disposition and intelligent. Above all, they appreciate and enjoy the finer aspects of life, such as food.

Example 6.7 John Templeton (born November 29, 1912, died July 8, 2008), Billionaire

Hour	Day	Month	Year
?	己 Yin Earth	辛 Yin Metal	壬 Yang Water
?	酉 Rooster	亥 Pig	子 Rat

3	13	23	33	43	53
壬 Yang Water	癸 Yin Water	甲 Yang Wood	乙 Yin Wood	丙 Yang Fire	丁 Yin Fire
子 Rat	丑 Ox	寅 Tiger	卯 Rabbit	辰 Dragon	巳 Snake

63	73	83	93
戊 Yang Earth	己 Yin Earth	庚 Yang Metal	辛 Yin Metal
午 Horse	未 Sheep	申 Monkey	酉 Rooster

This is a highly auspicious Follow the Children chart. We can see why it produced such an extremely successful person.

John Templeton and Warren Buffett were two of the 20th and the 21st century's most successful mutual fund gurus. While Buffett has a Dominant chart and is in the spotlight for his achievements, Templeton had a Follow the Children chart and was extremely low key and discreet while establishing his mutual fund empire. Similarly, the discretion extended to his charitable and philanthropic activities which he carried out through the Templeton Foundation. Templeton was always a good student. He graduated from Yale and attended Oxford University as a Rhodes Scholar. At the age of 27, he started working in the finance industry and was successful in reaching the upper echelons of his industry.

Templeton's chart is one of Children producing Grandchildren, a Special Configuration. There are two chains of 'Children producing Grandchildren' taking place concurrently in his chart. Within the Branches, the Yin Earth Day Master produces Rooster (which contains Yin Metal). The Rooster then produces the Pig and Rat, both of which contain water. Within the Stems, the Yin Earth produces Yin Metal which then gives birth to Yang Water.

We can ascertain that the few difficult periods in Templeton's life were due to the negative influence of earth. In the Ox (Yin Earth) period, Templeton played poker to finance his tuition while studying in Yale. By all accounts, he was an excellent poker player. We should also note the prevailing energy on the day he died.

The Day Templeton Died: July 8, 2008

Hour	Day	Month	Year
?	己 Yin Earth	己 Yin Earth	戊 Yang Earth
?	酉 Rooster	未 Sheep	子 Rat

On the day Templeton died, there were four earth Stems and Branches (the Day, Month and Year Stems and the Month Branch). They served as Competitors that disrupted his prevalent flow. As a result, he paid the price.

Other negative incidents involved the Clashing or breaking down of the production chain in his Branches. In 1939 (Yin Earth Rabbit year) at the age of 27, he borrowed heavily to purchase shares. In 1951 (Yin Metal Rabbit year) during the Rabbit Luck Cycle, two Rabbits (in the Luck Cycle and year) clashed with his Rooster (Spouse Palace). Templeton's wife passed away in a motorbike accident. The Rabbit disrupted the Rooster from producing.

Templeton passed away at the age of 95. His Special Configuration suggested a life that was extremely stable in terms of career and health, and Templeton did not experience much misfortune in his life apart from the death of his first wife. His philanthropic activities also served to nullify some of the negative influences.

Example 6.8 Sir Isaac Newton (born December 25, 1642, died March 20, 1727)

Note: The Date of Birth used here conforms to the Julian Calendar. The Gregorian Calendar was only introduced in the United Kingdom in 1752. I have compared this chart with the converted date of January 4, 1643. I stand by the chart provided here as I can use this to match the events in his life.

Hour	Day	Month	Year
丙	庚	壬	壬
Yang Fire	Yang Metal	Yang Water	Yang Water
子	子	子	午
Rat	Rat	Rat	Horse

1	11	21	31	41
癸	甲	乙	丙	丁
Yin Water	Yang Wood	Yin Wood	Yang Fire	Yin Fire
丑	寅	卯	辰	巳
Ox	Tiger	Rabbit	Dragon	Snake

51	61	71	81
戊	己	庚	辛
Yang Earth	Yin Earth	Yang Metal	Yin Metal
午	未	申	酉
Horse	Sheep	Monkey	Rooster

Newton is a Yang Metal Day Master born in the Rat month when water is strong. There is a strong presence of water in his chart that dominates even though there is no Combination formed. Newton's chart is considered a Follow the Children chart, with water being his best element and earth his worst element.

The Horse present in his Year Pillar contains fire and earth. Newton's teenage years were difficult as he lost his father during this period. The other element that Newton should avoid is metal which represents Competitors. If his chart had the wood element, it would have fulfilled the Children generating Grandchildren Configuration, but its absence meant that he had to look for this favorable element in the Luck Cycles or years.

Let us consider the negative influence of metal on the Yang Metal Day Master. In 1645 (Yin Wood Rooster year) at the age of 3, Newton's mother remarried and left him in the care of his paternal grandmother. In 1657 (Yin Fire Rooster year) at the age of 15, Newton started working as a farmer on the family farm. This was a job which he detested. In 1660 (Yang Metal Horse year), Newton lost all his sheep while shepherding. At the age of 50 in 1693 (Yin Water Rooster year) during the Snake Luck Cycle (which contained fire, earth and metal), he contracted a severe skin allergy. It can be ascertained that metal and earth created issues for Newton. For a Follow the Children chart, having Competitors is detrimental.

In contrast, the effects of wood on Newton tell a different story. Wood represents the children of water and its presence turns Newton's chart into a Children Producing Grandchildren situation. In 1685 (Yin Wood Snake year) at the age of 22 during the Yin Wood Luck Cycle, he graduated from Cambridge University and became a lecturer. Newton made breakthrough discoveries on 'light' physics in the years when water and wood were strong during the Rabbit Luck Cycle. They were 1672 (Yang Water Rat year) and 1675 (Yin Wood Rabbit year). In 1687 (Yin Fire Rabbit year) at 45, his thesis on Gravity shook the world.

We will now consider a lesser Follow the Children chart, that of 1930s actress Hu Die 蝴蝶 or Butterfly .

127

Example 6.9 Hu Die 蝴蝶 Buttefly Hu (born March 26, 1903, between 01:00 and 03:00 hours, died April 23, 1989)

Hour	Day	Month	Year
癸	癸	乙	癸
Yin Water	Yin Water	Yin Wood	Yin Water
丑	丑	卯	卯
Ox	Ox	Rabbit	Rabbit

4	14	24	34	44
丙	丁	戊	己	庚
Yang Fire	Yin Fire	Yang Earth	Yin Earth	Yang Metal
辰	己	午	未	申
Dragon	Snake	Horse	Sheep	Monkey

54	64	74	84
辛	壬	癸	甲
Yin Metal	Yang Water	Yin Water	Yang Wood
酉	戌	亥	子
Rooster	Dog	Pig	Rat

Butterfly Hu is a Yin Water Day Master who is born in the Rabbit month when wood dominates. The three Wood Stems and Branches in her chart (Yin Wood and two Rabbits) means that wood is the prevalent energy in her chart. This makes her a Follow the Children chart. It is however, not a strong Follow the Children chart as there are no Combinations. Wood and fire are the favorable elements. Metal (which attacks the best element wood) has to be avoided.

The two other Yin Water Stems in the chart compete with the Day Master and make it a False Follow the Children chart. There are also two Ox Branches in her chart. They contain metal which threatens the flow of wood. The negative elements created frustrations in her life.

How to determine the good or bad years of a movie star with mixed flows? I believe the most objective way would be to count the number of movies released each year. I have used this method to analyze the fortunes of several Hollywood stars and discovered that the number of films released tend to be higher in the favorable years and lower in the negative ones.

Buttefly Hu's golden period was between 1930 and 1940. Her peak occurred between 1931 and 35, when she was going through the Horse (fire) Luck Cycle. This is precisely the scenario of 'water giving rise to wood and wood giving rise to fire' Configuration, which is the 'Children Producing Grandchildren' Configuration.

Let us check out Hu's movie production throughout her career.

From 1931 to 1934, Hu was in the Horse Luck Cycle and she released between four and seven movies each year. It was the most productive Luck Cycle in her lifetime. Her two most productive years were 1926 (Yang Fire Tiger year) with 11 movies and 1927 (Yin Fire Rabbit year) with eight movies. Wood and fire dominated these years.

In contrast, metal exerted the opposite effects. Hu did not make any movies between 1954 and 1958 and between 1960 and 1965. Why? They all fell within her metal Luck Cycles. During the tough times, the influence of the year helped usher in some good fortune. In 1959 (Yin Earth Pig year), a year in which wood was strong during the metal Luck Cycle, Hu was in four movies. There was a Partial Three Harmony Wood Combination in her system that year. She could still utilize the good years in a bad Luck Cycle to attain a degree of success.

We should not underestimate her activities in 1935 (Yin Wood Pig year) as she was occupied with film festivals in Moscow and Europe. This gave her less time to film. The Yin Earth Luck Cycle that followed was also favorable as the Power element earth controlled her water Competitors.

Table 6.1 Butterfly Hu's Movie Output

Year	Stem Branch	Movies
1926	Yang Fire Tiger	11
1927	Yin Fire Rabbit	8
1928	Yang Earth Dragon	6
1929	Yin Earth Snake	3
1930	Yang Metal Horse	2
1931	Yin Metal Sheep	7
1932	Yang Water Monkey	4
1933	Yin Water Rooster	5
1934	Yang Wood Dog	7
1935	Yin Wood Pig	3
1936	Yang Fire Rat	1
1937	Yin Fire Ox	1
1938	Yang Earth Tiger	1
1939	Yin Earth Rabbit	1
1940	Yang Metal Dragon	1
1941	Yin Metal Snake	1
1942	Yang Water Horse	0
1943	Yin Water Sheep	0
1944	Yang Wood Monkey	0
1945	Yin Wood Rooster	0
1946	Yang Fire Dog	0
1947	Yin Fire Pig	2
1948	Yang Earth Rat	0
1949	Yin Earth Ox	0
1950	Yang Metal Tiger	0
1951	Yin Metal Rabbit	0
1952	Yang Water Dragon	0
1953	Yin Water Snake	1
1954	Yang Wood Horse	0
1955	Yin Wood Sheep	0
1956	Yang Fire Monkey	0
1957	Yin Fire Rooster	0
1958	Yang Earth Dog	0
1959	Yin Earth Pig	4
1960	Yang Metal Rat	0
1961	Yin Metal Ox	0
1962	Yang Water Tiger	0
1963	Yin Water Rabbit	0
1964	Yang Wood Dragon	0
1965	Yin Wood Snake	0
1966	Yang Fire Horse	6
1967	Yin Fire Sheep	Retired

Hu's chart has mixed energies due to the Competitors and Resource elements present amongst the Children or Output element. To fully utilize the Output element, it is better for the chart to be Dominant, like that of Example 3.7 Ingrid Bergman. We cannot say that Hu's chart is a weak chart even though there are many Competitors in her chart. This is because she achieved success in her wealth Luck Cycles when the Children element in her chart generated Grandchildren (her Wealth element). Hu's useful elements are wood and fire.

Here is an exercise. Adolf Hitler also belongs to the Follow the Children category, but the energy present within his chart is mixed and not pure. This may account for his destructive behavior. What can you see from Hitler's Four Pillars Chart?

Example 6.10 Adolf Hitler (born April 20, 1889, 18:30 hours), German dictator

Hour	Day	Month	Year
丁	丙	戊	己
Yin Fire	Yang Fire	Yang Earth	Yin Earth
酉	寅	辰	丑
Rooster	Tiger	Dragon	Ox

D) Follow The Resource (Many Mothers, One Child)

Charts that follow the Resource element are known traditionally as the chart of Many Mothers, One Child. In ancient China, it was not unusual for a man to have a few wives concurrently and yet have only one son or male heir for the family. All the mothers realized that they had to depend on this son for their future, so everyone would try their best to protect and nurture him. The child himself would also have an implicit understanding of the situation and ensure that he got along with all the mothers in order to maintain harmony in the household.

Those with this type of chart are accustomed to being looked after and have refined tastes. They have high expectations in terms of lifestyle. Pleasant and demure, they have good observational abilities, academic skills and possess sharp minds. They are reluctant to perform manual labor and menial tasks.

The Follow the Resource or Many Mothers, One Child charts are most vulnerable to the appearance of Siblings (Competitors or Rivals for the family title). A Yang Wood Day Master would prefer not to have another wood Stem or Branch present in the Chart, Luck Cycle or year. Yang Wood, Yin Wood, Rabbit, Pig, Tiger and Sheep will create issues (we have to take into account all the Hidden Stems to establish this). For Yang Metal Day Masters, they also prefer not to encounter Yang Metal or Yin Metal.

What is the basis for this? With more Siblings in the family, there will be more Competitors for the family's resources. This may result in the many mothers being unsure of which child to support, and they may temporarily withdraw their support for this child. When the Follow the Resource chart encounters this situation, they may lose their job, have financial setbacks, get divorced or become separated from their family.

Scheming will be involved when Siblings are aware of the Competitors or Rivals as they know that only one of them will succeed.

We will have to analyze the strength of the Day Master with regard to the Competitors. If the Self is unable to compete with the Rivals, there may be loss of wealth, divorce, injury, sickness or even death. At the lesser end of the spectrum, the person may change schools or homes. There is also a higher incidence of committing suicide during the Sibling Rivalry or Competitor Luck Cycle. However, if the Day Master is strong, it will only experience frustration prior to its eventual triumph.

As the Resource element is favorable, the element that produces the Resource element (the Power element) is also favorable. Let us consider some examples of Follow the Resource charts.

Example 6.11 Soong Ching Ling 宋慶齡 (born January 27, 1893, between 21:00 and 23:00 hours, died May 29, 1981), Wife of Dr. Sun Yat Sen

Hour	Day	Month	Year
乙 Yin Wood	甲 Yang Wood	癸 Yin Water	壬 Yang Water
亥 Pig	子 Rat	丑 Ox	辰 Dragon

7	17	27	37	47
壬 Yang Water	辛 Yin Metal	庚 Yang Metal	己 Yin Earth	戊 Yang Earth
子 Rat	亥 Pig	戌 Dog	酉 Rooster	申 Monkey

57	67	77	87
丁 Yin Fire	丙 Yang Fire	乙 Yin Wood	甲 Yang Wood
未 Sheep	午 Horse	巳 Snake	辰 Dragon

Soong Ching Ling 宋慶齡 was the second wife of Dr. Sun Yat Sen. She was one of the famous Soong sisters. All of them married famous men who shaped modern Chinese history. Soong is also revered as the mother of modern China.

The Yang Wood Day Master sits above the Directional Water Combination (Pig, Rat and Ox). There is also support from Yang Water and Yin Water in the Year and Month Pillars. The Yang Water in the Year Pillar also brings out the water hidden within the Dragon Branch. Water is the strongest element in this chart. The wood receives the assistance of the Resource element or Many Mothers. This is a Follow the Resource chart.

There is a Yin Wood Rival present in the Hour Pillar. However, it lies outside the sphere of water and is weaker than the Yang Wood Day Master. Even though it is not a significant threat, it can result in the Yang Wood Day Master being on guard at all times from any potential threats or obstacles. Soong's life was full of challenges despite the wealth from her immediate family and her high position attained through her marriage to Dr. Sun.

The mixed energies within Soong's chart manifested itself in Soong's turbulent relationship with her family. Her parents opposed her marriage to Dr. Sun, who was 26 years her senior and married at that time. To complicate matters further, he had to divorce his first wife to marry Soong. This was an issue as the general public at that time regarded divorce as immoral. The Yin Wood Rival present in Soong's chart can account for this, i.e. a Competitor that makes life difficult for her. This Rival could be traced back to Dr. Sun's first wife.

Soong married in 1915 at the age of 22 during the Pig Luck Cycle. There is a Yang Wood hidden in the Pig, which meant that it was a Rivalry Luck Cycle for Soong. Her relationship with her parents and siblings were adversely affected during this Luck Cycle.

Another negative element for Soong is earth as it confuses the flow of water. In the Dog (earth) Luck Cycle when she was 32 years old, she lost her husband to liver cancer. In 1927 (Yin Fire Rabbit year) during the Yang Earth Monkey month, Soong exiled herself to Europe for several years. Symbolically, it was like the child being kicked out of the home by angry mothers (due to the effect of earth disrupting the flow of her best element water). It was only in the favorable Rooster Luck Cycle that she re-established herself in China.

In 1949, the favorable Monkey Luck Cycle combined with the Dragon Year Branch to form water. Soong returned to Chinese politics. During this period, Soong was held in high esteem by the Communists who saw her as a link between their movement and Dr Sun. Soong maintained her influence in Chinese politics until her death at the age of 88.

Example 6.12 Qi Baishi 齊白石 (born January 1, 1864, died September 16, 1957), Chinese Painter

Hour	Day	Month	Year
辛 Yin Metal	乙 Yin Wood	甲 Yang Wood	癸 Yin Water
巳 Snake	丑 Ox	子 Rat	亥 Pig

8	18	28	38	48
癸 Yin Water	壬 Yang Water	辛 Yin Metal	庚 Yang Metal	己 Yin Earth
亥 Pig	戌 Dog	酉 Rooster	申 Monkey	未 Sheep

58	68	78	88
戊 Yang Earth	丁 Yin Fire	丙 Yang Fire	乙 Yin Wood
午 Horse	巳 Snake	辰 Dragon	卯 Rabbit

The Yin Wood Day Master is sitting above the Directional Water Combination (Pig, Rat and Ox) and there is additional support from Yin Water. The Yin Metal in the Hour Pillar also supports the flow of water. The Yin Wood relies on the Resource element water for survival. This is a Follow the Resource chart.

A stronger Yang Wood in the Month Pillar is challenging the Yin Wood Day Master as the heir for the family title. This Yang Wood Competitor can easily triumph over the Day Master and places the Yin Wood in a precarious position. After all, the strength of a tree is always greater than that of a plant.

Under such circumstances, the Yin Wood Day Master finds it difficult to enjoy peace of mind or a good life until the Yang Wood Competitor is removed. Let's see how his life shifted with the flows.

Qi was born to a farming family. Throughout his early years, he worked on the farms and performed other manual labor. At the age of 14 during the Pig Luck Cycle (which contained a Yang Wood Competitor), Qi lost the support of his family and had to work as a carpenter to support himself. For a long period of time, he studied art and painting on a part-time basis.

Qi's luck began to change in his late 30s when the Yang Metal Luck Cycle came along to control the Yang Wood Competitor. He was able to support himself then through selling his artwork. It was a time when Qi enjoyed some peace and stability in his life.

At the age of 41, he was in the favorable Monkey Luck Cycle. Qi was able to work full time as a painter. When the Resource element was prevalent, he led a more leisurely and relaxed life. After 1949 when Qi was 85 in the Dragon Luck Cycle, the Resource element became prevalent once again. It was akin to waiting for his Siblings or Rivals to pass away before he could enjoy good fortune.

Both Soong and Qi are wood Day Masters that had the Water Directional Combination in their charts. Soong was a Yang Wood Day Master with a Yin Wood Competitor. She was able to fight and lead. In contrast, Qi was a Yin Wood Day Master with a Yang Wood Competitor. He succumbed to the Rival who prevented him from leading. However, Soong and Qi both enjoyed acclaim and protection throughout their long lives. Such are the benefits enjoyed by those who have a Follow the Resource chart.

Example 6.13 Gary Cooper (born May 7, 1907, died May 13, 1961)

Hour	Day	Month	Year
?	乙 Yin Wood	壬 Yang Water	辛 Yin Metal
?	酉 Rooster	辰 Dragon	丑 Ox

6	16	26	36	46	56
辛 Yin Metal	庚 Yang Metal	己 Yin Earth	戊 Yang Earth	丁 Yin Fire	丙 Yang Fire
卯 Rabbit	寅 Tiger	丑 Ox	子 Rat	亥 Pig	戌 Dog

Cooper's chart is unusual. There is only one water Stem in his chart. However, there is a considerable amount of metal within the Branches that strengthens the water and makes it a Follow the Resource chart. There is also a possibility that Cooper's chart may be a Follow the Power (metal) chart as there is a Partial Three Harmony Metal Combination. In this case, Yang Water would be a negative element as it revives the Original Self. To ascertain whether water is a useful or negative element, the most objective method would be to analyze the films that Cooper released in each year.

If Cooper's chart were a Follow the Power (metal) chart, then earth would be a favorable element as it empowers metal and also controls water. Cooper did not fare well in the earth Luck Cycles. In the Yin Earth Luck Cycle between the ages of 21 and 26, he was doing odd jobs on the family ranch. In the Yang Earth Luck Cycle between the ages of 31 and 36, his movie output was hardly prolific with only three movies released in 1933 and 1934. In the other strong earth years 1929 (Yin Earth Snake year) and 1939 (Yin Earth Rabbit year), he only starred in two to three films per year.

Looking at Table 6.2, the water Luck Cycles were the most favorable. In 1932 (Yang Water Monkey year) and 1936 (Yang Fire Rat year), Cooper starred in four and five films respectively. This was due to the positive influence of water even though it was during the difficult Yang Earth Luck Cycle. His most famous film 'High Noon' was released in 1952, the Yang Water Dragon year when the water energy was prevalent. We can now confirm his best elements are metal and water. This makes his chart Follow the Resource rather than Follow the Power.

Table 6.2 Gary Cooper's Movie Output

Year	Stem Branch	Movies	Year	Stem Branch	Movies
1925	Yin Wood Ox	7	1938	Yang Earth Tiger	3
1926	Yang Fire Tiger	4	1939	Yin Earth Rabbit	2
1927	Yin Fire Rabbit	6	1940	Yang Metal Dragon	2
1928	Yang Earth Dragon	7	1941	Yin Metal Snake	3
1929	Yin Earth Snake	3	1942	Yang Water Horse	2
1930	Yang Metal Horse	5	1943	Yin Water Sheep	1
1931	Yin Metal Sheep	5	1944	Yang Wood Monkey	2
1932	Yang Water Monkey	4	1945	Yin Wood Rooster	2
1933	Yin Water Rooster	3	1946	Yang Fire Dog	1
1934	Yang Wood Dog	3	1947	Yin Fire Pig	1
1935	Yin Wood Pig	4	1948	Yang Earth Rat	1
1936	Yang Fire Rat	5	1949	Yin Earth Ox	4
1937	Yin Fire Ox	2	1950	Yang Metal Tiger	2

It is clear that metal is Cooper's useful element as he achieved his breakthrough in acting in the Ox Luck Cycle when the Ox combined with the Rooster in his chart to form metal.

Cooper passed away in the Dog Luck Cycle, his useful elements metal and water had undergone five years of weakening by fire and earth and the positive energy was eroded. Metal represents the lungs and Cooper succumbed to lung cancer at the age of 60.

Transformation Charts

Theory and Types

Charts that transform and follow are extremely auspicious. Day Masters of Follow charts surrender to the flow of the prevalent element. Charts that transform go one step further as they transform themselves into the prevalent element and pledge even more allegiance to the prevalent element than the Follow charts. Transformation charts are even more auspicious than Follow charts and are also seen less frequently.

While Transformation charts are more auspicious than Follow charts, keep in mind that there are also True and False Transformation charts.

How do we determine which category they fall into? The first step is to identify the Five Heavenly Stem Combinations. With each Combination, the Day Master has to be included. As shown in Table 6.3, there are five types of Transformation charts.

There are conditions for transformation to materialize. The prevalent element in the chart should be identical to the Transformed element, and the process should take place in the appropriate months as indicated in Table 6.3. An unsupported Transformed element or the inappropriate month will create a False Transformation.

Table 6.3 Transformation Charts and the Conditions Required

Type	Chart Classification	Combination Involving Day Stem	Final Element	Prevalent Energy in Chart	Timing (Month)
A	Earth Transformation	Yang Wood Yin Earth	Earth	Earth	Dragon, Dog, Ox, Sheep - the earth months of the four seasons
B	Metal Transformation	Yin Wood Yang Metal	Metal	Metal	Monkey, Rooster, Dog (Autumn Metal), Snake, Ox
C	Water Transformation	Yang Fire Yin Metal	Water	Water	Pig, Rat, Ox (Winter Water), Monkey
D	Wood Transformation	Yin Fire Yang Water	Wood	Wood	Tiger, Rabbit, Dragon (Spring Wood), Pig, Sheep
E	Fire Transformation	Yang Earth Yin Water	Fire	Fire	Snake, Horse, Sheep (Summer Fire) Tiger, Dog

For a True Transformation to occur, it will need to have the right time and the right supporting flow or place. After all, timing is a key condition in Chinese Metaphysics and the *I Ching*. The difference between success and failure lies in the timing. When you go with the flow of the right time and place, you will be successful in achieving your aims. Here are the conditions for a successful Transformation:

1. A partner who is loyal and faithful (e.g. Yang Wood paired with Yin Earth)
2. The environment or supporting flow in the chart has to be suitable and offer protection, i.e. the main energy flow within the chart should be the same as the transformed element
3. The Transformation should occur in one of the months indicated in the table.

The useful element in Transformation charts follows the newly materialized energy.

(1) When the Yang Wood Day Master combines with Yin Earth to form earth, the useful element will be earth. Fire will also be beneficial. The negative element would then be wood as it destroys the Transformed element earth.

(2) When Yin Wood and Yang Metal combine to form metal, the useful elements will be metal and earth. The negative element will be fire (which destroys the Transformed element).

We will consider several Transformation charts.

Example 6.14 District Governor from ancient China

Hour	Day	Month	Year
己	甲	壬	戊
Yin Earth	Yang Earth	Yang Water	Yang Earth
巳	辰	戌	辰
Snake	Dragon	Dog	Dragon

The Yang Wood Day Master encounters Yin Earth in the Hour Pillar and combines with it. The month of birth is the Dog month, which means the Transformation has the right timing. With five Earth Stems and Branches, the prevalent flow in the chart is also supportive. The Transformation meets all requirements. It is a superior Earth Transformation chart.

The chart above belongs to a District Governor in ancient China. It was a very important position as the country was divided into only nine districts at that time. He experienced difficulties during his childhood and early adulthood when he was in the Yin Water Pig and Yang Wood Rat Luck Cycles. This was due to the fact that wood and water threatened his useful elements earth and fire. His fortune began to change in the Ox (earth) Luck Cycle. In the Yang Fire Tiger Luck Cycle, the dominance of fire and earth saw him enjoy a good career and fulfilling life.

We now consider a Water Transformation chart which belongs to the Second Qing Emperor Qing Taizhong 清太宗.

141

Example 6.15 Qing Taizong 清太宗 (born November 8, 1592), Second Qing Emperor

Hour	Day	Month	Year
丙 Yang Fire	辛 Yin Metal	辛 Yin Metal	壬 Yang Water
申 Monkey	亥 Pig	亥 Pig	辰 Dragon

The Yin Metal Day Master combines with Yang Fire in the Hour Pillar and transforms into water. The Day Master is born in the Pig month in winter and has the right timing. The prevalent element (water) in the chart is also supportive. There is no fire or earth to interfere with the water flow. The Emperor was able to rule for almost two decades.

Next up is a Transformation chart that is more mixed. It belongs to the Fifth Qing Emperor Yongzheng 雍正.

Example 6.16 Yongzheng 雍正 (born December 13, 1678), Fifth Qing Emperor

Hour	Day	Month	Year
壬 Yang Water	丁 Yin Fire	甲 Yang Wood	戊 Yang Earth
寅 Tiger	酉 Rooster	子 Rat	午 Horse

The Yin Fire Day Master combines with Yang Water in the Hour Pillar and transforms into wood. His birth month, the Rat, is not one of the wood months. This means that the Transformation is misaligned in terms of timing and therefore less ideal. However, as water empowers wood, it offers some benefits. Does the chart have supportive wood elements? There is only the Yang Wood Month Stem which does not offer much support. The main issue with the chart is the Rooster (which contains metal) in the Day Branch which challenges the Wood Transformation and makes it a False Transformation.

Is this reflected in the Emperor's life?

As one of 14 princes, Yongzheng did not have an easy life when he was growing up. He had to prove himself through studying hard, excelling in martial arts and traveling to different districts to build and repair roads and bridges. Due to his hard work, Yongzheng finally gained his father's approval to inherit the throne. However, Yongzheng was 44 years old when he ascended to the throne. He ruled for only 13 years before his sudden death.

How did Yongzheng become the Emperor? The Directional Wood Combination was formed when the Rabbit year, the Dragon in the Luck Cycle and the Tiger in the Hour Pillar all came together. It truly reinforced his Wood Transformation chart. The Rabbit also clashed away the Rooster, his negative element and allowed Yongzheng to follow the flow of wood. He passed away in the Yang Metal Luck Cycle when his best element wood was under attack.

Now readers can differentiate between a False (Weak) and True (Strong) Transformation chart. The obstacles in a False case means assistance is required from external flows such as the year and Luck Cycles to clarify the flow so that the person can enjoy good fortune.

We now look at a Wood Transformation chart that is even more mixed than Emperor Yongzheng's. It belonged to the 11th Qing Emperor Guangxu 光緒

Example 6.17 Guangxu 光緒 (born August 14, 1871, died November 14, 1908).

Hour	Day	Month	Year
壬 Yang Water	丁 Yin Fire	丙 Yang Fire	辛 Yin Metal
寅 Tiger	亥 Pig	申 Monkey	未 Sheep

2	12	22	32
乙 Yin Wood	甲 Yang Wood	癸 Yin Water	壬 Yang Water
未 Sheep	午 Horse	巳 Snake	辰 Dragon

The Yin Fire Day Master combines with Yang Water in the Hour Pillar. The Tiger in the Hour Pillar is also supportive. However, the Monkey birth month is a time when metal is strong. This makes it the wrong time with regard to transformation. There could have been a Partial Wood Three Harmony Combination formed by the Pig and the Sheep, but this is intercepted by the Monkey. The supporting flow is flawed. To complicate matters further, there are two metal Stems and Branches that challenge the wood transformation. Significant cosmic help is required to clear the obstacles in this chart for the person to enjoy good fortune.

Let us take a look at Emperor Guangxu's life. The Emperor had many obstacles and was constantly manipulated and abused by Empress Dowager Cixi 慈禧太后. Guangxu was unable to make his own decisions. Although he was dedicated to his people and tried hard to be a good king, he ended up signing off the most humiliating treaty following the end of the First Sino-Japanese war. What was behind the event? Emperor Guangxu was in the Yin Water Luck Cycle, which attacked the positive Yang Fire Month Stem. The Yang Fire had combined with the Yin Metal in the Year Pillar to control it. With the Yang Fire compromised, the Yin Metal was then able to attack wood, his positive element.

In the Snake Luck Cycle, the Yang Fire was able to control the Yin Metal in the Year Pillar. However, the Snake clashed with the Pig (the Nobleman Star of the Yin Fire Day Master). Not only was the useful element wood being attacked, the Nobleman Star was also clashed. This explained why the conservatives within his court always blocked his plans for reforms.

Guangxu's best year proved to be 1898 (Yang Earth Dog year). At the age of 27, he pushed through the Hundred Days' Reform with the assistance of reformer Kang Youwei 康有為 . The successful event happened on June 11 that year. However, the reforms proved to be short lived as they only lasted 103 days. On September 21, 1898, Guangxu was stripped of his powers by the Empress Dowager Cixi and remained in exile until his death on November 14, 1908.

We will now look at the prevailing energies present on the day when the Emperor's reforms were pushed through and the day he was stripped of his powers.

June 11, 1898: Reforms Pushed Through

Hour	Day	Month	Year
?	乙 Yin Wood	戊 Yang Earth	戊 Yang Earth
?	巳 Snake	午 Horse	戌 Dog

September 21, 1898: Stripped of Power

Hour	Day	Month	Year
?	丁 Yin Fire	辛 Yin Metal	戊 Yang Earth
?	亥 Pig	酉 Rooster	戌 Dog

On June 11 1898, a fire team involving the Horse and Dog kept metal under control. This allowed the Wood Transformation to stay intact. He thrived and prevailed.

On September 21 1898, the prevalent metal energy attacked wood and prevented it from coming to his aid. He lost support and succumbed to his fate.

The Four Pillars charts of Emperors Yongzheng and Guangxu can only be explained through the False (Weak) Transformations charts. When encountering charts that have a mix of energies, the best way to analyze them would be to consider the life events of the individual in order to classify their charts. We have to approach the charts with an open mind and not try to force everyone into conforming to certain formulas.

While Transformation charts are rare, readers should keep in mind that some charts with mixed energies can sometimes be transformed suddenly, bringing forth short-lived fortune. This helps to explain the sudden upswings in a person's life.

Chapter Seven - Special Charts

Life is complicated as it involves many uncertainties. Every life is unique. Naturally, many Four Pillars charts do not fall into the patterns that were discussed in Chapters Five and Six. Ancient practitioners had noted down their observations and assigned a name for each special case. While some of the cases are scattered around in various Four Pillars documents, most can be found in the classics San Ming Tong Hui 三命通會 and Ming Li Zheng Zong 命理正宗. While some of these charts can be found in modern lives, deciphering their observations requires much time and verification. As a result, these special systems are seldom discussed in modern publications.

This chapter touches on some of the findings that arise in our modern time. By sharing this knowledge with readers, I hope to inspire more readers to delve deeper into Four Pillars. Together, we will discover more applications and cases to polish the theoretical basis of this system.

1) Same Division Heaven-Earth Union

The 60 Stem-Branch Pairs are divided into six Divisions of ten Pairs each (as discussed in Chapter Three). As shown in Table 7.1, within each Division, there are two Special Pairs whose Stems and Branches combine with each other.

Let us take a look at the Yang Wood Rat Division. The Special Pairs are Yang Earth Dragon and Yin Water Rooster. Between these Pairs, Yang Earth and Yin Water combine as part of the Five Stem Pairs, while Dragon and Rooster combine as one of the Six Harmony Combinations. Both the Stems and Branches combine between these two Pairs, making this a Heaven-Earth Union.

Having these Pairs in your chart is extremely auspicious. It suggests a special skill, way of thinking or position in society. The inter-changing Pairs can be located in any adjacent Pillars, not necessarily involving the Day Pillar. However, some may insist that the Day Pillar must be included.

Table 7.1 Same Division Heaven-Earth Union Pairs

Stems → / Six Divisions ↓	甲 Yang Wood	乙 Yin Wood	丙 Yang Fire	丁 Yin Fire	戊 Yang Earth	己 Yin Earth	庚 Yang Metal	辛 Yin Metal	壬 Yang Water	癸 Yin Water	Heaven-Earth Union
甲子 Yang Wood Rat	甲子 Yang Wood Rat	乙丑 Yin Wood Ox	丙寅 Yang Fire Tiger	丁卯 Yin Fire Rabbit	戊辰 Yang Earth Dragon	己巳 Yin Earth Snake	庚午 Yang Metal Fire	辛未 Yin Metal Sheep	壬申 Yang Water Monkey	癸酉 **Yin Water Rooster**	戊辰 癸酉 Yang Earth Dragon Yin water Rooster
甲戌 Yang Wood Dog	甲戌 **Yang Wood Dog**	乙亥 Yin Wood Pig	丙子 Yang Fire Rat	丁丑 Yin Fire Ox	戊寅 Yang Earth Tiger	己卯 **Yin Earth Rabbit**	庚辰 Yang Metal Dragon	辛巳 Yin Metal Snake	壬午 Yang Water Horse	癸未 Yin Water Sheep	甲戌 己卯 Yang Wood Dog Yin Earth Rabbit
甲申 Yang Wood Monkey	甲申 Yang Wood Monkey	乙酉 Yin Wood Rooster	丙戌 **Yang Fire Dog**	丁亥 Yin Fire Pig	戊子 Yang Earth Rat	己丑 Yin Earth Ox	庚寅 Yang Metal Tiger	辛卯 **Yin Metal Rabbit**	壬辰 Yang Water Dragon	癸巳 Yin Water Snake	丙戌 辛卯 Yang Fire Dog Yin Metal Rabbit
甲午 Yang Wood Horse	甲午 Yang Wood Horse	乙未 Yin Wood Sheep	丙申 Yang Fire Monkey	丁酉 Yin Fire Rooster	戊戌 **Yang Earth Dog**	己亥 Yin Earth Pig	庚子 Yang Metal Rat	辛丑 Yin Metal Ox	壬寅 Yang Water Tiger	癸卯 **Yin Water Rabbit**	戊戌 癸卯 Yang Earth Dog Yin Water Rabbit
甲辰 Yang Wood Dragon	甲辰 **Yang Wood Dragon**	乙巳 Yin Wood Snake	丙午 Yang Fire Horse	丁未 Yin Fire Sheep	戊申 Yang Earth Monkey	己酉 **Yin Earth Rooster**	庚戌 Yang Metal Dog	辛亥 Yin Metal Pig	壬子 Yang Water Rat	癸丑 Yin Water Ox	甲辰 己酉 Yang Wood Dragon Yin Earth Rooster
甲寅 Yang Wood Tiger	甲寅 Yang Wood Tiger	乙卯 Yin Wood Rabbit	丙辰 **Yang Fire Dragon**	丁巳 Yin Fire Snake	戊午 Yang Earth Horse	己未 Yin Earth Sheep	庚申 Yang Metal Monkey	辛酉 **Yin Metal Rooster**	壬戌 Yang Water Dog	癸亥 Yin Water Pig	丙辰 辛酉 Yang Fire Dragon Yin Metal Rooster

148

Note that for the Same Division Heaven-Earth Union, there are no Pairs involving Yin Wood/Yang Metal and Yin Fire/Yang Water. This is due to the fact that within the Same Division, the Branches involving these Pairs do not combine. For example, in the Yang Wood Rat Division, Yin Wood Ox and Yang Metal Horse do not have a Combination involving the Branches.

Example 7.1 Dr Albert Szent-Gyorg (born September 16, 1893), Polish Nobel Prize Winner for Medicine (1937)

Hour	Day	Month	Year
?	丙 Yang Fire	辛 Yin Metal	癸 Yin Water
?	辰 Dragon	酉 Rooster	巳 Snake

This is a Same Division Heaven-Earth Union Chart that involves the Day and Month Pillars.

Example 7.2 Ali Abdullah Saleh (born March 31 1946), Former President of Yemen

Hour	Day	Month	Year
?	甲 Yang Wood	辛 Yin Metal	丙 Yang Fire
?	辰 Dragon	卯 Rabbit	戌 Dog

This chart conforms to the Same Division Heaven-Earth Union but does not involve the Day Pillar.

I also have a client who has the Same Division Heaven-Earth Union in her chart involving the Day Pillar:

Example 7.3 Female (born November 6, 1961, between 07:00 to 09:00 hours)

Hour	Day	Month	Year
丙 Yang Fire	癸 Yin Water	戊 Yang Earth	辛 Yin Metal
辰 Dragon	卯 Rabbit	戌 Dog	丑 Ox

She is a successful manager in an IT company who enjoys a good family life and close relationships with her children.

2) Different Division Heaven-Earth Union

This type of Heaven-Earth Union does not have to involve Pairs from the same Division, but the Union has to include the Day Pillar. For example, Yin Wood Ox from the Yang Wood Rat Division can form a Different Division Heaven-Earth Union with Yang Metal Rat from the Yang Wood Horse Division.

Example 7.4 Donald Trump (born June 14, 1946, 10:54 hours)

Hour	Day	Month	Year
己	己	甲	丙
Yin Earth	Yin Earth	Yang Wood	Yang Fire
巳	未	午	丑
Snake	Sheep	Horse	Ox

While the Day and Month Pillars combine, they do not belong to the Same Division. However, with this Different Division Heaven-Earth Union, Trump is renowned for being one of the world's most successful property tycoons and entrepreneurs. He was born to a well-off family but achieved his success through his own hard work and talent. His Day Pillar Yin Earth Sheep is also one of the Six Talented Pillars (discussed in Chapter Four). Trump has a Follow the Resource (fire) chart. With all these Configurations, it is no wonder that he achieved the success he did.

Example 7.5 Camilo Jose Cela (born May 11, 1916), Spanish Nobel Laureate for Literature (1989)

Hour	Day	Month	Year
?	戊	癸	丙
	Yang Earth	Yin Water	Yang Fire
?	申	巳	辰
	Monkey	Snake	Dragon

There is also a Different Division Heaven-Earth Union between the Day and Month Pillars.

3) Mutual Exchange of Wealth, Power, Resource, Output and Siblings/Rivals Between Pillars

The Stem-Branch Exchange involves the Day Pillar and the adjacent two pillars (the Month and Hour Pillars). This Configuration within the Four Pillars chart represents special abilities and is seen in the charts of world leaders and those at the forefront of their field. When there are more elements exchanged (i.e. Power, Wealth, Resource), the person will have more skills and talents.

Example 7.6 Chiang Kai Shek 蔣介石 (born October 31, 1887, 12:20 hours)

Hour	Day	Month	Year
庚 Yang Metal	己 Yin Earth	庚 Yang Metal	丁 Yin Fire
午 Horse	己 Snake	戌 Dog	亥 Pig
丁 Yin Fire 己 **Yin Earth**	丙 Yang Fire 庚 **Yang Metal** 戊 Yang Earth	戊 **Yang Earth** 丁 Yin Fire 辛 Yin Metal	甲 Yang Wood 壬 Yang Water

Each Branch contains one or more Hidden Stems. They relate to the Day Master in different ways. How they exchange matters. In Chiang's chart, the Yin Earth Day Master has another Yin Earth Sibling present in the Horse Branch in the Hour Pillar. The Hour Stem Yang Metal also has a Yang Metal Sibling in the Day Pillar, resulting in a Sibling Exchange. This signifies the ability to rally help from trustworthy comrades whenever it is required.

The same exchange takes place between the Day and Month Pillars. The Yin Earth Day Stem finds Yang Earth in the Month Branch while the Yang Metal Month Stem finds another Yang Metal in the Day Branch. Chiang has a Double Sibling Exchange in his chart.

Example 7.7 Mao Zedong 毛澤東 (born December 26, 1893, 07:30 hours)

Hour	Day	Month	Year
甲 Yang Wood	丁 Yin Fire	甲 Yang Wood	癸 Yin Water
辰 Dragon	酉 Rooster	子 Rat	巳 Snake
癸 **Yin Water** 戊 Yang Earth 乙 Yin Wood	辛 **Yin Metal**	癸 **Yin Water**	丙 Yang Fire 庚 Yang Metal 戊 Yang Earth

The Yin Metal Stem within the Rooster controls the Yang Wood Month Stem while the Yin Water Stem within the Rat controls the Yin Fire Day Master. There is Mutual Exchange of the Power element between the Day and Month Pillars. This is highly auspicious for professional development.

The Yin Water within the Dragon in the Hour Pillar also controls the Yin Fire Day Master and the Yin Metal within the Rooster controls the Yang Wood in the Hour Pillar. There is also Mutual Exchange of the Power element between the Day and Hour Pillars. This makes Mao's chart an extremely Special Configuration.

Example 7.8 Lee Tsung-Dao 李政道 (born November 24, 1926), Nobel Prize Winner In Physics 1957

Hour	Day	Month	Year
?	丁 Yin Fire	己 Yin Earth	丙 Yang Fire
?	巳 Snake	亥 Pig	寅 Tiger
	丙 **Yang Fire** 戊 Yang Earth 庚 Yang Metal	甲 **Yang Wood** 壬 Yang Water	丙 Yang Fire 甲 Yang Wood 戊 Yang Earth

Lee became one of the youngest ever Nobel Prize winners at the age of 30. He was born in Shanghai and grew up during the Second Sino-Japanese War. Lee was only able to finish his education after the war ended. He left for graduate study in the US at the age of 20 and completed his Ph. D at 24. Lee also became Columbia University's youngest full time lecturer at the age of 30.

152

How do we account for such phenomenal success? Lee is incredibly resourceful. There is a Mutual Exchange of Resource between the Day and Month Pillars. Yang Wood in the Pig Month Branch supports his Yin Fire Day Stem while Yang Fire in the Snake Day Branch supports the Yin Earth Month Stem. This crossover pattern is a Mutual Exchange of the Resource element. It suggests assistance from mentors.

There is another Special Configuration in Lee's chart. It contains three of the four Traveling Horse Branches, the Tiger, Snake and Pig. The Monkey is the only one missing from his chart. As we cannot verify whether Lee was born in the hour of the Monkey, I'll just mention here that those with four of the Traveling Horse Branches within their chart are innovative, ambitious, self-aware and highly creative. While this Configuration is occasionally mentioned in some of the classic texts, no examples were given.

In 1956 (Yang Fire Monkey year), Lee became the youngest full time member of the Columbia University teaching faculty. He was also nominated for the Nobel Prize which he won the following year (1957, Yin Fire Rooster year). The Monkey completed the full Traveling Horse Branches within Lee's chart and brought him much success.

Here is another example that has three of the four Traveling Horse Branches.

Example 7.9 Michael Dell (born February 23, 1965), Founder and CEO of Dell Inc.

Hour	Day	Month	Year
?	戊 Yang Earth	戊 Yang Earth	乙 Yin Wood
?	申 Monkey	寅 Tiger	巳 Snake

Dell's chart is missing the Pig to form the full set of the Traveling Horse Branches. When he entered the Pig Luck Cycle at the age of 31, he formed Dell Inc. which became one of the world's leading sellers of personal computers. His business prospered during this auspicious period.

The Mutual Exchange of Power, Resource, Wealth, Output or Siblings is also an indication of special ability that may translate into financial success. Note that it is not the only criterion required for success. When we look at the Forbes list of millionaires, there is a significant number of Follow and Dominant charts.

Example 7.10 Edward Johnson the 3rd (born June 29, 1930), Chairman and CEO of Fidelity Investments

Hour	Day	Month	Year
?	庚 Yang Metal	癸 Yin Water	庚 Yang Metal
?	戊 Dog	未 Sheep	午 Horse
	戊 Yang Earth 辛 Yin Metal 丁 **Yin Fire**	乙 **Yin Wood** 丁 Yin Fire 己 Yin Earth	丁 Yin Fire 己 Yin Earth

The Wealth element of the Yang Metal Day Master is Yin Wood, which is hidden in the Sheep Month Branch. The Wealth element of Yin Water Month Stem is Yin Fire, which is hidden in the Dog Day Branch. There is a Mutual Exchange of the Wealth element between the Day and Month Pillars. This suggests that the individual obtains wealth from various sources and in different forms. Fidelity Investment is one of the largest mutual funds and financial services companies in the world.

4) Auspicious Stars Combining with Useful Elements

Auspicious Stars include the Heavenly and Monthly Virtue, the Nobleman and Academic Stars. When one or more of these Auspicious Stars are present with other Special Stars in the same palace, there will be multiple benefits for the person. This can be in the form of unexpected good news or helpful individuals. The best way to understand the positive benefits would be to find our own Auspicious Days or Months in the *Ten Thousand Year Calendar* and observe what the positive developments are.

Example 7.11 Bill Gates (born October 28, 1955)

Hour	Day	Month Heavenly and Monthly Virtue	Year
?	壬 Yang Water	丙 Yang Fire	乙 Yin Wood
?	戌 Dog	戌 Dog	未 Sheep

Bill Gates is a Yang Water Day Master. In his Month Pillar there is Yang Fire, which is both the Wealth element of Yang Water and also his Heavenly and Monthly Virtue Star. This makes him both wealthy and altruistic. He established the Bill Gates Charitable Foundation after making his fortune.

The founders of Facebook (Mark Zuckerberg, born May 14, 1984), Dell (Michael Dell, born February 23, 1965) and Intel (Gordon Moore, born January 3, 1929) all have the same Day Pillar: Yang Earth Monkey. The Monkey contains the Wealth element (Yang Water) for the Yang Earth Day Stem. It is also the Academic Star. All of them established highly successful companies as their Wealth element brought them great benefits. Everyone differed in terms of the benefits received.

Soong Ching Ling 宋慶齡, the wife of Dr Sun Yat Sen, is a Yang Wood Day Master who sits on the Directional Water Combination of Pig, Rat and Ox (as discussed in Chapter Six). The Ox is the Yang Wood Day Master's Nobleman Star. This means that her Resource element contains the Nobleman Star which contributed to her position as the First Lady.

Richard Nixon (born January 9, 1913) is a Yang Metal Day Master with the Ox in the Month Pillar. The Ox is the Nobleman Star of Yang Wood. Nixon has the Resource element containing the Nobleman Star which brought him a powerful position.

Example 7. 12 Richard Nixon (born January 9, 1913, between 19:00 and 21:00 hours)

Hour	Day	Month	Year
丙	庚	癸	壬
Yang Fire	Yang Metal	Yin Water	Yang Water
戌	寅	丑	子
Dog	Tiger	Ox	Rat
		Nobleman	

George Washington (born February 22, 1732) is a Yin Wood Day Master which had the Rat in the Year Pillar. This Rat contains both the Resource element and the Nobleman Star, which bestowed upon him a very prominent position.

Example 7.13 George Washington (born February 22, 1732, between 09:00 and 11:00 hours)

Hour	Day	Month	Year
辛	乙	壬	壬
Yin Metal	Yin Wood	Yang Water	Yang Water
已	酉	寅	子
Snake	Rooster	Tiger	Rat
			Nobleman

5) Other Configurations

Here are some other Configurations for readers to consider. Most of them involve the Power or Resource element and the Nobleman Star.

5a) Flanking Noblemen

These are Nobleman Stars that flank the Day Master in both the Hour and Month Pillars. This is a highly auspicious Configuration. It is seen in the chart of Jacqueline Kennedy Onassis (born July 28, 1929). The Sheep is one of the Nobleman Stars for her Yang Wood Day Master and is located both in the Hour and Month Pillars of her chart. The Yin Earth found within the Sheep supported the Yin Metal located above. This is the Power element of the Yang Wood Day Master. The two prominent and well supported Yin Metal Stems in the Month and Hour Pillars suggested that Kennedy Onassis married two very influential and successful

156

men.

Example 7.14 Jacqueline Kennedy Onassis (born July 28, 1929), Former First Lady of the United States

Hour	Day	Month	Year
辛 Yin Metal	甲 Yang Wood	辛 Yin Metal	己 Yin Earth
未 Sheep	戌 Dog	未 Sheep	巳 Snake
Mentor		Mentor	

The Day Masters of her two husbands were the Yin Metal Sheep (John F. Kennedy, born May 29, 1917) and Yin Earth Sheep (Aristotle Onassis, born January 15, 1906).

5b) Hidden Nobleman

The Nobleman Star of the Day Master can be hidden within two or more Branches in the Four Pillars chart. This Configuration is known as the Hidden Nobleman. Below is the chart of Qing Emperor Kangxi 康熙 (born May 4, 1654). It has the Dragon, Snake, Horse, (Sheep is a Hidden Nobleman) and Monkey Branches. The Nobleman Star Sheep is not actually present in the chart. It is concealed between the Horse and Monkey. Such a Configuration brings forth much benefit.

Example 7.15 Emperor Kangxi 康熙 (born May 4, 1654)

Hour	Day	Month	Year
丁 Yin Fire	戊 Yang Earth	戊 Yang Earth	甲 Yang Wood
巳 Snake	申 Monkey	辰 Dragon	午 Horse

5c) Year Stem repeated in the Hour Branch

When the Year Stem of the chart reappears in the Hour Pillar, it suggests that the individual is highly responsible and completes all his endeavors. It is seen in the chart of Qing Emperor Qing Taizong 清太宗 (born November 28, 1592).

The Monkey in the Hour Pillar contains Yang Water which is also found in the Year Pillar.

Example 7.16 Qing Taizong 清太宗 (born November 28, 1592)

Hour	Day	Month	Year
丙 Yang Fire	辛 Yin Metal	辛 Yin Metal	壬 Yang Water
申 Monkey	亥 Pig	亥 Pig	辰 Dragon
庚 Yang Metal 壬 **Yang Water** 戊 Yang Earth			

5d) Resource Reducing the Indirect Officer (Power element)

The Indirect Officer refers to the controlling element that is of the same polarity as the Day Master. For example, Yang Earth's Indirect Officer is Yang Wood while Yin Metal's Indirect Officer is Yin Fire. It is normally the driving force that pushes the Day Master to achieve. Many high achievers have a strong Indirect Officer. However, the Power element can become too oppressive at times and this results in a difficult life. What is the difference?

The key lies in the Resource element. If the Resource element is strong and well positioned in the chart, it gradually drains the Power element, transforming it into strength for growth. Such a scenario signifies that the person is able to work under great pressure and succeed in his or her goals. People who are able to surmount such obstacles would naturally leave a mark.

Example 7.17 Mao Zedong 毛澤東 (born December 26, 1893, 07:30 hours)

Hour Resource	Day	Month Resource	Year Indirect Officer
甲 Yang Wood	丁 Yin Fire	甲 Yang Wood	癸 Yin Water
辰 Dragon	酉 Rooster	子 Rat	巳 Snake
		Indirect Officer	

The Yin Water (in the Year Stem and the Rat Month Branch) is too strong for the Yin Fire Day Master. Without any remedy, it could kill the fire. Fortunately, a Yang Wood is positioned between the Yang Water Stem and the Rat Branch. It drains both from different directions and shields them from the Day Master. The Resource element is strong with another Yang Wood in the Hour Pillar.

To enjoy universal recognition, the Power element should be present in the Year Pillar. Having this configuration does not necessarily mean that the person will become a celebrity. At the very least, he or she will be recognized amongst his or her peers.

Here is another example with the Resource in the Year Pillar.

Example 7.18 Lily Chung (born July 3, 1937, between 11:00 and 13:00 hours)

Hour	Day	Month Indirect Officer	Year
甲 Yang Wood	辛 Yin Metal	丙 Yang Fire	丁 Yin Fire
午 Horse	卯 Rabbit	午 Horse	丑 Ox
丁 Yin Fire 己 Yin Earth	乙 Yin Wood	丁 Yin Fire 己 Yin Earth	己 Yin Earth 癸 Yin Water 辛 Yin Metal

The Yin Metal Day Master is born during the summer and is enfeebled by four fire Stems and Branches. However, she has a strategically positioned Ox as her Resource. It is very strong because of its location in the Year Pillar, right below the powerful Yin Fire and next to the Horse Month Branch. As such, the person is able to live a healthy and productive life. She also has a Flanking Nobleman chart with two Horses in the Month and Hour Pillars.

5e) Hurting Officer With Resource in the Same Pillar

This occurs when the Hurting Officer of the Day Master and the Resource element are in the same Pillar or Branch. In the chart below, the Hurting Officer of the Yin Metal Day Master is Yang Water and the Dragon contains the Resource Element Yang Earth. This Configuration is found in the Year Pillar.

Example 7.19 Chinese Writer (born October 12, 1952, between 19:00 and 21:00 hours)

Hour	Day	Month	Year Hurting Officer
戊 Yang Earth	辛 Yin Metal	己 Yin Earth	壬 Yang Water
戌 Dog	卯 Rabbit	酉 Rooster	辰 Dragon
			戊 **Yang Earth** 乙 Yin Wood 癸 Yin Water

5f) Study Hall Star In Harmony

The Harmony here refers to either the Three Harmony or the Six Harmony Combinations. When either the Three Harmony or Six Harmony Combinations involve the Study Hall Star, the person is likely to receive a promotion or recognition. Physicist Lee Tsung-Dao 李 政 道 (born November 24, 1926) is a good example. His Day Pillar is Yin Fire Snake, with the Rooster as his Study Hall Star. In 1957 (Yin Fire Rooster year), he won the Nobel Prize for Physics. The Rooster in that year combined with his Snake Day Branch, creating a Partial Three Harmony Metal Combination.

When the Study Hall Star is combined, the effects will vary depending on
(1) whether the Star belongs to a useful element and
(2) the flow of the chart.

Regardless of the effects, there will be a certain degree of recognition. The Rooster is also Lee's Nobleman Star and together with the Study Hall Star, it made the occasion doubly auspicious. When the Study Hall Star is present in the Luck Cycle, a person can take advantage of this period. To monitor the effects of this Configuration, you should note the events that occur on the Study Hall days.

5g) Talent Star with Resources - Great Administrator

The Talent Star 華蓋 is determined by the Day Branch, as shown in Table 7.2. Note that some masters use the Year Branch to determine the Talent Star.

Table 7.2 Talent Star as determined by the Day Branch

Day Branch	Talent Hua Gai 華蓋
子 Rat 辰 Dragon 申 Monkey	辰 Dragon
丑 Ox 巳 Snake 酉 Rooster	丑 Ox
寅 Tiger 午 Horse 戌 Dog	戌 Dog
卯 Rabbit 未 Sheep 亥 Pig	未 Sheep

The Talent Star represents different types of talent, which the person will need to cultivate through hard work, usually alone, thereby implying a degree of isolation from others. Those who have this Star will prefer a quiet and simple existence and should avoid verbal and legal disputes. The Talent Star can also alleviate negative developments and is considered positive. When it is present in the Luck Cycle or year, a person's talent will reveal itself. When the Talent Star is associated with an Empty Branch, the individual will have an interest in studying and understanding religion or spiritual matters.

The Talent with Resource Configuration is formed when the Talent Star 華蓋星:
(1) contains the Resource element,
(2) is the Resource element or
(3) is in the same Pillar as the Resource Element.

We will consider the chart of Ming Dynasty Statesman Zhang Juzheng (born 1525).

Example 7.20 Zhang Juzheng 張居正 (born 1525), Ming Dynasty statesman

Hour	Day	Month	Year
辛	辛	辛	乙
Yin Metal	Yin Metal	Yin Metal	Yin Wood
卯	酉	巳	酉
Rabbit	Rooster	Snake	Rooster

The Talent Star for Zhang (with the Rooster Day Branch) is the Ox. Zhang has a Dominant Metal chart and benefits from the Ox as it reinforces his dominance by completing the Three Harmony Metal Combination in his chart. The Rooster in Zhang's Day and Year Pillars already form a Partial Three Harmony Metal Combination with the Snake in the Month Pillar. The Ox also contains Yin Earth, which is Zhang's Resource element.

5h) Early Success In Life

Also known as Prosperity present in the Hour Pillar, this occurs when the element of the Day Master is also in the Hour Pillar. The Hour Branch corresponds to the directional sectors of the Day Master as seen in Table 7.3. When the rest of the chart is favorable, the person will enjoy good career prospects throughout his or her life. Even if the chart has issues, the person will always be employed. However, the Power element should not be present in the chart.

Table 7.3 Day Master and Hour of Birth for Early Success in Life

Day Master	Yang Wood Yin Wood	Yang Fire Yin Fire	Yang Earth Yin Earth	Yang Metal Yin Metal	Yang Water Yin Water
Hour of Birth	Tiger Rabbit	Snake Horse	Snake Horse	Monkey Rooster	Pig Rat

5i) The Power element with the Heavenly or Monthly Virtue Stars that Combines with the Day Master - Fame and Fortune

When the individual's Power element contains the Heavenly or Monthly Virtue Stars and there is a Combination with the Day Master, the person will leave his or her mark on history.

Example 7.21 Zhou Yushan 周玉山, Qing Dynasty official

Hour	Day	Month	Year
		Monthly Virtue Star Power element of Yin Fire Combines with Yin Fire Day Master	
壬 Yang Water	丁 Yin Fire	壬 Yang Water	丁 Yin Fire
寅 Tiger	酉 Rooster	子 Rat	酉 Rooster

Zhou is a Yin Fire Day Master born in the Rat month. His Monthly Virtue Star is Yang Water, which is present in both the Month and Hour Pillars. Yang Water is also his Power element. The Monthly Virtue Star and the Power element occur concurrently in the same Stem. The Yang Water Stem also combines with the Yin Fire Day Master.

Zhou enjoyed 30 years as a highly respected national administrator.

Example 7.22 Stephen Chow 周星馳 (born June 22, 1962, between 07:00 and 09:00 hours), Hong Kong Actor

Hour	Day	Month	Year
		Monthly Virtue Star Power element of Yin Metal Combines with Yin Metal Day Master	
壬 Yang Water	辛 Yin Metal	丙 Yang Fire	壬 Yang Water
辰 Dragon	卯 Rabbit	午 Horse	寅 Tiger

5j) Yang Wood with Yin Earth that becomes prosperous - High Integrity.

This refers to the Yang Wood and Yin Earth Combination that transforms into earth and has both the support of the season and the rest of the chart (i.e. Branches). Under these circumstances, the person will be trustworthy. The person will also be honest and have integrity when:

163

1. there is a strong presence of earth in the chart and
2. earth is the useful element.

5k) When the Day and Month Stems are duplicated - Stressful Life

When a Yang Wood Day Master encounters a Yang Wood in the Month Pillar or when a Yang Fire Day Master has another Yang Fire in the Month Pillar, it creates very clear Rivals in the chart. They are constantly fighting for prosperity. The Day Master is likely to struggle hard for a living.

5l) The Peach Blossom Star encounters the Nobleman, Heavenly or Monthly Virtue Star in the same palace – High Status and Prosperity. It is preferable that the sign falls into a void position.

The Peach Blossom Star is considered inauspicious as it has associations with promiscuity. However, when the Nobleman, Heavenly or Monthly Virtue Stars are associated with these Peach Blossom Stars, any negativity is redressed. The chart should have a Special Configuration to attract the attention of helpful individuals and obtain benefits. When the Peach Blossom Star is associated with an Empty Branch, the benefits are magnified as the person will have a good sense of justice and not yield to temptation.

Example 7.23 Lily Chung (born July 3, 1937, between 11:00 hours and 13:00 hours)

Hour	Day	Month	Year
甲	辛	丙	丁
Yang Wood	Yin Metal	Yang Fire	Yin Fire
午	卯	午	丑
Horse	Rabbit	Horse	Ox
Nobleman Empty/Void Peach Blossom		Nobleman Empty/Void Peach Blossom	

The Yin Metal Rabbit Day Pillar has its Empty (Void) Branches at Horse and Sheep. The Horse is also the Nobleman of the Yin Metal Day Master as well as the Peach Blossom Star for the Ox year of birth.

Chapter Eight - Five Elements And Health

Birth, aging, illness and death; these are the life stages that we all have to go through. Sadly, we were born unequal, with joy and sorrow, good health and illness not equally distributed. While some were born to enjoy good health, a few seem to be doomed to suffer illnesses. Why is this so? Globally, those skilled in metaphysics, philosophy or religion have endlessly sought to answer these questions.

Illness is the domain of medicine and science, and the success that Man has achieved in these fields is undeniable. I respect, depend on and am grateful to science for resolving many of Man's problems and restoring our health and well-being. I also believe in the objectivity of science and in its research procedures with respect to illnesses. However, among all the impressive observations and discoveries in the medical field, one puzzle remains. Why does a seemingly healthy person suddenly develop a fatal disease at a particular moment in time? Is it fate or destiny? How does one predict this?

Over the years, through practice and research, I have seen how people fell ill and passed on when negative elements from their Luck Cycle or external cosmic flows (i.e. the year) impacted their Four Pillars charts. Western medicine has never embraced any notion of the five elements. In contrast, Traditional Chinese Medicine practitioners use theories from the *I Ching* and place an emphasis on the five elements. In China, more Traditional Chinese Medicine practitioners are integrating their practice with Western medicine. So what is the role of the five elements in medicine and diagnosis?

Without any formal training in Western or Traditional Chinese Medicine, I am unable to offer any theoretical discussion on their merits. What I will do here is share some of my observations with you.

Stems, Branches and Illness

To understand the effects of the five elements on our health, we need to understand the different theoretical basis which is divided into two parts:

1. Stems, Branches and Corresponding Parts of the Body:

According to Chinese Metaphysics, there are indications in our Four Pillars charts regarding the illnesses and accidents to which we may be vulnerable. There are 22 Stems and Branches. Each represents different body parts and organs. Illness can strike any part of the body. Table 8.1 lists the Stems and Branches with their corresponding body parts so that we can objectively assess what may potentially harm a person.

Table 8.1 combines Traditional Chinese Medicine theory with Four Pillars principles, both from my own experience and from the following books: You Da Ren's 尤達人 Ming Li Tong Jian 命理通鑑 (1984) and Kun Yuan's 堃元 Biao Zun Wan Nian Li Bie Ce 標準萬年曆別冊 (1986). In Table 8.1, the Traditional Chinese Medicine organ associations are listed at the top of each section with the Four Pillars organ relationships below.

Table 8.1 Association between the Five Elements and Body Organs and Parts

Stem	甲 Yang Wood	乙 Yin Wood	丙 Yang Fire	丁 Yin Fire	戊 Yang Earth	己 Yin Earth	庚 Yang Metal	辛 Yin Metal	壬 Yang Water	癸 Yin Water
Body Part	Gall Bladder Head	Liver Neck	Small Intestine Shoulder	Heart	Stomach Pelvis	Spleen	Large Intestine Navel	Lung Pelvis	Bladder Head Back	Kidney Foot

Branch	子 Rat	丑 Ox	寅 Tiger	卯 Rabbit	辰 Dragon	巳 Snake	午 Horse	未 Sheep	申 Monkey	酉 Rooster	戌 Dog	亥 Pig
Body Part	Bladder Back	Spleen Abdomen	Gallbladder Neck Shoulder	Liver Eye Hand	Stomach Brain Chest Back	Heart Face Teeth	Small Intestine Abdomen	Spleen Pelvis Chest	Large Intestine	Lung	Stomach Head Neck Lung	Kidney Liver Head

167

Here are some observations from my own study and research on how the five elements affect our health:

- Properly balanced elements in a chart will keep one in good health.
- Mixed and conflicting elements in a chart may give rise to multiple illnesses.
- A prevalent element leading a person's chart will shield him or her from the onset of illness. The prevalent element has to stay intact; otherwise there will be no protection, which may result in health issues.
- A weak self supported by a strong Resource element stays in good health.
- The following are triggers for health issues:
  1. Sibling Rivalry for the Resource, Wealth, Power or Output elements.
  2. Clashes involving useful elements
  3. Competition between Stems and Branches for Combinations, e.g. between Three Harmony and Six Harmony Combinations

In Chinese medicine:

1) The kidney affects reproductive ability and overall well- being.

2) The liver relates to the soul (hun 魂) and the gallbladder courage.

3) The heart relates to a person's intelligence (shen 神).

4) The spleen relates to a person's energy levels (qi 氣).

2) The Five Elements, Personality Traits, Parts of the Body and Illness:

Wood
- Wood is associated with benevolence. The presence of strong functional wood in a chart suggests a kind and loving person.
- It is associated with the liver, sinews and the four limbs (arms and legs).
- When wood is harmed by metal, the person may be prone to liver and gall bladder disease, eye problems and convulsions.
- Prevalent metal within a chart could hurt the liver or gall bladder.

Fire

- Fire symbolizes courtesy, as well as a person's talents and skills.
- A strong fire individual is courteous, obliging and intelligent.
- When the fire element is the useful element and is supported by wood within a chart, the person will be kind and talented.
- Fire represents the heart and eye.
- Excessive water in the chart hurts fire, giving rise to vision issues.
- Excessive fire harms the skin, lungs and large intestine.

Earth

- Earth signifies trust and integrity.
- When there is hollow earth depleted by excessive metal within a chart, the person may have integrity issues and is not to be trusted.
- Those with earth and metal as useful elements within their chart will be intelligent and are likely to hold a high position.
- Earth represents the abdomen, spleen and digestive system.
- Excessive wood within a chart injures the earth, causing issues in the spleen, gall bladder, stomach, abdominal distension and diarrhea.

Metal

- Metal stands for a sense of justice, courage and principles.
- Dominant Metal charts or those with metal as their useful element will be just, courageous and decisive.
- When metal within a chart is cleansed by water, the person will be confident, refined and attractive.
- Metal represents the lungs, hair and skin.
- Excessive fire within a chart will harm the body parts associated with metal, i.e. the lungs, bones and skin.

Water

- Water represents wisdom and intelligence.
- It also signifies the kidney, bladder and ear.
- Unfavorable earth pollutes water, creating issues for the kidney, reproductive organs, ears, psychological disorders or learning disabilities.
- Excessive water may cause coughing, abdominal pain and diarrhea.

We focus on the useful element when assessing the types of illnesses in the following charts. When the useful element is under attack, issues arise.

Cancer

Example 8.1 Steve Jobs (born February 24, 1955, 19:15 hours, died October 5, 2011, between 17:00 and 19:00 hours)

Date of Birth			
Hour	**Day**	**Month**	**Year**
戊 Yang Earth	丙 Yang Fire	戊 Yang Earth	乙 Yin Wood
戌 Dog	辰 Dragon	寅 Tiger	未 Sheep

Date of Death			
Hour	**Day**	**Month**	**Year**
辛 Yin Metal	癸 Yin Water	戊 Yang Earth	辛 Yin Metal
酉 Rooster	巳 Snake	戌 Dog	卯 Rabbit

7	17	27	37	47
丁 Yin Fire	丙 Yang Fire	乙 Yin Wood	甲 Yang Wood	癸 Yin Water
丑 Ox	子 Rat	亥 Pig	戌 Dog	酉 Rooster

Jobs is a Yang Fire Day Master standing alone in an environment with abundant wood. He follows the flow of wood. Jobs is also born in spring when wood is in season and strong. As wood fuels or supports fire, it is the Resource element. Jobs has a Follow the Resource chart, or a Many

Mothers, One Child chart.

The useful element is wood. Metal is the negative element. While Jobs thrived during the wood and water Luck Cycles, he was challenged during the metal Luck Cycles. As Jobs is a Yang Fire Day Master, his flow is threatened during the fire Luck Cycles. The Day Master encounters Competition or Rivalry. This scenario may result in illness and even death.

Here are some developments in Jobs' life that support our reasoning:

- In 2006 (Yang Fire Dog year), the Yang Fire Rival appeared and disrupted the flow of the chart. At 51, Jobs entered the Rooster Luck Cycle that contained Yin Metal. The wood in his chart came under attack. The liver is represented by wood. Jobs was diagnosed with liver cancer during this period of time.
- In 2009 (Yin Earth Ox year), when the Ox in the year combined with the Rooster Luck Cycle to form a Partial Three Harmony Metal Combination, his liver cancer worsened. The increased metal flow further damaged his useful element wood. Jobs had a liver transplant at the age of 54 towards the end of this Luck Cycle.
- On October 5, 2011, Jobs passed away when the metal element was extremely strong. He died during the last three days of the festival marker White Dew, which has the strongest metal flow. On the day Jobs died, there was a Partial Three Harmony Metal Combination (Snake in the Day Pillar and Rooster in the Hour Pillar). There were also three additional metal Stems and Branches.

Jobs died in autumn, when metal is at its peak. There is an ancient Chinese formula that goes: *Illness in the liver, should recover in the summer* (fire curtails metal, which spares wood). *If it does not worsen in the summer, it will last till the autumn. If the person survives the autumn, he can hold on and tide over the winter.* Jobs passed away in the autumn.

While the wood element is strong in Jobs' chart, there are no Three Harmony, Six Harmony or Directional Wood Combinations. The wood Branches are the Tiger, Dragon and

Sheep, all of which contain other elements such as earth, fire and water. The energy is mixed and it is difficult to fully tap into the wood energy. This may account for his bad temper and melancholia. However, when the Rabbit appears in the Luck Cycle or year, a Wood Directional Combination is formed between the Tiger in the Month Pillar, the Rabbit and the Dragon in the Day Pillar. The appearance of a Pig in the Luck Cycle or year will form a Partial Three Harmony Wood Combination with the Sheep in the Year Pillar. Both these scenarios result in the flow of wood, which will make the individual calmer and more relaxed in his approach to life.

Example 8.2 Michael Milken (born July 4, 1946, 07:31 hours), American financier

Hour	Day	Month	Year
戊	己	乙	丙
Yang Earth	Yin Earth	Yin Wood	Yang Fire
辰	卯	未	戌
Dragon	Rabbit	Sheep	Dog

4	14	24	34	44
丙	丁	戊	己	庚
Yang Fire	Yin Fire	Yang Earth	Yin Earth	Yang Metal
申	酉	戌	亥	子
Monkey	Rooster	Dog	Pig	Rat

54	64	74	84
辛	壬	癸	甲
Yin Metal	Yang Water	Yin Water	Yang Wood
丑	寅	卯	辰
Ox	Tiger	Rabbit	Dragon

Milken is a Yin Earth Day Master that follows the prevalent element wood. Wood is the useful element. The negative elements are metal (which destroys wood) and earth (his Competitors or Rivals). The period marked by the Year Pillar Yang Fire Dog indicated the time from childhood up till his late teenage years. By the age of 20, Milken's chart became a Follow the Power (wood) chart.

- In the Pig Luck Cycle (1980 to 1985), the full Three Harmony Wood Combination was formed (with the Rabbit in his Day Pillar and the Sheep in his Month Pillar). Milken built a thriving enterprise in junk bonds.
- In 1989 (Yin Earth Snake year with a hidden Yang Metal Stem) during the Yang Metal Luck Cycle, Milken was found guilty of insider trading and sentenced to ten years imprisonment.
- In 1991 (Yin Metal Sheep year), when the Sheep strengthened his wood flow, Milken was released after serving only two years of his prison sentence.
- In 1993 (Yin Water Rooster year), the metal within the Rooster attacked Milken's useful element wood, and specifically, his Three Harmony Wood Combination. The Combination is crucial for his overall well-being as a Follow the Wood chart. Milken was diagnosed with prostate cancer at the age of 47. When the metal energy of the year waned, he was able to recover with the protection of his useful element wood in 1994 (Yang Wood Dog year) and 1995 (Yin Wood Pig year).

The conflicting metal and wood in Milken's chart mixed with the earth elements manifested itself as an illness associated with the pelvis and lower abdomen.

So why were the issues different in the two examples when metal clashed with wood? When the useful element is attacked, it will only indicate problems. The magnitude and nature of the problems will vary from place to place, from time to time and from person to person.

Example 8.3 Ingrid Bergman (born August 29, 1915, 03:30 hours, died August 29, 1982)

Date of Birth			
Hour	**Day**	**Month**	**Year**
壬 Yang Water	壬 Yang Water	甲 Yang Wood	乙 Yin Wood
寅 Tiger	辰 Dragon	申 Monkey	卯 Rabbit

Date of Death			
Hour	**Day**	**Month**	**Year**
?	甲 Yang Wood	戊 Yang Earth	壬 Yang Water
?	申 Monkey	申 Monkey	戌 Dog

3	13	23	33	43	53	63
乙 Yin Wood	丙 Yang Fire	丁 Yin Fire	戊 Yang Earth	己 Yin Earth	庚 Yang Metal	辛 Yin Metal
酉 Rooster	戌 Dog	亥 Pig	子 Rat	丑 Ox	寅 Tiger	

As discussed in Chapter Three Example 3.7, Bergman's chart uses the Output element wood. With wood as her useful element, Bergman is vulnerable to metal which attacks wood. In the Yin Metal Luck Cycle, she was diagnosed with breast cancer. Bergman passed away towards the end of this Luck Cycle after fighting the disease for almost five years.

In Traditional Chinese Medicine theory, the breast is under the domain of the liver channel, which is represented by wood. On the day Bergman died, the metal element was extremely strong.

Example 8.4 Anita Mui 梅艷芳 (born October 10. 1963, died December 30, 2003), Hong Kong singer and actress

Date of Birth			
Hour	**Day**	**Month**	**Year**
?	丙 Yang Fire	辛 Yin Metal	癸 Yin Water
?	戌 Dog	酉 Rooster	卯 Rabbit

Date of Death			
Hour	**Day**	**Month**	**Year**
辛 Yin Metal	丁 Yin Fire	甲 Yang Wood	癸 Yin Water
丑 Ox	丑 Ox	子 Rat	未 Sheep

10	20	30	40
壬 Yang Water	癸 Yin Water	甲 Yang Wood	乙 Yin Wood
戌 Dog	亥 Pig	子 Rat	

Mui is a Yang Fire Day Master born in the Rooster month in autumn, when the metal element is strong. Fire in autumn is weak. As a result, metal becomes the Dominant flow. Two developments prevent Mui's chart from becoming a Follow chart:

(1) The Day Master is supported by wood present in the Month Pillar.
(2) Fire is hidden in the Dog Branch in the Day Pillar.
Mui is a strong self in control of wealth.

However, the system is shaky. The powerful metal is too robust and requires much energy to control it. Under constant pressure to make money, Mui needs to control the Wealth element to achieve this. As a result, she is in constant need for more Resource (wood) to give her additional strength. Mui's chart would be a borderline case as at times, she is able to follow metal, the Wealth element. She first became famous in 1981 (Yin Metal Rooster year) at the age of 18, during the Dog Luck Cycle.

175

What does wood do? Mui enjoyed the peak of her career during the Pig Luck Cycle (1988 to 1993). The Pig combined with the Rabbit in her Year Pillar to strengthen her. It was the strongest wood Luck Cycle. She became a strong wood self who fully controlled the Wealth element metal and was able to use it. While Mui continued to be in the public eye for the rest of her life, it was tumultuous due to the constant tussle between metal and wood in her chart.

Metal represented her opportunities for wealth, which also consistently motivated her to fight for it. At the age of 35, she entered the Rat Luck Cycle which weakened her Day Master Fire energy. In 2003 (Yin Water Sheep year), the Sheep combined with the Rabbit in her Year Pillar to form wood. Unfortunately, wet wood cannot ignite a fire. Rather, this increased her stress and disrupted her peace of mind. The fire within her chart was weakened. Mui was diagnosed with cervical cancer. The cervix is governed by the wood element that also represents the liver.

On the day she died, metal was extremely strong as there were two Oxen clashing with the Sheep of the year. Her useful element wood was attacked. Mui's Fire self was trapped in a battle between metal and wood in which metal triumphed. The Fire self lost the support of wood and succumbed to the cancer. Both Bergman's and Mui's charts have the conflict between metal and their useful element wood.

Example 8.5 Robert Taylor (born August 5, 1911, 07:00 hours, died June 8, 1969)

Date of Birth			
Hour	**Day**	**Month**	**Year**
甲 Yang Wood	丁 Yin Fire	乙 Yin Wood	辛 Yin Metal
辰 Dragon	未 Sheep	未 Sheep	亥 Pig

Date of Death			
Hour	**Day**	**Month**	**Year**
?	甲 Yang Wood	己 Yin Earth	己 Yin Earth
?	寅 Tiger	巳 Snake	酉 Rooster

10	20	30	40	50
甲 Yang Wood	癸 Yin Water	壬 Yang Water	辛 Yin Metal	庚 Yang Metal
午 Horse	巳 Snake	辰 Dragon	卯 Rabbit	寅 Tiger

Taylor has a Follow the Resource or a Many Mothers, One Child chart. The Partial Three Harmony Combination between the Pig and Sheep in his chart produces his Resource element wood. Wood is also his useful element. However, this Combination is very fragile. If a Tiger appears (e.g. in the Luck Cycle), the Partial Three Harmony Combination will be broken up as it combines with the Pig in the Year Pillar to form a Six Harmony Combination. Taylor is also vulnerable to metal, which attacks the useful element wood.

In the Tiger Luck Cycle (at the age of 58), Taylor was diagnosed with lung cancer. He passed away on a Tiger day, when the Tiger interfered with the Three Harmony Wood Combination within his chart. In addition, in 1969 (Yin Earth Rooster year), metal was strong and attacked wood. Metal is associated with the lung.

Metal is clearly the negative element for Taylor. His mother passed away due to a terminal illness when he was ten during the Yin Metal Luck Cycle. Taylor's Hollywood career did not fare well in the metal years. In 1945 (Yin Wood

177

Rooster year), 1957 (Yin Fire Rooster year) and 1961 (Yin Metal Ox year), he did not appear in a single film. This was due to Taylor's useful element wood being attacked.

Our career, wealth and health are all related to the strength of our useful elements. Knowing and protecting our useful elements is crucial for our success and overall well-being.

Example 8.6 Gary Cooper (born May 7, 1901, 0545 hours, died May 31, 1961)

Date of Birth			
Hour	**Day**	**Month**	**Year**
己 Yin Earth	乙 Yin Wood	壬 Yang Water	辛 Yin Metal
卯 Rabbit	酉 Rooster	辰 Dragon	丑 Ox

Date of Death			
Hour	**Day**	**Month**	**Year**
?	甲 Yang Wood	癸 Yin Water	辛 Yin Metal
?	子 Rat	巳 Snake	丑 Ox

6	16	26	36	46	56
辛 Yin Metal	庚 Yang Metal	己 Yin Earth	戊 Yang Earth	丁 Yin Fire	丙 Yang Fire
卯 Rabbit	寅 Tiger	丑 Ox	子 Rat	亥 Pig	戌 Dog

As discussed in Chapter Six Example 6.3, Cooper passed away due to lung cancer in the final year of the Dog Luck Cycle. Cooper's situation is similar to Taylor's as both their useful elements are under attack. While Taylor's useful element wood is under attack by metal, Cooper's useful elements metal was compromised by hidden fire. The Fire within the Dog destroys metal, which represents the lung.

Example 8.7 Susan Hayward (born June 30, 1917, 16:01 hours, died March 4, 1975)

Date of Birth			
Hour	**Day**	**Month**	**Year**
庚	癸	丙	丁
Yang Metal	Yin Water	Yang Fire	Yin Fire
申	卯	午	巳
Monkey	Rabbit	Horse	Snake

Date of Death			
Hour	**Day**	**Month**	**Year**
?	己	戊	乙
	Yin Earth	Yang Earth	Yin Wood
?	酉	寅	卯
	Rooster	Tiger	Rabbit

3	13	23	33	43	53
丁	戊	己	庚	辛	壬
Yin Fire	Yang Earth	Yin Earth	Yang Metal	Yin Metal	Yang Water
卯	辰	巳	午	未	申
Rabbit	Dragon	Snake	Horse	Sheep	Monkey

Hayward is a Yin Water Day Master born in the Horse month in summer when fire is strong. The fire is further strengthened by the Rabbit in the Day Pillar, rendering Hayward's chart a Follow the Wealth (fire) chart. Fire is the useful element. Water is the negative element as it destroys fire.

At the age of 58, during the Yang Water Luck Cycle, the strong water disrupted the flow of fire in her chart and she died of a brain tumor. From Table 8.1, we can see that Yang Water represents the head. On the day Hayward died, the Rooster day clashed with the Rabbit in her Day Pillar. The Rabbit is the Nobleman Star for the Yin Water Day Master. When the Nobleman Star is involved in a Clash, problems arise.

The examples above encompassed clashes involving all five elements. In each case, the useful element is under attack and the body part involved can be traced to the Stems and Branches. When the useful element is under attack, there can be other manifestations such as losing one's job or having financial problems. For those who are well off, losing their job or some of their wealth may not be too challenging. However, when it comes to health issues, everyone is affected regardless of socio-economic background.

AIDS

AIDS or Acquired Immunodeficiency Disease Syndrome is caused by HIV, the Human Immunodeficiency Virus. The body's immune system is compromised, resulting in a person being vulnerable to a range of secondary infections and diseases. From a Four Pillars perspective, the governing energy of the chart will be weakened and the useful element damaged or destroyed. Its effect is different from that of cancer, as can be seen in the following examples:

Example 8.8 Rock Hudson (born November 17, 1925, 02:15 hours, died October 2, 1985)

Date of Birth			
Hour	**Day**	**Month**	**Year**
丁	乙	丁	乙
Yin Fire	Yin Wood	Yin Fire	Yin Wood
丑	巳	亥	丑
Ox	Snake	Pig	Ox

Date of Death			
Hour	**Day**	**Month**	**Year**
?	甲	乙	乙
	Yang Wood	Yin Wood	Yin Wood
?	戌	酉	丑
	Dog	Rooster	Ox

3	13	23	33	43	53
丙	乙	甲	癸	壬	辛
Yang Fire	Yin Wood	Yang Wood	Yin Water	Yang Water	Yin Metal
戌	酉	申	未	午	巳
Dog	Rooster	Monkey	Sheep	Horse	Snake

Hudson is a Yin Wood Day Master sitting on a Partial Three Harmony Metal Combination within his Branches. The Snake in the Day Pillar combines with the Ox in the Year and Hour Pillars. The roots of the Yin Wood Day Master are cut

180

by metal. Fortunately, two Yin Fire Stems keep the metal under control, and another Yang Wood hidden in the Pig offers support. Hudson's chart is weak requiring the assistance of fire and wood. Metal is negative as it damages his useful element wood.

All his key life events demonstrate how metal created issues for him.

- In the Rooster Luck Cycle, the full Three Harmony Metal Combination of Rooster, Ox and Snake trimmed his roots dramatically. Hudson was not doing well financially, wandering from one odd job to another. Symbolically, his Yin Wood Day Master had no foothold as it was without any roots. Hudson could not gain admission into any college.
- During the Yang Wood Luck Cycle from the age of 23, additional wood flow gave Hudson his breakthrough into acting with the help of friends.
- He became famous in the years 1954 (Yang Wood Monkey year) to 1956 (Yang Fire Monkey year), when the favorable wood and fire elements were able to help him. Fire controls the negative element metal.
- In 1978 (Yang Fire Horse year) at the age of 53, he entered the Yin Metal Luck Cycle and started having health issues associated with his drinking. Hudson also found it difficult to get acting roles.
- In 1983 (Yin Water Pig year) at 58, Hudson entered the Snake Luck Cycle, which combined with the Ox Branches in his chart to form a Partial Three Harmony Metal Combination. He was diagnosed HIV positive.
- In 1985 (Yin Wood Ox year), in the Rooster month, when the Full Three Harmony Metal Combination was present, he succumbed to AIDS.

The clash between metal and the useful element wood in Hudson's chart manifested as AIDS.

Example 8.9 Arthur Ashe (born July 10, 1943, 12:55 hours, died February 6, 1993)

Date of Birth			
Hour	**Day**	**Month**	**Year**
戊 Yang Earth	己 Yin Earth	己 Yin Earth	癸 Yin Water
午 Horse	巳 Snake	未 Sheep	未 Sheep

Date of Death			
Hour	**Day**	**Month**	**Year**
?	戊 Yang Earth	甲 Yang Wood	癸 Yin Water
?	午 Horse	寅 Tiger	酉 Rooster

1	11	21	31	41
丙 Yang Fire	乙 Yin Wood	甲 Yang Wood	癸 Yin Water	壬 Yang Water
午 Horse	巳 Snake	辰 Dragon	卯 Rabbit	寅 Tiger

Ashe is a Yin Earth Day Self surrounded by six Earth Stems and Branches. He is also supported by the Directional Fire Combination (Snake, Fire and Sheep). Ashe is a Dominant Earth chart, whose useful elements are fire and earth. Ashe is vulnerable to wood and water which damage his useful elements. There are two Sheep Branches that contain wood – they could easily turn into the Partial Three Harmony Wood Combination with the onset of a Pig or Rabbit. When that occurs, Ashe's earth team will be broken up, undermining his total well-being. As the saying goes: *Hidden killers are waiting for the opportune moment to pounce.* This is an extremely frail and fragile chart.

All these observations showed up in Ashe's key life events:

- Before Ashe turned 32, his Luck Cycles were mostly fire and earth, which bestowed upon him good fortune. The peak of his career was in 1975 (Yin Wood Rabbit year) when he won the Wimbledon singles title.
- Once he entered the Rabbit Luck Cycle (1979 to 1984), the Partial Three Harmony Wood Combination came along. Ashe suffered from various health issues.
- In 1979 (Yin Earth Sheep year) when the Sheep in the year further reinforced the Three Harmony Wood Combination in his chart, he underwent heart surgery following a heart attack at the age of 36.
- In 1980 (Yang Metal Monkey year) at 37, Ashe announced his retirement from tennis after his heart surgery.
- In 1983 (Yin Water Pig year), he had a second round of heart surgery to correct the previous surgery. Ashe and his doctors believed that he contracted HIV at that time through a blood transfusion. There was a Full Three Harmony Wood Combination that year.
- In 1988 (Yang Earth Dragon year), Ashe was diagnosed HIV positive at the age of 45 during the Yang Water Luck Cycle after experiencing paralysis in his right arm.
- On the day Ashe died, the negative wood and water energies were strong. They attacked his useful elements earth and fire.

Ashe succumbed to AIDS when his useful elements earth and fire were attacked by wood and water. This is different from Hudson's chart, which had the metal-wood clash. What the two charts have in common is that the useful elements are under attack.

Example 8.10 Isaac Asimov (born January 2, 1920, 14:00 hours, died April 6, 1992)

Date of Birth			
Hour	**Day**	**Month**	**Year**
辛 Yin Metal	己 Yin Earth	丙 Yang Fire	己 Yin Earth
未 Sheep	未 Sheep	子 Rat	未 Sheep

Date of Death			
Hour	**Day**	**Month**	**Year**
?	壬 Yang Water	甲 Yang Wood	壬 Yang Water
?	子 Rat	辰 Dragon	申 Monkey

10	20	30	40	50	60	70
乙 Yin Wood	甲 Yang Wood	癸 Yin Water	壬 Yang Water	辛 Yin Metal	庚 Yang Metal	己 Yin Earth
亥 Pig	戌 Dog	酉 Rooster	申 Monkey	未 Sheep	午 Horse	

Asimov is a Yin Earth Sheep Day Master. His Day Pillar Yin Earth Sheep is one of the six Talented Pillars that signifies intelligence. This was discussed in Chapter Four. Asimov wrote 400 books and was a member of MENSA.

With another Yin Earth in the Year Pillar and three more Yin Earth Branches, Asimov has an Earth Sibling Rivalry chart. The threat comes from the identical Yin Earth in the Year Pillar as both are equal in strength. This results in stressful battles of long duration that end in stalemates. The Rat in the Month Branch that contains the Wealth element water is tempting the Siblings to fight amongst themselves. Asimov did not have a peaceful life.

This conflict may manifest as emotional instability. Asimov was afraid of flying and also preferred small, confined spaces.

What is Asimov's useful element? It has to be Yang Wood which combines with the other Yin Earth in his chart. He did very well during the Yang Wood Luck Cycle in his graduate studies. There were no more wood Luck Cycles after the age of 24.

- Asimov became a professor of chemistry at the age of 28 and enjoyed a good reputation for both his academic and literary careers.
- In 1977 (Yin Fire Sheep year) during the Sheep Luck Cycle at 57, the onset of additional fire from the year empowered the earth Competitors within his chart. Asimov suffered a heart attack that required surgery. Four earth Competitors were fighting.
- In 1983 (Yin Water Pig year), Asimov had further heart surgery and it was believed that he contracted HIV during this procedure. Additional water created battles among the earth Rivals.
- From 1990 (Yang Metal Horse year), Asimov entered the Yin Earth Luck Cycle. With two earth Rivals (in the Year Pillar and Luck Cycle) competing for water (Wealth), his heart condition worsened.
- On the day Asimov died, there was the Full Three Harmony Water Combination that caused the Yin Earth Rivals to battle hard for wealth. This resulted in his death.

Why is the Wealth Luck Cycle so lethal to the Competitive charts? Money has always been the source of conflict or battle. On many occasions, Man has lost his life due to wealth. Most successful tycoons belong to either the Dominant or Follow charts rather than the Sibling Rivalry chart.

As we can see from our three examples, AIDS-related cases can be due to Competitors fighting over Wealth or the useful element being injured. Here are three cases for readers to consider, all of them male actors or singers.

185

1) Anthony Perkins, (born April 4, 1932, died September 12, 1992)
2) John Hargreaves, (born November 28, 1945, died January 8, 1996)
3) Liberace (born May 16, 1919, 23:15 hours, died February 4, 1987)

Other Illnesses

We will now consider some unusual health issues. As there are only one or two examples for each illness, the explanations will be more detailed.

Psychological Illness:

When the energy of the chart is weak, it may manifest as mental or psychological illness such as depression, dementia or others.

Example 8.11 Ted Kaczynski (born May 22, 1942), the Unabomber

Hour	Day	Month	Year
?	乙 Yin Wood	乙 Yin Wood	壬 Yang Water
?	亥 Pig	巳 Snake	午 Horse

5	15	25	35	45
丙 Yang Fire	丁 Yin Fire	戊 Yang Earth	己 Yin Earth	庚 Yang Metal
午 Horse	未 Sheep	申 Monkey	酉 Rooster	戌 Dog

55	65	75
辛 Yin Metal	壬 Yang Water	癸 Yin Water
亥 Pig	子 Rat	丑 Ox

Kaczynski is a Yin Wood Day Master born in the Snake month, when the metal element is strong. The Snake can form a Partial Three Harmony Metal Combination when it encounters the Rooster or Ox. The metal formed will trim the roots of the plants and cause it to wither. The best chance to thrive in such an environment is to have a Follow chart.

There is not much chance for Kaczynshi to become a Follow Chart. There is a Yin Wood in the Month Pillar and another Yang Wood hidden underneath the Pig Day Branch. There is also Yang Water in the Year Pillar that empowers all of them. He is a weak self vulnerable to the attack of metal.

Kaczynski was a child prodigy in mathematics and entered Harvard at the age of 16. When he was 25, he became an assistant professor at Berkeley after earning a Ph. D from the University of Michigan. Below is a brief chronology of his life events:

- In 1969 (Yin Earth Rooster year), Kaczynski suddenly resigned from his teaching position at 27. He started living as a recluse in the wilderness of Montana, learning survival skills in an attempt to be self-sufficient.
- From 1978 (Yang Earth Horse year) to 1994 (Yang Wood Dog year), Kaczynski sent out 14 mail bombs to universities and airlines, killing three and injuring 23 in the process. This period was governed by the Rooster and Yang Metal Luck Cycles.
- He was finally apprehended on April 3, 1996 (Yang Metal Horse Day, Yin Metal Rabbit month, Yang Fire Rat year).

So can the five elements explain his skewed thinking? Why did a talented mathematician carry out such horrific acts of terrorism? From examining his Four Pillars chart, we can see that it is due to the Clash between metal and wood. In 1969 (Yin Earth Metal year), Kaczynski resigned when the Snake in his Month Pillar combined with the Rooster in the year to snap off the roots of his wood self. His Yin Wood Day Master was unable to stand firm or survive. In 1970 (Yang Metal Dog year) and 1971 (Yin Metal Pig year) when metal was strong during the Yang Earth Luck Cycle, Kaczynski lived as a recluse in the wild.

187

His thoughts became more bizarre over time. In the metal Luck Cycles, Kaczynski wanted to inflict pain and suffering on computing intellectuals by bombing them. The majority of bombs appear to have been posted on days when the metal element was extremely strong. Readers can look up the dates the bombs were posted out and investigate the energy present on those days.

Example 8.12 Thomas Edison (born February 11, 1847, died October 18, 1931)

Hour	Day	Month	Year
壬	戊	壬	丁
Yang Water	Yang Earth	Yang Water	Yin Fire
子	寅	寅	未
Rat	Tiger	Tiger	Sheep

1	11	21	31	41
辛	庚	己	戊	丁
Yin Metal	Yang Metal	Yin Earth	Yang Earth	Yin Fire
丑	子	亥	戌	酉
Ox	Rat	Pig	Dog	Rooster

51	61	71	81
丙	乙	甲	癸
Yang Fire	Yin Wood	Yang Wood	Yin Water
申	未	午	巳
Monkey	Sheep	Horse	Snake

Edison's Luck Cycles are the opposite of Kaczynski's. The latter attained success when he was young and then floundered as an adult, unable to deal with the challenges of life. Edison went through difficult Luck Cycles as a child and performed poorly at school. Being used to hardship early on, he had the inherent strength to carry on despite the challenges in life.

Edison is a Yang Earth Day Master born in the Tiger month in spring, when wood (representing the Power element) is strong. There is much wood and water in his chart (three Stems and Branches each), which means that wood is prevalent. Edison has a Follow the Power (wood) chart. His useful elements are water and wood, while the negative elements are earth, metal and fire. Those with Follow the Power charts are focused on their work and do not give up easily. They also have a very clear perception of right and wrong.

At age 2, he entered 15 years of metal Luck Cycles. Edison had multiple childhood illnesses. At the age of 6 in 1853 (Yin Water Ox year), he started school but performed so badly that he had to leave. Edison's mother home schooled him until the age of 12. After that, Edison sold newspapers on a train. At the age of 17 in 1864 (Yang Wood Rat year), he entered the water Luck Cycle, and started working at Western Union before patenting the telegraph. Edison became renowned for his inventions and in the Pig Luck Cycle he enjoyed the peak of his career.

Example 8.13 Franklin Roosevelt (January 30, 1882, 20:15 hours, died April 11, 1945, 15:15 hours)

When the useful element is under attack, accidents and mishaps are likely to occur. This is a good example of metal undermining earth, disabling the legs of the person.

Date of Birth			
Hour	**Day**	**Month**	**Year**
甲 Yang Wood	己 Yin Earth	辛 Yin Metal	辛 Yin Metal
戌 Dog	巳 Snake	丑 Ox	巳 Snake

Date of Death			
Hour	**Day**	**Month**	**Year**
甲 Yang Wood	庚 Yang Metal	庚 Yang Metal	乙 Yin Wood
申 Monkey	戌 Dog	辰 Dragon	酉 Rooster

8	18	28	38	48	58
庚 Yang Metal	己 Yin Earth	戊 Yang Earth	丁 Yin Fire	丙 Yang Fire	乙 Yin Wood
子 Rat	亥 Pig	戌 Dog	酉 Rooster	申 Monkey	

Roosevelt is a Yin Earth Day Master born in the Ox month when metal is strong. There is also a Partial Three Harmony Combination of Snake and Ox involving the Day,

189

Month and Year Branches. Two Yin Metal Stems in the Month and Year Pillars reinforce the metal flow. It could be a Follow the Children chart, but the Dog in the Hour Pillar creates problems for the flow of metal. The earth covers the metal and prevents it from functioning. At some stages of Roosevelt's life, he had a Follow the Children chart. Roosevelt was the longest serving President of the United States. He served for three terms even though he was wheelchair bound.

Looking at Roosevelt's life events, metal created problems for him:

- In 1921 (Yin Metal Rooster year) at the age of 39 during the Yin Fire Luck Cycle, Roosevelt was stricken by polio resulting in both his legs being paralyzed. Can this be explained through the five elements? The additional metal acted as the last straw exhausting his earth. As a result, the self was undermined.
- On the day Roosevelt died, the Directional Metal Combination was present.

Example 8.14 Roland Reagan (born February 6, 1911, 04:16 hours, died June 5, 2004)

Date of Birth			
Hour	Day	Month	Year
壬	丁	庚	辛
Yang Water	Yin Fire	Yang Metal	Yin Metal
寅	未	寅	亥
Tiger	Sheep	Tiger	Pig

Date of Death			
Hour	Day	Month	Year
?	乙	己	甲
	Yin Wood	Yin Earth	Yang Wood
?	卯	巳	申
	Rabbit	Snake	Monkey

Here is another chart with the metal-wood conflict. Unlike Kaczynski, Reagan was more fortunate with regard to metal cutting into his useful element wood. The structure of his Four Pillars chart made the difference. The best way to glide over accidents and mishaps is through the help of Auspicious Stars. Regan has a Nobleman Star (Pig) in the Year Branch and a Heavenly Virtue Star in the Day Master, the best position for it to be.

Reagan is a Yin Fire Day Master born in the Tiger month in spring. There are two possible wood Combinations within the chart. The Pig in the Year Pillar can form a Partial Three Harmony Wood Combination with the Sheep in the Day Pillar. The Tiger in the Month Pillar can also form a Six Harmony Combination with the Pig in the Year Pillar. Regardless of which Combination takes precedence, wood is definitely the prevalent flow and the useful element.

The two metal Stems in the Year and Month Pillars are challenging the leadership of the wood. The Day Master has a hard time moving along his life path and must deviate to avoid confrontations.

The metal flow accounts for a major incident in Reagan's life and also his eventual demise.

Reagan survived an assassination attempt on March 30, 1981, which left his Press Secretary permanently disabled. It took place towards the end of the Sheep Luck Cycle. Here is the energy on that day:

Hour	Day	Month	Year
?	丁 Yin Fire	辛 Yin Metal	辛 Yin Metal
?	未 Sheep	卯 Rabbit	酉 Rooster

1	11	21	31	41	51	61	71	81
己 Yin Earth	戊 Yang Earth	丁 Yin Fire	丙 Yang Fire	乙 Yin Wood	甲 Yang Wood	癸 Yin Water	壬 Yang Water	辛 Yin Metal
丑 Ox	子 Rat	亥 Pig	戌 Dog	酉 Rooster	申 Monkey	未 Sheep	午 Horse	巳 Snake

Adding the Rabbit Month Branch to Reagan's chart, the full Three Harmony Wood Combination (Pig, Rabbit and Sheep) was present at that time. This meant that wood was prevalent. While there were three metal Stems and Branches present on the day, they did not form a team. The incident also occurred in spring when wood was strong and metal was weak. Wood had the upper hand and was able to survive the challenges posed by metal. It explained why the assassination failed to hit its target. Other positive developments supporting Reagan were his Nobleman Star, the Heavenly Virtue Star and the favorable Sheep Luck Cycle he was in.

When the negative metal energy returned, Reagan was not so fortunate. In June 1994 (Yang Wood Dog year) in the Yin Metal Luck Cycle, he was diagnosed with Alzheimer's disease at the age of 83. Reagan suffered for a decade before he passed away in June 2004 during the Yang Metal Luck Cycle. On the day he died, metal and wood were in conflict once again. This time round, metal won due to the influence of the Luck Cycle that strengthened and supported it.

This is a good example that illustrates the importance of timing with regard to the strength of elements.

Example 8.15 Intellectually Challenged Male (born August 26, 1989, 22:00 hours)

Hour	Day	Month	Year
癸	戊	壬	己
Yin Water	Yang Earth	Yang Water	Yin Earth
亥	午	申	巳
Pig	Horse	Monkey	Snake

6	16	26	36	46	56	66	76
辛	庚	己	戊	丁	丙	乙	甲
Yin Metal	Yang Metal	Yin Earth	Yang Earth	Yin Fire	Yang Fire	Yin Wood	Yang Wood
未	午	巳	辰	卯	寅	丑	子
Sheep	Horse	Snake	Dragon	Rabbit	Tiger	Ox	Rat

This is the chart of an intellectually challenged person who has the mental age of a six-year old child as determined by medical specialists. Why is this so?

He is a Yang Earth Day Master born in the Monkey month in autumn when water and metal are strong. There are three water Stems and Branches in the chart and one wood Branch that undermines his earth self. This makes him extremely weak. It could well make a Follow case.

However, there are some obstacles within his chart that prevent it from becoming a Follow Chart. There is a Yin Earth Rival in the Year Pillar and another hidden in the Snake Year Branch. The Horse Day Branch contains fire and earth. These elements are intense as they are located directly underneath. This prevents him from following any prevalent element. There is no useful element.

Example 8.16 Intellectually Challenged Female (born September 3, 1981 19:30 hours)

Hour	Day	Month	Year
甲	甲	丁	辛
Yang Wood	Yang Wood	Yin Fire	Yin Metal
戌	申	酉	酉
Dog	Monkey	Rooster	Rooster

2	12	22	32	42	52	62	72
戊	己	庚	辛	壬	癸	甲	乙
Yang Earth	Yin Earth	Yang Metal	Yin Metal	Yang Water	Yin Water	Yang Wood	Yin Wood
戌	亥	子	丑	寅	卯	辰	巳
Dog	Pig	Rat	Ox	Tiger	Rabbit	Dragon	Snake

She is a Yang Wood Day Master born in the Rooster month in autumn when metal is strong. The full Directional Metal Combination (Monkey, Rooster and Dog) is present in her chart. It looks like a good candidate for a Follow the Power (metal) chart.

However, there is a Yang Wood Competitor present in the Hour Pillar that prevents this development. The Yin Fire in the Month Pillar is also challenging metal and interferes with the Day Master surrendering to the prevalent flow. It becomes a feeble Day Self surviving on her own strength.

At the age of 14, she had the physical stature of a five-year old with deformed legs, making it difficult for her to walk. There is no useful element.

The Day Master is like a tree whose roots are constantly being trimmed or cut by strong metal underneath. There is no possibility of being nurtured. The tree barely grows and her deformed body and legs reflect the situation.

Chapter Nine - Identifying The Useful Element In A Four Pillars Charts

Our main motivation for learning the Four Pillars is to analyze and understand our lives better. The ultimate aim is to identify or "catch the useful element". Once we have identified the useful element(s), we can then focus on heading in the right direction or the right path in life. Even if we do not become renowned, at the very least we will not waste our time and energy in futile pursuits. The main danger to avoid is to "catch the incorrect element', as this will lead us on the wrong path.

What is a useful element and why is it important? The useful element protects the person and brings forth benefits and good fortune. It refers to one of the five elements in the Cosmos (our surroundings) and is entirely free for us to harness its benefits. There are 22 Chinese characters in the Four Pillars charts (10 Branches and 12 Stems) that encompass the five elements.

There is usually more than one character that will be useful or beneficial. In contrast, there are also several characters that are inauspicious and these are known as the negative elements. We can harness the favorable energy to create better fortune or mitigate the unfavorable energy to avoid mishaps.

While some charts are harmonious or beneficial, we can also find charts with mixed energies. There are many different categories of charts. Interestingly, these charts reflect the complexity of life. After all, we cannot apply a universal formula to all individuals.

For charts that are clear, the useful element can be identified immediately. Even for charts that are mixed or complicated, it is possible to identify the useful element. In these multifaceted examples, the useful element will vary with the onset of new elements either from the Luck Cycle or the year. Unfortunately, there are also charts where there is no apparent useful element for many different reasons. At times, these charts cannot be salvaged. Two such examples were discussed in Chapter Eight.

Chinese Metaphysicians who are riding on a good Luck Cycle will encounter clear charts. This allows them to make accurate predictions that will make their clients prosperous and happy. Their productive work contributes to their reputation. In contrast, Metaphysicians in bad Luck Cycles will be confronted with challenging and impossible charts. As a result, they will struggle to achieve clarity with their readings.

The strength of the useful element will also vary from case to case. It may be strong, weak or even helpless or powerless at times. The worst are those charts where the useful element is being clashed or compromised. So how do we identify the useful element from the charts that are mixed or complicated?

I have introduced an easy-to-follow procedure to analyze a Four Pillars chart. Here are the steps to follow:

- Mapping the chart: Each Stem or Branch is assigned a graphic symbol to create a visual display of how the Stems and Branches interact with the Day Master.
- Classifying the chart: Gather evidence from the key life events of the individual. The flow is then identified, tested and verified. This allows us to confirm their useful and negative elements.
- Taking measures to live with the flows: This includes determining the right Stems or Branches which will benefit or hurt the Day Master. Plan suitable ways to conduct your life and deploy Feng Shui design to enhance the good flows and avoid the bad ones.

As all charts are different with different flows and energies, the approach will also vary so we need to be flexible. We have to appreciate the uniqueness of Metaphysics. The study of how life interacts with the cosmos is too complicated to conform to a few formulas. I have chosen the following examples to demonstrate the different modes of analysis. I hope readers will gain insight from each case and apply the knowledge in their study of the Four Pillars.

A) Dominant Wood Chart and Follow the Resource (Water) Chart

We will start with a Dominant chart and a Follow chart. These contrasting examples should provide readers with useful guidelines that will help them differentiate charts. As both charts have clear energies, both individuals enjoyed successful lives. Clear, focused and powerful energy will result in the ability to innovate and accomplish major tasks.

Example 9.1 Sir Frederic Banting (born November 14, 1891, died February 22, 1941)

Dominant Wood Chart

Banting was honored as a Nobel Laureate in Medicine (1923) for discovering insulin. He was given a lifetime annuity by the Canadian government for his research and was also knighted by King George V. However, Banting died before the age of 50 in a plane crash.

Hour	Day	Month	Year
?	甲 Yang Wood	己 Yin Earth	辛 Yin Metal
?	辰 Dragon	亥 Pig	卯 Rabbit

2	12	22	32	42
戊 Yang Earth	丁 Yin Fire	丙 Yang Fire	乙 Yin Wood	甲 Yang Wood
戊 Dog	酉 Rooster	申 Monkey	未 Sheep	午 Horse

Figure 9.1 Pictorial Representation of Sir Frederic Banting's Four Pillars chart

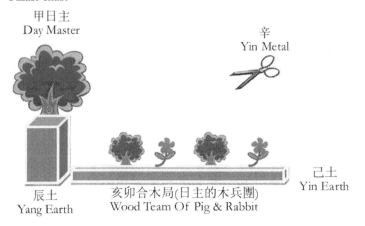

甲日主
Day Master

辛
Yin Metal

己土
Yin Earth

辰土
Yang Earth

亥卯合木局(日主的木兵團)
Wood Team Of Pig & Rabbit

Analysis

Banting is a Yang Wood Day Master, symbolically a big tree. He is born in the Pig month, when wood is growing. Banting was born at the right time, with good seasonal support. The Pig Month Branch combines with the Rabbit in the Year Pillar to form a Partial Three Harmony Wood Combination. This can be visualized as a forest. The Wood Day Master is like a leader leading his loyal troops who are dedicated to bringing him wealth.

A Dominant chart is associated with successful leaders noted for their intelligence, self-belief and courage. As wood represents benevolence, these individuals perform their tasks with kindness and consideration towards others.

Are there issues with this chart? There is no water (we are not absolutely certain as we do not have the Hour Pillar) in the chart to provide irrigation. This makes the forest short-lived. There is also a Yin Metal in the Year Stem waiting for the opportune moment to chop down the plants and trees. As a rule, a Dominant Wood chart has problems keeping his health, marriage and family intact. What is the logic behind this? A forest is an open asset which is extremely accessible and inviting to invaders. With a metal in the chart, such possibilities are increased. Banting passed away in the prime of his life.

Assessing the Elements

The useful elements for Dominant charts are their own element and the Resource element that generates them. We can conclude that water and wood are Banting's useful elements. As metal destroys wood, it is his number one enemy. For Banting, it is critical to control metal by enhancing fire. To verify our conclusions, we need to check on his key life events as shown in Table 9.1:

Table 9.1 Life Events of Sir Frederic Banting

Age	Year/flow	Luck Cycle	Life Events
18	1909 己酉 Yin Earth Rooster	酉 Rooster	Confused by the metal energy, Banting wasted two years studying theology before transferring to medicine.
26	1917 丁巳(庚) Yin Fire Snake (Yang Metal hidden in the Year Branch)	申(壬, 庚) Monkey (Yang Water, Yang Metal)	Suffered an arm injury while working in the army.
29	1920 庚申 Yang Metal Monkey	申(壬, 庚) Monkey (Yang Water, Yang Metal)	He had to close his surgical instrument shop and suffered heavy financial losses.
32	1923 癸亥 Yin Water Pig	乙(Yin Wood)	Received the Nobel Prize in Medicine.
41	1932 壬申 Yang Water Monkey	未 (Sheep)	Divorced his first wife Marion Robertson.
50	1941 辛巳 Yin Metal Snake	午 (Horse)	Died when his private plane ran out of gas and crashed.

So how did the wood element assist Banting? Medicine is a profession associated with wood and water. His prevalent wood energy ensured that he achieved recognition in the medical field. In 1923 (Yin Water Pig year), a year when water and wood were strong during the Yin Wood Luck Cycle, he received the Nobel Prize in Medicine for his research into insulin. He enjoyed universal acclaim when he entered the Yang Wood Luck Cycle at the age of 42.

The useful elements for Banting are wood and water (which sustains it). They are seen in the following Stems and Branches: Yang Wood, Yin Wood, Yang Water, Yin Water, Rat, Tiger, Rabbit, Sheep and Pig. Each of these Stems or Branches differs in the degree of benefits. The most useful Stems or Branches are those that strengthen the energy of wood. These would be the Branches that constitute the Directional Wood Combination (Tiger, Rabbit and Dragon) and the Three Harmony Wood Combination (Pig, Rabbit and Sheep). The Tiger and Sheep are not found in Banting's chart. This means that the Sheep Luck Cycle turned out to be the best period of his life. The Sheep was also Banting's Nobleman Star. The Tiger and Sheep are therefore the most auspicious characters for him.

The negative element for Banting is metal, which is seen in the following Stems and Branches: Yang Metal, Yin Metal, Snake, Rooster and Ox. The Rooster is the most lethal as it can easily form a Partial Three Harmony Metal Combination with the Ox or Snake.

To maximize benefits and minimize harm, readers should identify the positive and negative Stems and Branches in the Luck Cycle, year or day before making recommendations in terms of Date Selection and Feng Shui.

Maximizing Benefits Minimizing Risks

If we have a chart like Banting's, we cannot avoid normal activities on metal days but we can avoid buying and wearing metal items, flying planes or carrying out high-risk activities on these days. Apart from working in wood-related fields and occupations, we can also plant more trees around our garden, keep some indoor plants, use green in home decoration or hang pictures of wood and water. For those who require significant wood energy, they can also live in heavily wooded areas.

Interventions

When working in a field or occupation that belongs to the

useful element, success will come easily. When you are in the wrong line of work, achievement will be difficult to come by and despite much effort, there will be limited success.

The timing of the elements is extremely important. When the time or season supports your useful element, the chances of success will be higher. When there is no seasonal support, the possibility of failure is high.

To fully understand a person's life, the Special Stars should be identified as well. Banting was born on a Yang Wood Dragon day which belongs to the Smart Group of Ten (discussed in Chapter Four). His Study Hall Star, the Pig, is sitting in the Month Branch. Banting excelled academically and became a lecturer. Yang Wood is his Monthly Virtue Star. It also happens to be his Day Master. So why was Banting's Monthly Virtue Star unable to rescue him from the plane crash? While his Monthly Virtue Star did pull Banting away from theology and guided him to pursue medicine where he thrived and succeeded, we cannot expect it to solve all issues.

Example 9.2 Bill Clinton (born August 19, 1946, 08:51 hours)

Follow the Resource (Water)

Hour	Day	Month	Year
庚 Yang Metal	乙 Yin Wood	丙 Yang Fire	丙 Yang Fire
辰 Dragon	丑 Ox	申 Monkey	戌 Dog

6	16	26	36	46
丁 Yin Fire	戊 Yang Earth	己 Yin Earth	庚 Yang Metal	辛 Yin Metal
酉 Rooster	戌 Dog	亥 Pig	子 Rat	丑 Ox

56	66	76
壬 Yang Water	癸 Yin Water	甲 Yang Wood
寅 Tiger	卯 Rabbit	辰 Dragon

Figure 9.2 Pictorial Representation of Bill Clinton's Four Pillars chart

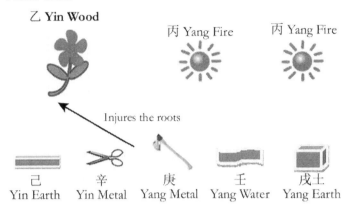

乙 **Yin Wood**

丙 Yang Fire   丙 Yang Fire

Injures the roots

己   辛   庚   壬   戌土
Yin Earth   Yin Metal   Yang Metal   Yang Water   Yang Earth

Analysis

Like Banting, Clinton's Day Master is also wood, but his chart is the total opposite of Dominant Wood. The Yin Wood is born in the Monkey month in autumn when metal is strong, cutting into the wood. To enjoy good fortune, the Yin Wood has to take shelter under the prevalent element for provision and protection. It satisfies the conditions for a Follow chart.

However, it is hard to identify the prevalent flow. Metal seems to lead but it is locked up within the Dog and Ox Branches. There are two fire Stems on top and one hidden in the Dog Branch. This curtails the metal and prevents it from leading the flow.

Could earth lead? Although there are three earth Branches supported by two fire Stems, is it powerful enough? The flow of earth is unlikely as earth is hollow in autumn when metal is strong. With regard to fire, both Yang Fire Stems are weak as fire is feeble in autumn and unable to lead.

What is the potential of water leading the flow? The Monkey Branch is the only water Branch and it is extremely strong during autumn. With additional assistance from water and/or metal, it can become the prevalent flow. The strength of fire fades after Clinton's youth as it is located in the Year Pillar. This situation lends further credence to water being the prevalent flow.

How do we confirm that water is Clinton's useful element?

We will need to check out his key life events to verify this.

Assessing the Elements

Table 9.2 Life Events of Bill Clinton

Age	Year/flow	Luck Cycle	Life Events
5-10		丁 Yin Fire	Unhappy childhood. Stepfather was a gambler and alcoholic who physically abused Clinton's mother.
16-26		戊 Yang Earth and 戌 Dog	Lived in the South, East Coast and also in Oxford as he pursued his tertiary studies.
27	1973 癸丑 Yin Water Ox	己 Yin Earth	Graduated from Yale Law School and worked as a lawyer.
31-35		亥 Pig	Won his first term as Governor of Arkansas but lost his position after 2 years.
36	1982 壬 戌 Yang Water Dog	庚 Yang Metal	Successfully re-elected as Arkansas Governor, a position he held for 10 years.
46	1992 壬申 Water Monkey	辛 Yin Metal	Elected as President of United States.
50	1996 丙子 Yang Fire Rat	辛 Yin Metal and 丑 Ox	Elected to his 2nd term as President of United States.
52-53	1998, 1999 戊寅,己卯 Yang Earth Tiger, Yin Earth Rabbit	丑 Ox	Had to contend with allegations of sexual misconduct.
58	2004 甲申 Yang Wood Monkey	壬 Yang Water	Had successful quadruple coronary artery bypass surgery.
59	2005 乙酉 Yin Wood Rooster	壬 Yang Water	Had successful follow-up surgery to remove scar tissue

			and fluid from his chest.
64	2010 庚寅 Yang Metal Tiger	寅 Tiger	Underwent surgery to place two stents in a coronary artery.

Let us begin with water. Clinton's biggest accomplishments in his life thus far are graduating from Yale Law School, being re-elected as Governor of Arkansas and his two terms as President of the United States. All these events took place in years when metal or water were strong or during his metal Luck Cycles. Clinton's chart benefited from water, his Resource element and metal, his Power element which in turn empowers his Resource element. Clinton has a Follow the Resource chart or a Many Mothers, One Child chart.

Wood representing Competitors is his worst element. What is the evidence? In the Pig Luck Cycle (when wood is strong) from the age of 32 to 37, Clinton won his first term as Governor of Arkansas. Even though he worked very hard to prove himself, Clinton lost his position after only two years. In November (Pig month) of 1995 (Yin Wood Pig year), his "improper relationship" with intern Monica Lewinsky began. In 1998 (Yang Earth Tiger year) and 1999 (Yin Earth Rabbit year), impeachment proceedings were filed against Clinton for his alleged sexual misconduct with Lewinsky.

In other wood years, there were health issues. In 2004 (Yang Wood Monkey year), Clinton had quadruple coronary artery bypass surgery after experiencing chest pains. In March (Yin Earth Rabbit month) 2005 (Yin Wood Rooster year), he had follow-up surgery to drain some fluid and to remove scar tissue from his chest. In February (Yang Earth Tiger month) 2010 (Yang Metal Tiger year), Clinton had two coronary stents implanted in his heart after complaining of chest pains. The operations were successful, occurring during the favorable Yang Water Luck Cycle. Clinton was fortunate that there were no complications after placement of the stents in 2010 as he was in the Tiger Luck Cycle. We can clearly see that Clinton is not a weak wood person who needs additional wood.

From analyzing Clinton's life, we can verify that he is a Follow the Resource (water) chart. He is most vulnerable to wood, which represents his Competitors or Rivals. When the wood Luck Cycle approaches, issues arise. This is in contrast to a Dominant Wood chart as it would benefit from additional wood flows.

Maximizing Benefits Minimizing Harm

Clinton suffered some health issues and weathered the sex scandal during the negative wood years and months. If you were forewarned about the negative elements approaching, would you be able to minimize any harm? For those of us who understand our Four Pillars charts, we can employ the *Ten Thousand Year Calendar* and take precautions.

Interventions

While a clear Dominant chart attains success from its own strength and hard work, Follow charts will achieve their success through external assistance. Once we know the flow of energy within our chart, we can plan our career accordingly and maximize our chances of success.

For instance, if water is the useful element, then we should work in aquatic engineering or study water-related subjects such as marine biology and ship building. We should also observe the events that occur on days when the water energy is strong. Those with Follow the Resource, charts possess strong instincts and will naturally gravitate towards careers that are suited to them. For Clinton, politics was a suitable choice as it is represented by his favorable elements metal and water.

B) Competitive Sibling Rivalry Chart, Supported by Resources

We will now consider a Competitive or Sibling Rivalry chart that is prone to problems with the onset of the Resource element. However, this Sibling Rivalry example is unique because the Resource element is the useful element.

Example 9.3 Leslie Cheung 張國榮 (born September 12, 1956, died April 1, 2003, 18:41 hours), Actor and Singer

Hour	Day	Month	Year
?	壬 Yang Water	丁 Yin Fire	丙 Yang Fire
?	午 Horse	酉 Rooster	申 Monkey

9	19	29	39
戊 Yang Earth	己 Yin Earth	庚 Yang Metal	辛 Yin Metal
戌 Dog	亥 Pig	子 Rat	丑 Ox

Figure 9.3 Pictorial Representation of Leslie Cheung's Four Pillars chart

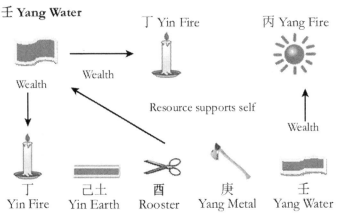

壬 **Yang Water**

丁 Yin Fire   丙 Yang Fire

Wealth

Wealth

Resource supports self

Wealth

丁   己土   酉   庚   壬
Yin Fire   Yin Earth   Rooster   Yang Metal   Yang Water

Cheung was born in Hong Kong. He was a superstar in the 80s and 90s noted for his acting and singing. Cheung became famous internationally for his role in Chen Kaige's Farewell My Concubine. In spite of the fame and adulation he enjoyed, Cheung committed suicide by leaping from the 24th floor of the Mandarin Hotel in Hong Kong at the age of 46.

Analysis

Cheung is a Yang Water Day Master who is born in a Monkey year. With a Yang Water Stem hidden in the Year Branch, he is a Competitive or Sibling Rivalry Water chart. Unlike other Competitive charts, Cheung's chart is superior as there is abundant wealth to go around without causing

Competition among Siblings. The Day Master also enjoys far more financial opportunities than his Siblings. There are two Yin Fire Wealth Stems (one in the Month Stem and the other hidden in the Horse in the Day Branch) that naturally pair up with the Day Master. Cheung was able to enjoy significant income from his career.

Why is the Yang Water Rival in the Monkey Year Branch quietly staying in his place? The Rival is content with his share of wealth as he is able to reach the Yang Fire located in the Year Stem. Cheung will have to stay competent and strong to use his financial assets. His strength comes from the Rooster in the Month Pillar. With metal as his useful element, whatever clashes with or attacks the metal will create issues for him. Cheung acknowledged that he loved white, the color that is associated with metal. Instinctively, he was aware that metal was his best element.

Assessing The Elements

Metal also represents melody and music and those with a strong metal flow in their chart tend to have beautiful singing voices. Not surprisingly, a significant number of singers such as Leslie Cheung have metal as their useful element.

From Table 9.3, we can see that the metal in Cheung's chart was not sufficient in accounting for his success. He required external support from the Luck Cycles or years. Without additional support from metal, Cheung could lose control of his Wealth and invite Competition from his Rival.

In 2003 (Yin Water Sheep year), at 46 in the Ox Luck Cycle, Cheung was enjoying the benefits brought upon by the Ox and the Rooster in his Month Pillar. However, after reaching the peak, the only way to go was down. Cheung did not enjoy his good fortune for long.

As 2003 started, an unwelcome Yin Water Rival came along and threatened his security. Cheung was emotionally unstable as he experienced mood swings and started to question his life goals. Concurrently, the Sheep in the year clashed with the Ox in the Luck Cycle and disrupted the Partial Three Harmony Metal Combination between the Ox and Rooster. Cheung lost the protection he gained from metal. As mentioned above, the metal in Cheung's chart was insufficient and for him to succeed, Cheung required the assistance of metal in the Luck Cycle or year. Without external support, the lone metal in Cheung's chart could not give him sufficient strength to cope with the challenges he encountered.

In March (Yin Wood Rabbit month) of 2003, the Rabbit in the month also clashed away the Rooster in his chart and left him helpless. His Yang Water Rival which was hidden in the Monkey Year Branch overwhelmed him. On the day Cheung committed suicide (April 1, 2003), the energy was as follows:

Hour	Day	Month	Year
癸	甲	乙	癸
Yin Water	Yang Wood	Yin Wood	Yin Water
酉	辰	卯	未
Rooster	Dragon	Rabbit	Sheep

The powerful wood flow (as seen in the Month and Day Pillars) was strengthened by abundant water and it clashed away the last traces of metal. The Rooster hour did not contain enough metal to fight the Rabbit.

Table 9.3 Life Events of Leslie Cheung

Age	Year/flow	Luck Cycle	Life Events
21	1977 丁巳 Yin Fire Snake	己 Yin Earth	The Snake in the year combined with the Rooster present in his Month Pillar to form a Partial Three Harmony Metal Combination. Cheung was the runner-up in an Asian Music contest held by Rediffusion Television, launching his career in the entertainment industry.
24	1981 辛 酉 Yin Metal Rooster	亥 Pig	The strong metal present that year saw him nominated for Best Supporting Actor in the Hong Kong Film Awards.

31-33	1987 丁卯 Yin Fire Rabbit to 1989 己巳 Yin Earth Snake	庚 Yang Metal	In the favorable Yang Metal Luck Cycle, Cheung became one of the top Cantopop singers in Hong Kong. In 1989 (Yin Earth Snake year), the Snake in the year combined with the Rooster in his chart to form a Partial Three Harmony Metal Combination. Cheung sang for 33 consecutive nights in the Hong Kong Coliseum as part of his retirement concert series.
35	1990 庚午 Yang Metal Horse	子 Rat	Without the support of the metal Luck Cycle, Cheung emigrated to Vancouver at the peak of his success.
39	1995 乙亥 Yin Wood Pig	辛 Yin Metal	With the favorable Yin Metal Luck Cycle, he returned to Hong Kong full-time to re-establish his singing and acting career.
44	2000 庚辰 Yang Metal Dragon	丑 Ox	Cheung enjoyed the peak of his singing and acting career.

Maximizing Benefits Minimizing Harm

Was it possible for Cheung to escape his fate? In reality, there are others who shared his birthday but they did not commit suicide on that day. I have a client who was born on the same day, month and year as Cheung. He consulted me not long after Cheung's suicide as his wife had suddenly asked him for a divorce on the same day that Cheung died.

At that time, the client was doing well in his career and was pursuing a hobby in classical music on weekends. This client also has a good singing voice and loves performing. A decade after Cheung's death, the client remains healthy and happy even though his career has had some setbacks over the years.

So why is his destiny different from Cheung's even though they share the same birthday? We all have our own destiny (and perhaps karma) and my client is living an ordinary life. When a person has never reached a peak, he or she will not have the inevitable fall. By reaching the peak, we exhaust our own vital energy. We need to return goodwill to the universe in order to achieve karmic balance and continue to enjoy our good fortune. This philosophy is found in the *I Ching*, the book of changes.

Interventions

Cheung 's preference for wearing white was well known. This meant that he was attuned to the influences of the five elements. His decision to retire and then re-enter his industry was also consistent with the flow of his favorable element. Unfortunately superstars in the entertainment industry are probably too engaged in living up to their public roles to allow them time for spiritual pursuit.

Multiple Flows with Multiple Useful Elements

Example 9.4 Teresa Teng (born January 29, 1953, died May 8, 1995), Taiwanese Singer

Hour	Day	Month	Year
?	庚 Yang Metal	癸 Yin Water	壬 Yang Water
?	辰 Dragon	丑 Ox	辰 Dragon

9	19	29	39
壬 Yang Water	辛 Yin Metal	庚 Yang Metal	己 Yin Earth
子 Rat	亥 Pig	戌 Dog	

Teresa Teng was a renowned Taiwanese singer who died at the age of 42.

Figure 9.4 Pictorial Representation of Teresa Teng's Four Pillars chart

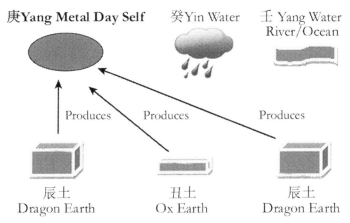

庚**Yang Metal Day Self**   癸Yin Water   壬 Yang Water River/Ocean

Produces   Produces   Produces

辰土   丑土   辰土
Dragon Earth   Ox Earth   Dragon Earth

Analysis

So why is Teng's chart considered one with multiple flows and useful elements? The structure of flows (Stems and Branches) in her chart changes with the onset of external influences from the Luck Cycles or years. This allows Teng's chart to fall into different classifications at different times during the input of a new flow. Her life events as shown in Table 9.4 clearly demonstrate these changes.

Table 9.4 Life Events of Teresa Teng

Age	Year/flow	Luck Cycle	Life Events
19	1972 壬子 Yang Water Rat	辛 Yin Metal	Teng was one of Hong Kong's top ten female singers
26	1979 己未 Yin Earth Sheep	亥 Pig	The Pig in the Luck Cycle combines with the Sheep in the year to form a Partial Three Harmony Wood Combination. She was barred briefly from entering Japan for using a fake Indonesian passport and had to

			fly to the United States following the setback.
27	1980 庚申 Yang Metal Monkey	亥 Pig	The Monkey year combined with the Dragon in her Year and Day Pillars to form a Partial Three Harmony Water Combination. Teng was chosen as Asia's most popular female singer.
28	1981 辛酉 Yin Metal Rooster	庚戌 Yang Metal Dog	The Yang Metal Dog Pillar in her Luck Cycle gave Teng three Kui Gang or Commanding Pillars in her chart. Her live concerts in Hong Kong broke all previous attendance records.
29	1982 壬戌 Yang Water Dog	庚 Yang Metal	Her engagement to the son of Malaysian billionaire Robert Kuok was called off due to parental disapproval.
30-31	1983 癸亥 Yin Water Pig	庚戌 Yang Metal Dog	A highly successful concert at Hong Kong's Hung Hom stadium.
36	1989 己巳 Yin Earth Snake	戌 Dog	Teng moved to Paris because of the Tiananmen Incident. This corresponded to the Clash between the Dog and the Dragon in the Commanding Pillars.
37	1990 庚午 Yang Metal Horse	戌 Dog	Death of her father.
42	1995 乙亥 Yin Wood Pig	己 Yin Earth	Died from an asthma attack.

Assessing the Elements

Teng's chart can be evaluated under four different classifications.

(1) Commanding Pillar System

Commanding Pillars were discussed in Chapter Four. Teng has two Commanding Pillars in her chart. The Yang Metal Dragon is present in the Day and Year Pillars. Two Commanding Pillars are likely to make one wealthy and successful. With three Commanding Pillars, there is certainty of success. Teng's chart proves this.

On April 14, 1981 (Yin Metal Rooster year), Teng was 28 and entering the start of the Commanding Pillar Yang Metal Dog Luck Cycle. She had the highest grossing concert ever for a solo singer in Hong Kong. This was also the decade when Teng was at the peak of her earning capacity. The additional metal flow from 1981 also boosted the impact of her record breaking concert.

(2) Mentor Assistance

Having assistance from Special Stars will also create a positive chart. Her Yang Metal Day Master represents both the Heavenly and Monthly Virtue Stars. The Dragon Day Branch is her Talent Star. Her Day Pillar not only bestows Teng with talent, it also shields her from danger. There is also a Nobleman Star in the Ox in the Month Pillar.

(3) Follow the Children

Teng is a Yang Metal Day Master who has both Yang Water and Yin Water Stems. Water represents her Output or Children element. The two Dragon Branches can easily form a Partial Three Harmony Water Combination when a Monkey or Rat is present. She then becomes a Follow the Children chart. In the Rat Luck Cycle from the age of 13 to 18, Teng achieved fame in her native homeland Taiwan. In 1972 (Yang Water Rat year), at the age of 19, she was already one of the top 10 most popular singers in Hong Kong. In 1980 (Yang Metal Monkey year), Teng was rated Asia's top female singer.

When the Follow the Children (water) chart encounters wood (the product of water) it becomes a chart that produces Grandchildren from Children. This suggests even more success. This configuration appeared in 1983 (Yin Water Pig year) and 1984 (Yang Wood Rat year) when Teng was 30 and 31 during the Yang Metal Luck Cycle. On December 29, 1983, Teng had another highly successful concert at Hung Hom Stadium in Hong Kong.

Hour	Day	Month	Year
?	辛 Yin Metal	甲 Yang Wood	癸 Yin Water
?	卯 Rabbit	子 Rat	亥 Pig

The strong flow of wood that day brought her much success. The Yang Wood in the Month Pillar was supported by the Rat underneath (which contains water). The Pig in the Year Branch and Rabbit in the Day Branch also formed a Partial Three Harmony Wood Combination. As Teng's case has Multiple Flows, wood is only positive during the years when the flow of water is strong so that she can fulfill the condition of a Follow the Children chart.

(4) Follow the Resource

Teng was born in the Ox month that is predominantly an earth month. With the two earth Dragon Branches in her chart, she could well qualify as a Follow the Resource (earth) chart. Teng possessed all the qualities associated with a Follow Chart: beautiful, delicate and elegant. She was also able to acquire money easily. However, Teng was vulnerable to the attack of wood.

When she entered the Yin Earth Luck cycle at the age of 38, she became a Follow the Resource chart. In 1995 (Yin Wood Pig year) when wood was strong, her useful element earth was under attack. On the day she died, May 8, 1995, the chart was as follows:

Hour	Day	Month	Year
?	己 Yin Earth	辛 Yin Metal	乙 Yin Wood
?	亥 Pig	巳 Snake	亥 Pig

214

The strong wood flow present on that day (Yin Wood, the Pig in the Day and Year Pillars) challenged the earth element and interfered with the support for Teng's Yang Metal Day Master.

Teng's chart is dynamic and changes according to the Luck Cycle and year. Her useful element changes with the periods in her life as well. This suggests that Teng's adaptable and flexible approach in life facilitated her phenomenal success. Unfortunately, it was also difficult to control the downturns in her life.

Maximizing Benefits Minimizing Risk

Even though Teng had multiple useful elements in her life, her chart maintained a distinct direction. What she needed to avoid was the Clash with the Dog and the attack of wood when she was a Follow the Resource chart. Her chart is considered superior in terms of the energy flow and Special Stars.

Other Individuals Born on the Same Day, Month and Year

I have always been curious about the lives of people born on the same day, month and year. From my research, I managed to find three famous individuals who were born on the same day, month and year as Teng, the highest number in my many years of research. For example, I found two other famous people who are born on the same day, month and year as Steve Jobs.

So why did Teng die early? Some might say that it was due to the conflicts within her chart or her weakened energy. The three examples we consider here are those who share the same Three Pillars as Teng and are still alive almost two decades after Teng's death. We are indeed fortunate to have three further examples to deepen our understanding in the destinies of people who share similar birth data. However, we do not include the Hour Pillar.

Some Chinese Metaphysicians insist on the uniqueness of a Four Pillars chart. They contend that the time of birth will undeniably alter the flow of the entire chart. It is therefore vital in analysis. While I do not refute their claims, I can safely state that having only Three Pillars gives a reasonably accurate picture. From my years of experience, I have discovered that the Hour Pillar only affects the later stages of our lives, i.e. after our 40s. It does not have an overpowering influence on the rest of the chart. The Day and Month Pillars are more important as they are with us throughout our entire lives. The influence of the Year Pillar wanes when we reach middle age.

Let us look at the charts of three different individuals who share the same Three Pillars and see how each one of them can have different lives from Teng's.

Example 9.4.1 Hwang Woo-Suk (born January 29, 1953), South Korean scientist

Hour	Day	Month	Year
?	庚 Yang Metal	癸 Yin Water	壬 Yang Water
?	辰 Dragon	丑 Ox	辰 Dragon

2	12	22	32
甲 Yang Wood	乙 Yin Wood	丙 Yang Fire	丁 Yin Fire
寅 Tiger	卯 Rabbit	辰 Dragon	巳 Snake

42	52	62	72
戊 Yang Earth	己 Yin Earth	庚 Yang Metal	辛 Yin Metal
午 Horse	未 Sheep	申 Monkey	酉 Rooster

Hwang is a South Korean veterinarian and Professor of Biotechnology in Seoul University. He is known for his stem cell research. Being a man, Hwang's Luck Cycles are different from those of Teng as they progress in a forward rather than backward fashion.

There is a considerable amount of earth (Hwang's Resource element) to support his Yang Metal Day Master. The Children or Output element is also prominent. This suggests that Hwang is ambitious and enjoyed high status in his career. From the age of 22, he enjoyed success during the fire and earth Luck Cycles, which strengthened his Follow the Resource or Many Mothers, One Child chart.

In 2004 (Yang Wood Monkey year) at the age of 51, when the Monkey in the year combined with the Dragon present in his Day and Year Pillars, Hwang's chart was transformed into a Follow the Children chart. The wood energy in that year represented the Output element of water. Water is his Yang Metal Day Master's Output element. This meant that Hwang's Follow the Children (water) chart generated Grandchildren (wood). This is highly auspicious. Hwang became a global celebrity with his breakthrough in stem cell research. As the flow was short-lived (for that year only), Hwang's fame did not last long.

In 2006 (Yang Fire Dog year), the Dog in that year clashed with the two Dragons present in Hwang's chart and compromised his Resource element. He was charged with embezzlement and it transpired that much of his stem cell research findings were fake. Hwang was dismissed from his position in Seoul University and all his teaching and research work was terminated. It was akin to being kicked out by his mother from his own house.

In 2009 (Yin Earth Ox year), Hwang's entered the Sheep Luck Cycle at the age of 56. The two Oxen (his Nobleman Star) in the Year and his Month Pillar clashed with the Sheep in the Luck Cycle. Hwang was found guilty of embezzlement and bio-ethical violations and given a two year suspended sentence.

In 2011 (Yin Metal Rabbit year), Hwang went to Libya to establish a stem cell research facility but the project was abandoned following the outbreak of civil war. The Rabbit in that year combined with the Sheep Luck Cycle to form a Partial Three Harmony Wood Combination which attacked his favorable element earth.

Was Hwang able to avoid the scandal and his prison sentence? For someone like him who was highly capable with multiple opportunities in his life, the temptations were too great to resist. I am sure Teng encountered similar situations in her life. However, I am confident that we will all react to the situation differently due to our different values and principles in life. The right principles will keep us on the right track and prevent us from committing offenses with undesirable consequences.

The Dog year would have appeared earlier in Hwang's life, so why did it only create issues later on in his life? With his Follow the Resource chart, the Resource element would have protected Hwang for a significant period of time and assisted him in overcoming numerous obstacles. However, there came the day when Hwang pushed the boundaries too far. Even if it was his first major offence, it occurred later in life when Hwang's energy was weaker than in his younger days. Hwang was unable to face up to the same challenges.

Example 9.4.2 Paulin Bordeleau (born January 29, 1953), Canadian Ice Hockey player

Hour	Day	Month	Year
?	庚 Yang Metal	癸 Yin Water	壬 Yang Water
?	辰 Dragon	丑 Ox	辰 Dragon

2	12	22	32
甲 Yang Wood	乙 Yin Wood	丙 Yang Fire	丁 Yin Fire
寅 Tiger	卯 Rabbit	辰 Dragon	巳 Snake

42	52	62	72
戊 Yang Earth	己 Yin Earth	庚 Yang Metal	辛 Yin Metal
午 Horse	未 Sheep	申 Monkey	酉 Rooster

Bordeleau is an ice hockey player who represented France in the 1988 Winter Olympics. As a man, his Luck Cycles move in the same direction as Hwang's. I have reproduced both the chart and Luck Cycles here for easy reference.

Bordeleau was born in Vancouver. In his early 20s in 1973 (Yin Water Ox year) and 1974 (Yang Wood Tiger year), he was already making a million Canadian dollars per year. With his intelligence and athletic prowess, it is hardly surprising that Bordeleau achieved success early in life like Teng. The chart clearly reflects their abilities.

In 1974 (Yang Wood Tiger year) during the Rabbit Luck Cycle, the Directional Wood Combination was formed (Tiger, Rabbit and Dragon). Bordeleau's chart transformed from Follow the Resource (earth) into Follow the Wealth (wood). This change of flow was supported by the Yang Water and Yin Water in the Year and Month Pillars. As he became a Follow the Wealth chart, Bordeleau's annual salary jumped up to 4.2 million Canadian dollars. In 1975 (Yin Wood Rabbit year), the Directional Wood Combination was no longer present and his salary fell to 1.6 million Canadian dollars. Such are the swift changes that are seen in charts that have multiple flows and useful elements.

The next 15 years consisted of Fire and Earth Luck Cycles, and Bordeleau's chart reverted to using Resource as its useful element. In 1988 (Yang Earth Dragon year) during the Yin Fire Luck Cycle when he was 35, Bordeleau represented France in the Olympics. At the age of 36, Bordeleau entered the Snake Luck Cycle which combined with the Ox in his Month Pillar to form metal. He retired from playing ice hockey to focus on coaching when the earth in his chart was drained and weakened.

Example 9.4.3 Lynne McGranger (born January 29, 1953), Australian actress

Hour	Day	Month	Year
?	庚 Yang Metal	癸 Yin Water	壬 Yang Water
?	辰 Dragon	丑 Ox	辰 Dragon

2	12	22	32	42	52	62	72
壬 Yang Water	辛 Yin Metal	庚 Yang Metal	己 Yin Earth	戊 Yang Earth	丁 Yin Fire	丙 Yang Fire	乙 Yin Wood
子 Rat	亥 Pig	戌 Dog	酉 Rooster	申 Monkey	未 Sheep	午 Horse	巳 Snake

McGranger had her initial training in acting in 1975 (Yin Wood Rabbit year) during the Pig Luck Cycle. She had her big break at the age of 39 in 1992 (Yang Water Monkey year) when she joined the cast of Australian soap opera 'Home and Away'. McGranger is still playing the same character today (at time of printing) and is the second longest serving cast member.

Her success in 1992 (Yang Water Monkey year) at the age of 39 was due to the Monkey year combining with the Dragon in her Day and Year Pillars to form a Partial Three Harmony Water Combination. McGranger enjoyed the benefits of a Follow the Children chart. Even though she was in the Yin Earth Luck Cycle, she did not have the same issues as Teng.

The four examples presented here are based on the same Three Pillars. All of them share common traits such as being talented, leading a life in the public eye and enjoying distinguished careers and financial success. Their Output element, which impacts public visibility, is prominent and useful. All of them enjoyed the benefits of a Follow chart at some point. The versatility of the system and the magnitude of the benefits vary from case to case. The impact of the five elements on individuals is undeniable. How do we adapt to or anticipate their impact for our own best interests is a matter of personal choice.

While Teresa Teng's achievements surpassed those of the other three examples, she also expended the greatest amount of energy. This may have accounted for her early demise.

Intervention

Individuals who have charts with multiple flows lead eventful lives. However, as a result of the multiple changes in their charts, they also lack a source of constant support. This means that their lives are more fragile and at times difficult to control. If you fully understand your flow, you can use the positive times accordingly. Charts with multiple flows are becoming increasingly common in current times, so flexibility in analyzing them is required.

Example 9.5 Robert Kennedy (born November 20, 1925, 15:11 hours, died June 6, 1968, 02:00 hours)

Hour	Day	Month	Year
庚 Yang Metal	戊 Yang Earth	丁 Yin Fire	乙 Yin Wood
申 Monkey	申 Monkey	亥 Pig	丑 Ox

4	14	24	34	44
丙 Yang Fire	乙 Yin Wood	甲 Yang Wood	癸 Yin Water	壬 Yang Water
戌 Dog	酉 Rooster	申 Monkey	未 Sheep	午 Horse

Figure 9.5 Pictorial Representation of Robert Kennedy's Four Pillars chart

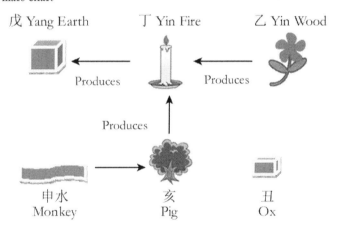

Robert Kennedy was a US Senator, Attorney General and the brother of President John F. Kennedy. He was assassinated during his presidential campaign.

Analysis

Kennedy is a Yang Earth Day Master who is born in the Pig month, when the wood element is growing and extremely strong. Earth is extremely weak and requires the support of the Resource element. Fortunately, there is a Yin Fire in the Month Pillar close by to provide support. This Yin Fire is vital for Kennedy. As shown in Figure 9.5, it is fueled by a Yin Wood in the Year Pillar and another Yang Wood in the Pig. This makes it a strong fire that supports the Yang Earth Day Master. Kennedy's chart is a Follow the Resource or Many Mothers, One Child chart. Kennedy was born into a famous and successful family. He received love and support from his parents and siblings when he was growing up.

Unfortunately, the Yang Water present in the Monkey in the Day Pillar is interfering with the supportive Yin Fire. The Wealth element water is also a focus of Competition among Rivals. There was always the potential for conflicts.

So why are the Rivals such an issue for Kennedy's chart? As previously discussed, in a Follow the Resource or Many Mothers, One Child chart, the onset of a Stem or Branch of the same element as the Day Master will start a fight. This results in the weaker Day Master being kicked out of the home or eliminated. In reality, it could translate into the loss of a job, home, family member or in the worst case scenario, life.

Kennedy's auspicious elements are fire and wood including the Branches Tiger, Rabbit, Pig and Sheep. His negative element is earth which represents Competition for his Resource element. This includes the Branches Dog and Dragon. Water is also a problem as it extinguishes the Resource element fire. This will cause him to lose his support. Kennedy has to be wary of the Branches Rat and Monkey, especially if the Three Harmony Water Combination is formed.

Assessing the Elements

We will now have a look at the events in Kennedy's life. As the flow in Kennedy's chart is very distinct, I have divided the chart into two sections. The first half focuses on challenging events and the second half depicts auspicious events.

Table 9.5 Life Events of Robert Kennedy

Age	Year/flow	Luck Cycle	Life Events
13	1938 戊寅 Yang Earth Tiger	戌 Dog	At the outbreak of World War II, Kennedy returned home from London, where his father was serving as the US ambassador.
23	1948 戊子 Yang Earth Rat	酉 Rooster	Enrolled at the University of Virginia Law School after graduating from Harvard.
33	1958 戊戌 Yang Earth Dog	申 Monkey	Had a confrontation with Teamsters Union President Jimmy Hoffa during his testimony when working as chief counsel for the Senate Labor Rackets Committee.
43	1968 戊申 Yang Earth Monkey	未 Sheep	Died shortly after being shot at close range while campaigning to be President.
34	1960-63	癸 Yin Water	Attorney General of the United States
38	1964-68	未 Sheep	Senator for the state of New York

Kennedy's chart is favorable as most of the Stems and Branches are working in tandem to assist him. There were just a few obstacles from the negative Stem and Branches.

223

The best period of Kennedy's life was the Yin Water Luck Cycle from the age of 34 to 39. The Yin Water was able to combine with any Yang Earth Competitor. Between 1960 and 1963, Kennedy helped his brother, John, in his Presidential election campaign. He was then appointed Attorney General of the United States. Kennedy had to depend on his siblings and family for this appointment as he lacked the experience to take on such a demanding role. The Sheep Luck Cycle combined with the Pig in his Month Pillar to form wood which strengthened his Resource element. Kennedy then became the Senator for the state of New York.

The most damaging Stem is the Yang Earth Competitor which was present in several challenging years, including the last year of his life when he was assassinated. We will now consider the energy present when he was shot:

June 6, 1968, shortly after midnight			
Hour	**Day**	**Month**	**Year**
庚	丁	戊	戊
Yang Metal	Yin Fire	Yang Earth	Yang Earth
子	未	午	申
Rat	Sheep	Horse	Monkey

There were two Yang Earth Competitors that confronted Kennedy's Yang Earth Day Master. The Yang Earth Horse Stem-Branch Pair was very strong. The weaker Day Master was in danger of injury or death. The Yin Fire Day Stem, which symbolized the Resource element, set off a battle among the three Yang Earth Stems as they competed for its support.

The Rat in the Hour and the Monkeys in the Year and Kennedy's Day Pillar also formed a Partial Three Harmony Water Combination which extinguished the auspicious element fire. Kennedy lost the protection he gained from his Resource element.

You may think that the analysis here looks like a fairy tale, but we should never underestimate the consequences of Rivals. It is not possible to ascertain the exact nature of the misfortune but financial losses, illness, injury and death are all possible. The nature and magnitude of the misfortune vary amongst individuals. Some believe that karmic issues are part of our destinies.

Maximizing Benefits Minimizing Harm

According to Four Pillars theory, Kennedy's run for the US Presidency was not supported by the cosmic flow. He died at 43 and the following Yang Water Luck Cycle would have combined with his vital Yin Fire Stem. This would have left his Yang Earth Day Master without any support and unable to handle any important positions.

Could Kennedy have escaped the fatal attack? It is possible if he was aware of his energy flow and stayed away from the limelight. He could lead a low-key life for several years and prepare for a comeback when the good Luck Cycle returned. Following the Yang Water Luck Cycle would be the Horse Luck Cycle, which contained the useful Yin Fire Stem. Kennedy did not reach his golden period. Rather, during an unfavorable year, he contested the Democratic ballot for the US Presidency, the most powerful position globally and was assassinated in the process.

An individual's personality and approach to life clearly plays a part in his or her destiny.

Intervention

How do we survive an unfavorable Luck Cycle? We need to refrain from vices, continue to work hard and exercise adequately if possible. For those of us who possess charts with conflicting flows, apart from practicing the above, we may have to go the extra mile by helping others in need. The energy we expend on others will return to us tenfold. Our positive energy will be increased in the process. We could also increase our levels of auspicious energy by using the favorable elements and working with others who contribute to our positive flows. Above all, we should not forget our values and principles and yield to easy short cuts or other types of temptations.

Conclusion

I have used celebrity examples with clear flows in this chapter for a number of reasons. Firstly, we need to choose familiar cases to prove our points with credibility. Secondly, these charts have identifiable useful elements and distinct responses to changes of flow. Finally, with the advances in technology and communication, celebrity examples offer readers the opportunities to investigate the accuracy of our analyses.

Chapter Ten - Conclusion

As can be seen from the previous chapters, the Four Pillars charts provide us with reliable messages on our quality of life and the changes in our life path. The accuracy of the messages varies with the structure and nature of the chart. You cannot deny its efficacy. The Four Pillars system makes a unique contribution to our lives.

Let us sum up the issues in the following categories.

Reliability:

Chapters Three to Nine cited different examples using the procedures and steps I use to analyze charts. We were able to gather information about an individual's personality, ability and potential, health, success, favorable periods and so on. There were different approaches and no fixed formula can be applied to all cases with similar results. For example, we discovered that men and women who were born on the same day, month and year had different destinies and lives. I would like to point out that apart from the Four Pillars, other factors like genetics, family background, environmental influence (including pregnancy and upbringing), behavior, personal principles, values and beliefs, life and work experiences should also be taken into account. It is not possible to empirically measure or determine the role and influence of each of these factors.

However, there are two facts that we can be certain about:

1) Four Pillars charts clearly indicate our talents, personality, health and abilities. For charts that have a clearly defined flow, the indications are even more accurate.

2) The cyclical nature of cosmic flow is a proven fact confirmed by the Chinese wise men who devised Chinese Metaphysics. Scientists worldwide admit the reality of cosmic flow but no one has attempted to define it so far. Cosmic flow has a definite and clear impact on our lives, for better or for worse. Once we know how each of the Stems and Branches affects our daily activities, we will be guided to plan our actions and make our decisions accordingly. In this way, we

will be able to lead meaningful lives.

Accepting The Findings:

The Four Pillars gives us good and bad news which none of us can avoid. As the old saying goes: *the man of principle and wisdom asks only about bad news and does not worry about good news.* Wise people take precautions to guard against misfortune. Auspicious events are not worth worrying about.

In our modern times, astrologers are viewed as psychologists with clients who only want to seek solace in knowing the good news. When people are enjoying good Luck Cycles or are at the peak of their lives, they do not give much thought to the bad times that might be just around the corner. When the bad times hit, they have no strategy to cope with them. At times, when the truth is revealed, the messenger is blamed for the clients' misfortune and the reliability of the Four Pillars system is then criticized.

In reality, as Rudyard Kipling said, *treat triumph and disaster the same way.* Knowledge of impending calamity will allow us to prevent it. Being aware of future success means that we can motivate ourselves to use our time fully and take advantage of the right moment. We want to optimize the good and avoid the bad. After all, the only constant in life is change, which means that good and bad will take their turns in our lives. If we go with the flow of the universe, then we will not exhaust our energy by going down the wrong path. With the Four Pillars system, we can be thankful for its predictive ability and approach it with objectivity and open hearts.

Using The Information With Flexibility and Adaptability:

So how do we use the information provided by the Four Pillars method in a beneficial manner that is adaptable and flexible?

(1) In good times, we need to know in which direction is the favorable spring wind blowing so that we can take preventative measures before the rain falls. In bad times, we need to work harder on ourselves so as to welcome the good times when they arrive. As the *I Ching* states: *"At the extreme of happiness, sadness is born. After the worst times, the best will* *approach.*" I feel that I have quoted sufficient examples in the book of individuals who did not fully grasp the flow of their lives. This may have caused them to make mistakes that resulted in their early demise. We should avail ourselves to the ebb and flow of positivity and negativity from the Luck Cycles.

(2) Use the *Ten Thousand Year Calendar* to set up your chart and also some of the important dates of your life so far. Ascertain what type of chart you have, i.e. Follow, Dominant, Competitive etc and then identify the favorable and negative elements. Once you understand the flow in your chart, you can then direct your attention to strengthen the favorable influences. For instance, if water is a useful element, you can choose to live near water, work in an industry that is related to water or take up hobbies that are associated with it.

Observe your living and working environment and find colleagues or partners who have flows in their chart that are beneficial to you. Note that favorable and prevalent flows can bring about success in enterprises or projects. When making important decisions, be proactive and take risks on the favorable days. On difficult days, be discreet and remain low key.

(3) There are numerous Special Stars covered in this book. Familiarize yourself with the Stars that work for you. They have clear influences. Readers can apply the Stars in their daily lives. For example, we can use the Nobleman day to solve problems. We can also tailor our activities to the Stars. For instance, we can use the Academic Star when we are writing submissions, giving presentations or tendering contracts. The Peach Blossom Star is suitable for dates with our partners and events involving clients and colleagues. By understanding the Four Pillars, we can use our knowledge in selecting our auspicious days from the Chinese almanac.

Negative Stars can also be used. It would not be a good idea to get married or have romantic dates during the Isolation or Widow days. In contrast, the Loss or Condolence days can be used to conduct funerals.

We should start from small events to gain experience and confidence in Date Selection. This will allow us to go with the flow of energy and maximize our potential in life. We need to experiment for ourselves in order to truly understand the influence of the elements. After all, we have the power to determine our own lives.

The Challenges Of Life

Most of the Four Pillars charts covered in this book have clear and definite directions with flows and elements that are readily identifiable. Several of them have issues that can be solved and are considered auspicious charts. There are also those that have issues which can only be solved in the favorable Luck Cycle or year. These window periods allow them the opportunity to achieve success.

Sadly, there are charts with mixed flows where there is no useful element available. This results in problematic lives. The essential aim of Four Pillars is to find a useful element and ascertain its strength and efficacy. Even a weak useful element is better than not having one. In the event that a useful element is not identifiable, we can still use the favorable Special Stars as discussed. In the journey of life, we need all the help we can get.

The most challenging types of charts are those that are on the borderline with regard to being able or unable to Follow a prevalent element, or those having flows that are all tangled up. Those with such charts may be mired in disappointment or despair. They may be prone to destructive behavior such as alcoholism, drug use, gambling etc. There may also be difficulties in finding meaningful employment. The incidence of physical or mental disabilities is also higher.

Can Feng Shui be used to change a person's fortunes? Feng Shui is the study of an individual's response to the environment (i.e. the elements) and Feng Shui design depends on the person's reactions to harmonious energy. When there is no energy or element that we can use, then there will not be any favorable interactions. Feng Shui cannot salvage the situation. So what else can we do? We will have to depend on divine intervention. Heaven provides and nurtures, so how do we seek its assistance? We have to follow the natural way of life.

What is the natural way of life? How do we find it? Heaven's Way or the natural way to life refers to the laws that govern the objects in the Universe and it is found in the *I Ching*, the Book of Changes. The *I Ching* addresses the questions of life in 64 themes, expressed in the form of hexagrams.

The *I Ching* can provide assistance to those who require divine help or those who have difficulty making decisions in their lives. They may feel frustrated and helpless due to weak energy flows in their charts. I feel that if they apply the principles of the *I Ching* to their lives, they will be able to devise the appropriate life strategies and succeed naturally.

All of us have our share of ups and downs in life that are beyond our control. But at the very least, the *I Ching* allows us to accept reality and stay on the right path in life. When we focus our energy on what we do best and are happy about it, we naturally build up positive energy in the process. This reservoir of positive energy will lead us to bigger accomplishments.

Appendix

Appendix 1 Distribution of Energy in the Months

Table A1.1 Distribution of the Energy of the Five Elements in Each Month

Month	Agricultural Marker Festival	Energy	Energy	Energy
1st 寅 Tiger	Start of Spring	Day 1-7 戊 Yang Earth	Day 8-14 丙 Yang Fire	Day 15-Month End 甲 Yang Wood
2nd 卯 Rabbit	Insects Awakening	Day 1-10 甲 Yang Wood	Day 11- Month End 乙 Yin Wood	
3rd 辰 Dragon	Clear Bright	Day 1-9 乙 Yin Wood	Day 11-12 癸 Yin Water	Day 13- Month End 戊 Yang Earth
4th 巳 Snake	Start of Summer	Day 1-7 戊 Yang Earth	Day 8-14 庚 Yang Metal	Day 15- Month End 丙 Yang Fire
5th 午 Horse	Corn in Ear	Day 1-10 丙 Yang Fire	Day 11-19 己 Yin Earth	Day 20- Month End 丁 Yin Fire
6th 未 Sheep	Slight Heat	Day 1-9 丁 Yin Fire	Day 10-12 乙 Yin Wood	Day 13- Month End 己 Yin Earth
7th 申 Monkey	Start of Autumn	Day 1-7 戊 Yang Earth	Day 8-14 壬 Yang Water	Day 15- Month End 庚 Yang Metal
8th 酉 Rooster	White Dew	Day 1-10 庚 Yang Metal	Day 11- Month End 辛 Yin Metal	
9th 戌 Dog	Cold Dew	Day 1-9 辛 Yin Metal	Day 10-12 丁 Yin Fire	Day 13- Month End 戊 Yang Earth
10th 亥 Pig	Start of Winter	Day 1-7 戊 Yang Earth	Day 8-14 甲 Yang Wood	Day 15-Month End 壬 Yang Water
11th 子 Rat	Large Snow	Day 1-10 壬 Yang Water	Day 11- Month End 癸 Yin Water	
12th 丑 Ox	Slight Cold	Day 1-9 癸 Yin Water	Day 10-12 辛 Yin Metal	Day 13- Month End 己 Yin Earth

Table A1.1 shows the distribution of the five elements which starts from the beginning of a solar month as indicated by the Agricultural Marker Jie 節 (Festival). These markers are climate dividers that signal the initial change of climate so as to guide Chinese farmers in agricultural activities.

For the first seven days of the Tiger month (the first month of the Chinese Calendar), earth dominates the cosmos. As the Start of Spring coincides with February 4, the first seven days fall into the period from February 4 till 10. Fire is prevalent from the eighth till the 14th day (February 11 to 17). The energy of wood prevails for the rest of the month.

So how do we apply this ? The chart helps us to understand the nature of a Four Pillars chart since the month can have up to two or three different types of energy. For example, the Ox month contains the energy of Yin Water, Yin Metal and Yin Earth. This means that there will be different energies dominating different times of the month as seen in the three examples below:

Example A1.1 (born January 10, 2011)

Hour	Day	Month	Year
?	乙 Yin Wood	己 Yin Earth	庚 Yang Metal
?	丑 Ox	丑 Ox	寅 Tiger

Example A1.2 (born January 17, 2011)

Hour	Day	Month	Year
?	壬 Yang Water	己 Yin Earth	庚 Yang Metal
?	申 Monkey	丑 Ox	寅 Tiger

Example A1.3 (born February 2, 2011)

Hour	Day	Month	Year
?	戊	己	庚
	Yang Earth	Yin Earth	Yang Metal
?	子	丑	寅
	Rat	Ox	Tiger

All three people are born in the Ox month but the energy in the Month Pillar varies.

Example A1.1 is born within the first nine days of the month when the cosmos is dominated by the energy of water and would experience more water influence.

Example A1.2 is born in the next flow period and would have more metal flow.

Example A1.3 is born towards the end of the month and has more earth.

When analyzing a Four Pillars chart we need to take note of the strength of the Month Branch.

We also use a similar model to measure the year's energy. During the final months of the year, the strength of the year is weak. For example, if a person is born two days prior to the Start of Spring (as in Example A1.3), the energies of both the month and year are weak as it is towards the end of both periods. The flow of energy within the person's chart is therefore unstable with the potential of change and multiple opportunities. The person could be extremely flexible and adaptable. Having the same Month Branch does not mean that the same energy will prevail in all cases.

When we encounter charts of people born towards the end of the month or year, we need more verification to understand the flow of energy in the chart.

Appendix 2 Eight Trigrams

What is the relationship between the Eight Trigrams and the Four Pillars?

The *I Ching* or *Book of Changes* is the origin of Chinese Metaphysics. Its Yin-Yang philosophy marks the theoretical basis of all Chinese Metaphysical schools. The core teaching of the *I Ching* is how to implement the laws of nature so as to allow us to lead an error-free life to our best interests. In other words, living in harmony with cosmic flows.

This is what the Four Pillars is trying to achieve by identifying our potential and the elements that make our lives flow smoothly. This will allow us to go with the cosmic flow with what we have and what we do best. Without a good understanding of the *I Ching* to anchor the laws of nature, we may be prone to mishaps in our pursuit of harmony.

The Eight Trigrams place the vital components of the *I Ching* in a cohesive and coherent model. It reveals how all components of Heaven, Earth and Man are inter-related. Table A2.1 shows the different representations of the Eight Trigrams.

Table A2.1 The Different Aspects of the 8 Trigrams

Kua	Qian 6	Kun 2	Zhen 3	Xun 4	Kan 1	Li 9	Gen 8	Dui 7
Trigram	☰	☷	☳	☴	☵	☲	☶	☱
Direction	North West	South West	East	North East	North	South	North East	West
Family Member	Father	Mother	Eldest Son	Eldest Daughter	Middle Son	Middle Daughter	Youngest Son	Youngest Daughter
Body Part	Head	Abdomen	Foot	Pelvis	Ear	Eye	Hand	Mouth
Animal	Horse	Ox	Dragon	Rooster	Pig	Pheasant	Dog	Sheep
Nature	Heaven	Earth	Thunder	Wind	Water	Fire	Mountain	Lake
Element	Metal	Earth	Wood	Wood	Water	Fire	Earth	Metal
Season	End of Autumn	End of Summer	Spring	Start of Summer	Winter	Summer	End of Winter	Autumn
Time of Day	Night	Sunset	Sunrise	Afternoon	Midnight	Noon	Early Morning	Sunset
Virtue	Justice	Integrity	Kindness	Kindness	Intelligence	Courtesy	Integrity	Justice

The Eight Trigrams form an essential tool for Feng Shui practitioners to represent or codify the phenomena seen in the realm of Heaven, Man and Earth. Before understanding the Eight Trigrams, we need to know which sectors they govern on the compass. See Table A2.2 below.

Table A2.2 The Eight Trigrams and their Sectors on the Compass

North (Kan) 337.6-22.5	North East (Gen) 22.6-67.5
East (Zhen) 67.6-112.5	South East (Xun) 112.6-157.5
South (Li) 157.6-205.5	South West (Kun) 202.6-247.5
West (Dui) 247.6-292.5	North West (Qian) 292.6-337.5

Appendix 3 Polish Air Force Tu-154 Crash

On April 10, 2010, many of Poland's top officials and politicians (including the President) were on their way from Warsaw to Smolensk, Russia to commemorate the 70th anniversary of the infamous Katyn massacre. Their plane crashed, killing all 96 people on board. As news of the disaster reverberated across the world, Poland declared a state of national mourning. It was possibly the first time so many leaders of a country perished in a single event.

Was it possible to forecast the impending catastrophe from the charts of those on board? We will now analyze the Four Pillars charts of nine victims. The first factor to consider is the day of the crash (April 10, 2010, 10:44 hours). Here is the chart:

Hour	Day	Month	Year
辛	庚	己	庚
Yin Metal	Yang Metal	Yin Earth	Yang Metal
己	寅	卯	寅
Snake	Tiger	Rabbit	Tiger

It was a spring day when the wood energy dominated the cosmos. The Yang Metal present in the Day and Year Pillars (both with the Tiger underneath) symbolized two Competitors vying for the Wealth element (Yin Wood) that is located in the Rabbit Month Branch. No one wants to make the first move for the money as that would make the Self vulnerable to a Competitor of equal strength. There is also a Yin Metal Competitor supported by the Snake Branch in the Hour Pillar. The situation is fragile, a state that can easily be broken by the introduction of an external element.

Example A3.1 Jerzy Szmajdinski (born April 9, 1952), Former Defense Minister

Hour	Day	Month Heavenly, Monthly Virtue	Year
?	乙 Yin Wood	甲 Yang Wood	庚 Yang Metal
?	酉 Rooster	辰 Dragon	辰 Dragon
	Peach Blossom	Talent	Talent

9	19	29	39	49	59
乙 Yin Wood	丙 Yang Fire	丁 Yin Fire	戊 Yang Earth	己 Yin Earth	庚 Yang Metal
巳 Snake	午 Horse	未 Sheep	申 Monkey	酉 Rooster	戌 Dog

Szmajdinski, being a Yin Wood Day Master born in spring is further empowered by the additional wood and water in his chart. There was a strong presence of wood in his chart. This made him vulnerable to the two Yang Metal Stems present on the day of the accident.

What caused his misfortune were the two Roosters present on the day (one from his Day Branch and the other from his Luck Cycle). At 58, Szmajdinski was in the Rooster Luck Cycle. The two Roosters clashed with the Rabbit present in the Month Pillar of the day, which caused the two Yang Metal Stems on the day to retaliate. As a result, the Yin Wood Day Master was destroyed in the battle between the metal and wood elements.

Example A3.2 Franciszek Gagor (born September 8, 1951), Chief of Staff of the Polish Armed Forces

Hour	Day	Month	Year
?	辛 Yin Metal	丁 Yin Fire	辛 Yin Metal
?	亥 Pig	酉 Rooster	卯 Rabbit

1	11	21	31	41	51
丙 Yang Fire	乙 Yin Wood	甲 Yang Wood	癸 Yin Water	壬 Yang Water	辛 Yin Metal
申 Monkey	未 Sheep	午 Horse	己 Snake	辰 Dragon	卯 Rabbit

Gagor's chart is very similar to Szmajdinski's. At the age of 58, he was in the Rabbit Luck Cycle. There is also another Rabbit present in his Year Pillar. The Rooster in his Month Pillar clashed with the Rabbits in the Year Pillar and the month in which the accident took place. His Yin Metal Day Master was destroyed by the stronger Yang Metal Competitors present on that day.

Example A3.3 Przemyslaw Gosiewski (born May 12, 1964), Former Deputy Prime Minister

Hour	Day Heavenly Virtue	Month	Year
?	辛 Yin Metal	己 Yin Earth	甲 Yang Wood
?	酉 Rooster	己 Snake	辰 Dragon

8	18	28	38	48
庚 Yang Metal	辛 Yin Metal	壬 Yang Water	癸 Yin Water	甲 Yang Wood
午 Horse	未 Sheep	申 Monkey	酉 Rooster	戌 Dog

At the age of 45, Gosiewski was in the Rooster Luck Cycle. There were two Roosters (his Day Branch and Luck Cycle) that clashed with the Rabbit month. The Dominant Yin Metal Day Master would normally have served as a Rival to the two Yang Metal Stems present on that day. However, he lost the support of the Rooster in the Day Branch due to the Clash with the Rabbit month and was unable to compete with the two Yang Metal Stems on that day.

Example A3.4 Lech Kacynski (born June 18, 1949), President of Poland

Hour	Day	Month	Year
?	己 Yin Earth	庚 Yang Metal	己 Yin Earth
?	卯 Rabbit	午 Horse	丑 Ox

4	14	24	34	44	54
己 Yin Earth	戊 Yang Earth	丁 Yin Fire	丙 Yang Fire	乙 Yin Wood	甲 Yang Wood
巳 Snake	辰 Dragon	卯 Rabbit	寅 Tiger	丑 Ox	子 Rat

At the age of 61, Kacynski was in the Rat Luck Cycle which clashed with the Horse in his Month Pillar. On the day of the crash, the Yang Metal in his Month Pillar and a Rabbit from his Day Branch encountered more Metal Competitors and the Wealth element Wood.

Example A3.5 Slawomir Skrzypek (born May 10, 1963), President of National Bank of Poland

Hour	Day	Month	Year
?	癸 Yin Water	丁 Yin Fire	癸 Yin Water
?	丑 Ox	己 Snake	卯 Rabbit
		Mentor Literacy	

1	11	21	31	41
丙 Yang Fire	乙 Yin Wood	甲 Yang Wood	癸 Yin Water	壬 Yang Water
辰 Dragon	卯 Rabbit	寅 Tiger	丑 Ox	子 Rat

In 2010, Skrzypek was 46 and in the Rat Luck Cycle. He is a Yin Water Day Master who has a Follow the Resource or Many Mothers, One Child chart. On the day of the crash, the Resource element metal not only strengthened him, but also the two Yin Water Competitors present in the Year Pillar and Luck Cycle. The water Competitors strengthened the wood present on that day and made the Wealth element of the Yang Metal Day and Year more prominent. The three water Competitors fought for the Resource element metal present on the day. As a result, the Yin Water Day Master perished in this intense fight.

Example A3.6 Ryszard Kaczorowski (born November 26, 1919), Former President of Poland

Hour	Day	Month	Year
?	壬 Yang Water	乙 Yin Wood	己 Yin Earth
?	午 Horse	亥 Pig	未 Sheep

6	16	26	36	46
甲 Yang Wood	癸 Yin Water	壬 Yang Water	辛 Yin Metal	庚 Yang Metal
戌 Dog	酉 Rooster	申 Monkey	未 Sheep	午 Horse

56	66	76	86
己 Yin Earth	戊 Yang Earth	丁 Yin Fire	丙 Yang Fire
巳 Snake	辰 Dragon	卯 Rabbit	寅 Tiger

Kaczorowski has a Partial Three Harmony Wood Combination in his chart (the Pig in his Month Pillar and the Sheep in his Year Pillar). The amount of wood was too enticing for the Yang Metal Stems present on the day of the crash. At 90, the retired President was also in the Tiger Luck Cycle. This Tiger, the two Tigers present on the day of the crash and the Rabbit were all fighting to combine with the Pig in his Month Pillar. The Yang Water Day Master could not survive this conflict.

Example A3.7 Anna Walentynowicz (born August 13, 1929), Co-founder of Solidarity Trade Union

Hour	Day	Month	Year
?	庚 Yang Metal	壬 Yang Water	己 Yin Earth
?	寅 Tiger	申 Monkey	巳 Snake
			Academic

8	18	28	38	48	58	68	78
癸 Yin Water	甲 Yang Wood	乙 Yin Wood	丙 Yang Fire	丁 Yin Fire	戊 Yang Earth	己 Yin Earth	庚 Yang Metal
酉 Rooster	戌 Dog	亥 Pig	子 Rat	丑 Ox	寅 Tiger	卯 Rabbit	辰 Dragon

Walentynowicz is a Yang Metal Day Master and was in a Yang Metal Luck Cycle. On the day of the crash, there were four Yang Metal Stems fighting for one Rabbit, which was like four hungry animals fighting for a piece of meat. The Monkey in her Month Pillar also clashed with the three Tigers present on the day (in the day and year and also in her Day Pillar).

Example A3.8 Captain Arkadiusz Protasiuk (born November 13, 1974), Pilot

Hour	Day	Month	Year
?	戊 Yang Earth	甲 Yang Wood	甲 Yang Wood
?	午 Horse	戌 Dog	寅 Tiger

8	18	28
乙 Yin Wood	丙 Yang Fire	丁 Yin Fire
亥 Pig	子 Rat	丑 Ox

Protasiuk's chart has the Full Three Harmony Fire Combination (Tiger, Horse and Dog), which is further supported by the Yang Wood Month and Year Stems. His strongest element is fire, so he has a Follow the Resource (fire) chart. Protasiuk's negative elements are:

1) earth representing his original Self and Competitors,
2) water which extinguishes his best element fire and
3) metal which destroys his other useful element wood.

Protasiuk was going through the Ox Luck Cycle (which contains earth, metal and water) when the plane crashed. On the day of the crash, the metal-wood conflict also created issues for him.

Example A3.9 Major Robert Grzywna (born February 5, 1974), Co-Pilot

Hour	Day	Month	Year
?	己 Yin Earth	丙 Yang Fire	甲 Yang Wood
?	丑 Ox	寅 Tiger	寅 Tiger

10	20	30
丁 Yin Fire	戊 Yang Earth	己 Yin Earth
卯 Rabbit	辰 Dragon	巳 Snake

Grzywna's chart goes with the flow of his two best elements, fire and wood. There is fire hidden within the Tiger Month and Year Branches and the Yang Fire Month Stem receives support from the Yang Wood Year Stem. With fire as his strongest element, Grzywna has a Follow the Resource (fire) chart. Like Protasiuk, Grzywna's negative elements are earth, water and metal. Grzywna was going through the negative Snake Luck Cycle. The Snake combined with the Ox Day Branch to form the negative element metal that destroys his useful element wood. On the day of the crash, Grzywna's useful element wood was caught in the tussle between the Metal Competitors fighting for it.

Conclusion

This example illustrates how a major catastrophe involves Clashes between the elements and fighting between Competitors. However, misfortune could be averted, as seen in the decision of the President's twin brother who did not board the doomed fight.

Appendix 4 The Middle Eastern Leaders in 2011

How does the Four Pillars chart of a leader affect the destiny of his country? To answer this question, we can consider the charts of the leaders of the Arab countries caught up in the Arab Spring of 2011.

Example A4.1 Zine Al Abedine Ben Ali (born September 3, 1936), Second Tunisian President

Hour	Day	Month	Year
?	戊	丙	丙
	Yang Earth	Yang Fire	Yang Fire
?	子	申	子
	Rat	Monkey	Rat

2	12	22	32	42	52	62	72
丁	戊	己	庚	辛	壬	癸	甲
Yin Fire	Yang Earth	Yin Earth	Yang Metal	Yin Metal	Yang Water	Yin Water	Yang Wood
酉	戌	亥	子	丑	寅	卯	辰
Rooster	Dog	Pig	Rat	Ox	Tiger	Rabbit	Dragon

The Yang Earth Rat Day Pillar is noted for being a great strategist. The two Rats present in the Day and Year Pillars combine with the Monkey in the Month Pillar to form a Partial Three Harmony Water Combination. There are two Yang Fire Stems (representing the Resource element) that strengthen the Yang Earth Day Master. Ben Ali's chart is one of a strong self using the Wealth element water. With his Wealth element involving his ancestors, parents and spouse (the Year, Month and Day Pillars), Ben Ali was born to a wealthy family and trained at military schools in France and the United States.

The issue with Ben Ali's chart is that the Wealth element can become too overwhelming for him to control. He needs the support of the Resource element fire and is vulnerable to the onset of additional wood and metal. The former attacks his Earth Day Master and the latter weakens him. Earth Stems are also problematic as they serve as Competitors for his wealth and assets.

On January 14, 2011, Ben Ali fled to Saudi Arabic and relinquished his presidency. At 75, he was in the Yang Wood Luck Cycle. This unfavorable period started when Ben Ali was

72 and it suggested that he had been struggling to keep his country in order for a few years prior to the revolution.

Here is the chart of the fateful day:

January 14, 2011			
Hour	**Day**	**Month**	**Year**
?	己 Yin Earth	己 Yin Earth	庚 Yang Metal
?	巳 Snake	丑 Ox	寅 Tiger

The day had significant metal energy (the Snake in the Day Branch combines with the Ox in the Month Pillar), which undermined Ben Ali's fading earth energy. There was also the presence of four to five Earth Competitors that were stronger than the Yang Earth Day Master. As a result, Ben Ali was ousted. His negative Luck Cycle placed the country at risk.

Example A4.2 Hosni Mubarak (born May 4, 1928), Fourth Egyptian President

Hour	**Day**	**Month**	**Year**
?	甲 Yang Wood	丙 Yang Fire	戊 Yang Earth
?	辰 Dragon	辰 Dragon	辰 Dragon

1	**11**	**21**	**31**	**41**
丁 Yin Fire	戊 Yang Earth	己 Yin Earth	庚 Yang Metal	辛 Yin Metal
巳 Snake	午 Horse	未 Sheep	申 Monkey	酉 Rooster

51	**61**	**71**	**81**
壬 Yang Water	癸 Yin Water	甲 Yang Wood	乙 Yin Wood
戌 Dog	亥 Pig	子 Rat	丑 Ox

Mubarak is a Yang Wood Day Master born in the Dragon month. There are four earth Stems and Branches in his chart. Mubarak has a Follows the Wealth (earth) chart. His best elements are earth and fire (which strengthens earth). His negative element is wood, which symbolizes his Competitors.

On January 24, 2011, when Mubarak was 83 during the Yin Wood Luck Cycle, he resigned as President following 18 days of protest. Here is the flow of the day:

Hour	Day	Month	Year
?	己 Yin Earth	己 Yin Earth	庚 Yang Metal
?	卯 Rabbit	丑 Ox	寅 Rabbit

The Tiger in the Year and the Rabbit in the Day combined with the Dragon present in Mubarak's chart to form the Directional Wood Combination. His useful element earth came under extreme attack. Mubarak collapsed and yielded helplessly. Egypt descended into turmoil from which it has yet to recover.

Example A4.3 Muammar al-Gaddafi (born June 7, 1942), Libyan President

Hour	Day	Month	Year
?	辛 Yin Metal	丙 Yang Fire	壬 Yang Water
?	卯 Rabbit	午 Horse	午 Horse

10	20	30	40	50	60	70
丁 Yin Fire	戊 Yang Earth	己 Yin Earth	庚 Yang Metal	辛 Yin Metal	壬 Yang Water	癸 Yin Water
未 Sheep	申 Monkey	酉 Rooster	戌 Dog	亥 Pig	子 Rat	丑 Ox

Gaddafi is a Yin Metal Day Master born in the Horse month in summer when fire was strong. There are two Horses and a Yang Fire in his chart, which means the prevalent flow is fire. Gaddafi has a Follow the Power (fire) chart. He is highly intelligent and hardworking, a man of wealth and position. His useful elements are fire and wood (which supports fire). Gaddafi's negative elements are metal (his Competitors and original Self element) and water (which destroys his best element fire). The Resource element earth is also negative as it revives his original earth self.

Unfortunately, there is a Yang Water present in the Year Pillar that disrupts the flow of fire in the chart. Gaddafi was under constant stress and fear which at times translated into his extreme and disruptive behavior.

How did Gaddafi lose the reign of his country? It all started in the Rat Luck Cycle. The strong water in this period attacked his useful element fire. 2011 was a Yin Metal Rabbit year which introduced an equally strong adversary identical to Gaddafi's Day Pillar.

On September 16, 2011, Gaddafi lost the recognition of the United Nations as leader of his country and went into hiding:

Hour	Day	Month	Year
?	甲 Yang Wood	丁 Yin Fire	辛 Yin Metal
?	辰 Dragon	酉 Rooster	卯 Rabbit

Apart from the Yin Metal Rabbit in the Year Pillar that mirrored his own Day Pillar, there was also a Rooster in the month. This served as another Competitor for Gaddafi. On October 20, 2011, Gaddafi was assassinated and buried by thick earth.

Hour	Day	Month	Year
?	戊 Yang Earth	戊 Yang Earth	辛 Yin Metal
?	申 Monkey	戌 Dog	卯 Rabbit

(born September 11, 1965), Syrian President

Hour	Day	Month	Year
?	戊 Yang Earth	乙 Yin Wood	乙 Yin Wood
?	辰 Dragon	酉 Rooster	巳 Snake

1	11	21	31	41	51	61	71
甲 Yang Wood	癸 Yin Water	壬 Yang Water	辛 Yin Metal	庚 Yang Metal	己 Yin Earth	戊 Yang Earth	丁 Yin Fire
申 Monkey	未 Sheep	午 Horse	巳 Snake	辰 Dragon	卯 Rabbit	寅 Tiger	丑 Ox

Assad is a Yang Earth Day Master born in the Rooster month when metal is dominant. There is also a Partial Three Harmony Metal Combination involving the Snake in the Year Pillar and the Rooster in the Month Pillar. There are also two Yin Wood Stems that control the Yang Earth Day Master. Assad has a Follow the Children (metal) chart.

With the useful elements in the Month and Year Pillars, Assad was born into a wealthy and powerful family. His father Hafez was the President of Syria. Assad is also a qualified medical doctor. At 35 during the favorable Yin Metal Luck Cycle, he became President of Syria upon his father's death and his years in power progressed smoothly until 2011.

Assad embarked on the Dragon Luck Cycle in 2011 at 46 when another earth Competitor is introduced. Assad's use of force towards protesters escalated into an all-out civil war. As he struggles to maintain his reign over Syria, the next Luck Cycle is Yin Earth, so it appears that there are more challenging times ahead for Assad.

Example A4.5 Ali Abudullah Saleh (born March 21, 1946), Former President of Yemen

Hour	Day	Month	Year
?	甲 Yang Wood	辛 Yin Metal	丙 Yang Fire
?	午 Horse	卯 Rabbit	戌 Dog

4	14	24	34
壬 Yang Water	癸 Yin Water	甲 Yang Wood	乙 Yin Wood
辰 Dragon	己 Snake	午 Horse	未 Sheep

44	54	64	74
丙 Yang Fire	丁 Yin Fire	戊 Yang Earth	己 Yin Earth
申 Monkey	酉 Rooster	戌 Dog	亥 Pig

This is a Fire Transformation chart as the Yang Fire in the Year Pillar combines with the Yin Metal in the Month Pillar. This is further supported by the Horse in the Day Branch, which contains fire. The negative element is water as it extinguishes fire. Any Clashes that involve the Dog or Rabbit would also be problematic as the Fire Combination is destroyed. The Rabbit and Dog combine to form fire due to the Six Harmony Combination.

At the age of 60, in the Rooster Luck Cycle, Saleh was slowly losing his grip on the country as the Rooster clashed with the Rabbit in his Month Pillar. He finally resigned towards the end of November 2011 when the negative water element was strong and extinguished his useful element fire. Saleh was fortunate as he did not lose his life, family or assets.

From the charts of the five Arab leaders, readers can see that misfortune befell them during their unfavorable Luck Cycles.

We should always be aware of our positive flow and protect them as much as possible, so that we can stay on the right path and avert catastrophe when negative Luck Cycles approach. If some of these leaders had focused on serving their country justly, they would have had a degree of protection.

Appendix 5 The Story of Two Best-Selling Writers

In the 1930s, two best-selling books made a lasting impact on the American psyche and cultural landscape: Napoleon Hill's *Think and Grow Rich* (1937) and Dale Carnegie's *How To Win Friends And Influence People* (1936). Both books sold millions of copies worldwide and have also been translated into other languages. Hill's and Carnegie's books spearheaded the self-help book industry that focuses on improving our lives through understanding ourselves and others better.

Both authors share similarities. They were born to farming families in the South five years apart, Hill in Virginia and Carnegie in Missouri. From a young age, they both had to support themselves financially in order to complete their education. Most interesting of all, they both attributed their success to industrialist and philanthropist Andrew Carnegie. In 1908, Hill interviewed Andrew Carnegie and was inspired by the steel magnate to interview others in order to find the formula for their success. Hill considered this interview a turning point in his life. As for Dale Carnegie, he changed the spelling of his last name from Carnagey to Carnegie, a well regarded and revered name at that time due to Andrew Carnegie's renown as an influential industrialist. In 1916, Dale Carnegie had his first sell out seminar in Carnegie Hall that focused on public speaking.

The success of both best-selling authors was not only due to their hard work but also the alignment of favorable energies and the assistance of mentors. Hill spent years interviewing 500 successful individuals of his time. He was able to collate all his research and publish it in his best-selling book.

Dale Carnegie modeled himself after the Greek philosopher Socrates and other inspirational speakers from history to teach interpersonal and public speaking skills. Both were able to attain success through their diligence as well as their personal beliefs and values.

As the *I Ching* Hexagram Da Guo Large Excess (Number 28) suggests, *in order to succeed in a large enterprise and achieve our visions, we need to have ability, principle and position.* Ability and principle are achieved through our efforts. As for position, it refers to the proper timing of events and help from mentors.

For instance, when there is harmony between Heaven, Earth and Man, then success is inevitable. Without the influence of favorable Luck Cycles or years when one can tap the positive energy, I can confidently state that Hill and Carnegie would not have achieved the degree of success they had.

We will now consider the charts of Hill and Carnegie. As Hill is older by 5 years, we will analyze his chart first.

Example A5.1 Napoleon Hill (born October 26, 1883, died November 8, 1970)

Date of Birth			
Hour	**Day**	**Month**	**Year**
?	癸 Yin Water	壬 Yang Water	癸 Yin Water
?	卯 Rabbit	戌 Dog	未 Sheep
	Mentor		

Date of Death			
Hour	**Day**	**Month**	**Year**
?	壬 Yang Water	丁 Yin Fire	庚 Yang Metal
?	辰 Dragon	亥 Pig	戌 Dog

5	15	25	35	45
辛 Yin Metal	庚 Yang Metal	己 Yin Earth	戊 Yang Earth	丁 Yin Fire
酉 Rooster	申 Monkey	未 Sheep	午 Horse	巳 Snake

55	65	75	85
丙 Yang Fire	乙 Yin Wood	甲 Yang Wood	癸 Yin Water
辰 Dragon	卯 Rabbit	寅 Tiger	

In his book *Think and Grow Rich*, Hill states that a person can attain his or her goals by focusing on the greater good and eliminating negative thoughts. Is this the way to success?

Life History

Hill lost his mother at the age of nine and his father remarried two years later. At the age of 13, he worked as a reporter for several regional newspapers. In 1908 (Yang Earth Monkey year), Hill had a major turning point following his interview with Andrew Carnegie, who inspired him to interview 500 successful individuals to find out their secret to success. In 1925 (Yin Wood Ox year) when Hill was 42, he published *The Philosophy Of Achievement*. In 1937 (Yin Fire Ox year) at 54, Hill released the best selling *Think And Grow Rich*, which has sold more than 20 million copies and gone through 17 editions.

Analysis

Hill is a Yin Water Day Master born in the Dog month, when fire and earth are strong, leaving no room for water to thrive. A Partial Three Harmony Wood Combination is formed between the Rabbit in the Day Pillar and the Sheep in the Year Pillar. The prevalent element is wood, which makes Hill a Follow the Children chart.

The presence of Yang Water and Yin Water in the Month and Year Pillars complicates matters. Competitors or Rivals are introduced. For Hill to succeed, he needs to nullify these Rivals. His best elements are wood, fire and earth and his negative elements are metal and water.

There is another contradiction in Hill's chart. The Dog is located between the Rabbit and Sheep and stands in the way of the Three Harmony Combination. The Dog also combines with the Rabbit as part of the Six Harmony Combinations, so the Rabbit has the choice of combining with the Sheep or the Dog. The Dog is located in the sector associated with the mother. As it disrupts the flow of wood (the Rabbit-Sheep Combination), Hill did not have much opportunity to cultivate a relationship with his mother. She passed away when Hill was a child.

The Earth within the Dog also controls the Yin Water Day Master. For a man, the element that controls the self represents the Children. Hill had a son who was born without ears. However, not only did he learn to speak, he also graduated from college. Water also represents the ear and hearing. The two Water Stems (Yang Water and Yin Water) representing Competitors are negative. Hill needed to eliminate these two Competitors to achieve success.

From 1891 to 93, metal and water were dominant. In the Yin Metal Luck Cycle, Hill lost his mother and up till the age of 25, he had to work hard with little to show. However, when Hill entered the Yin Earth Luck Cycle in 1908 (Yang Earth Monkey year) at 25, he turned his life around following his interview with Andrew Carnegie. The strong fire, earth and wood Luck Cycles that followed saw him achieve success with his writing and teaching, especially in 1925 (Yin Wood Ox) and 1937 (Yin Fire Ox).

Hill's success was clearly influenced by the prevailing energy in his Four Pillars chart. When he was going through the metal and water Luck Cycles in his youth, his hard work barely paid off. It is clear that Hill worked harder during this time than in the earth and wood Luck Cycles later in life. Without the positive influence of his Luck Cycles, no matter how much Hill envisioned and thought about success and wealth, he could only be an excellent reporter.

Hill passed away at 87 in the third year of the unfavorable Yin Water Luck Cycle when he had to battle with Competitors. On the day Hill died, the negative metal and water elements were prominent and there was additional Competition for Combinations within his chart involving the Dog in the year.

Why was 1937 (Yin Fire Ox year) such a successful year for Hill? He was 54 at that time in the Yin Fire Luck Cycle. The Yin Fire in the year combined with the Yang Water in his Month Pillar, a major Competitor. The Ox in the year clashed away the Sheep in his Year Pillar, freeing the Dog to combine with the Rabbit to create a prevalent fire flow. Hill became a Follow the Wealth (fire) chart. He started reaping financial rewards through the sales of his book and finally received his pay off 28 years after being inspired by Andrew Carnegie.

The Ox in 1925 (Yin Wood Ox year) also brought him success as he published his course *The Philosophy of Achievement*, which taught students the secrets to success. The competition between the Dog and Sheep was solved by the Ox clashing away the Sheep. Both the breakthroughs he enjoyed were a

256

result of the Ox.

Example A5.2 Dale Carnegie (born November 24, 1888, died November 1, 1955)
(original surname Carnagey, changed in 1922)

Date of Birth			
Hour	**Day**	**Month**	**Year**
?	己 Yin Earth	癸 Yin Water	戊 Yang Earth
?	亥 Pig	亥 Pig	子 Rat
			Mentor

Date of Death			
Hour	**Day**	**Month**	**Year**
?	丙 Yang Fire	丙 Yang Fire	乙 Yin Wood
?	寅 Tiger	戌 Dog	未 Sheep

4	14	24	34	44	54	64
甲 Yang Wood	乙 Yin Wood	丙 Yang Fire	丁 Yin Fire	戊 Yang Earth	己 Yin Earth	庚 Yang Metal
子 Rat	丑 Ox	寅 Tiger	卯 Rabbit	辰 Dragon	巳 Snake	午 Horse

Carnegie's book *How To Win Friends And Influence People*, published in 1936, is a seminal work in the self-help field. What was the secret to his success?

Life History

Carnegie graduated from college in 1908 and worked as a salesperson. In 1912 (Yang Water Rat year), he became a lecturer in adult education. In 1914 (Yang Wood Tiger year), Carnegie became a much sought after lecturer, earning $500 a week (around $10 000 by today's standards). In 1936 (Yang Earth Rat year) when he was 48 during the Dragon Luck Cycle, Carnegie published *How To Win Friends and Influence People*, which was translated into 31 languages within a number of years and sold more than 50 million copies. He continued to enjoy the fruits of his success and traveled around the world to promote his philosophy and principles. On November 1, 1955, Carnegie died of uremia caused by Hodgkin's disease.

Analysis

Carnegie is a Yin Earth Day Master born in the Pig month, when water and wood are strong. The Rat in the Year Pillar provided further support to the wood present in his chart. The Self element earth is weak so Carnegie has a Follow the Power (wood) chart. Wood is his useful element and as water gives birth to wood, it is also useful. Negative elements would be the original Self element earth, and fire which empowers the original Self. Metal has to be avoided as it destroys his useful element wood. The wood and water within Carnegie's chart represents his skills and talents.

The presence of Yang Earth in the Year Pillar means that there is a Competitor present in his adolescence. This could account for the hardships he suffered then. The peak of Carnegie's career came in 1931 (Yin Metal Sheep year) when the full Three Harmony Wood Combination was formed. The Sheep in the year combined with the Rabbit Luck Cycle and the Pig in Hill's Month and Day Pillars.

The next 20 years included the Yang Earth and Yin Earth Luck Cycles. While Carnegie did not enjoy any more breakthroughs, he was able to travel around the world to promote his courses and philosophies. Even in his unfavorable Luck Cycles, Carnegie was able to enjoy the fruits of his labor, possibly due to his accumulation of goodwill and resources while at the peak of his success. Another point to note is that during unfavorable cycles, we can also depend on the energy of the year or Combinations between one's own chart and the year or Luck Cycle to achieve breakthroughs.

In 1939 (Yin Earth Rabbit year), when Carnegie was 51 during the Dragon Luck Cycle, he was able to achieve another peak in his career. The Rabbit of the year combined with the Pig in his Month and Day Pillars to form the Partial Three Harmony Wood Combination. The Dragon in the Luck Cycle also combined with the Rat in his Year Pillar to form water that strengthened the favorable element wood. Carnegie successfully introduced his courses to Japan. He continued to expand his influence to Korea, China and other Asian countries.

On November 1, 1955, Carnegie died of kidney failure. It was a day with excessive fire and earth.

Appendix 6 The Main Players of Google

Example A6.1 Larry Page (born March 26, 1973), Co-founder of Google

Hour	Day	Month	Year
?	辛 Yin Metal	乙 Yin Wood	癸 Yin Water
?	酉 Rooster	卯 Rabbit	丑 Ox

7	17	27	37	47	57	67	77
甲 Yang Wood	癸 Yin Water	壬 Yang Water	辛 Yin Metal	庚 Yang Metal	己 Yin Earth	戊 Yang Earth	丁 Yin Fire
寅 Tiger	丑 Ox	子 Rat	亥 Pig	戌 Dog	酉 Rooster	申 Monkey	未 Sheep

Page is a Yin Metal Day Master who has the Partial Three Harmony Metal Combination present in the Day and Year Pillars (Rooster and Ox). This makes him a Dominant Metal chart. Page is decisive, self-confident, intelligent and capable.

He is born in the Rabbit month (spring) when wood is dominant. This wood is further supported by the Yin Water Year Stem. Wood is the Wealth element for the metal Day Master. The strength of the Wealth element in Page's chart suggests that he will accumulate wealth successfully.

However, the Wealth element also brings negative issues for Page. In spring, both earth and metal are weak. The Wealth element is supported by both the season and the Stems. The extremely strong Wealth element can excessively drain his Yin Metal Day Master.

The negative elements for Page are:
1. wood (the Wealth element that he has sufficient amounts of)
2. water (the Output element further drains his Metal Day Master)
3. fire (the Power element destroys his Metal Day Master)

The positive elements for Page are:
1. earth (the Resource element strengthens his Metal Day Master)
2. metal (the Metal element works as Siblings to assist the Dominant Metal Day Master)

At the age of 25 during the positive Ox Luck Cycle, Page met Sergey Brin. The Ox Luck Cycle further strengthens Page's Yin Metal Day Master.

Example A6.2 Sergey Brin (born August 21, 1973)

Hour	Day	Month	Year
?	己 Yin Earth	庚 Yang Metal	癸 Yin Water
?	丑 Ox	申 Monkey	丑 Ox

4	14	24	34
己 Yin Earth	戊 Yang Earth	丁 Yin Fire	丙 Yang Fire
未 Sheep	午 Horse	已 Snake	辰 Dragon

44	54	64	74
乙 Yin Wood	甲 Yang Wood	癸 Yin Water	壬 Yang Water
卯 Rabbit	寅 Tiger	丑 Ox	子 Rat

Brin's chart has four metal Stems and Branches, all of which further strengthen Page's Dominant Metal Day Master. Brin's Day Master is Yin Earth. His prevalent element is metal, which makes him a Follow the Children (metal) chart. Together with Page, Brin founded Google.

Page entered ten years of water Luck Cycles at the age of 28 (Yang Water and Rat) and his Dominant Metal Self was weakened. Fortunately, in 2001 (Yin Metal Snake year), when the positive metal energy was strong, Page brought Eric Schimidt in as the CEO of Google.

Example A6.3 Eric Schmidt (April 27, 1955)

Hour	Day	Month	Year
?	戊 Yang Earth	庚 Yang Metal	乙 Yin Wood
?	午 Horse	辰 Dragon	未 Sheep

4	14	24	34
己 Yin Earth	戊 Yang Earth	丁 Yin Fire	丙 Yang Fire
卯 Rabbit	寅 Tiger	丑 Ox	子 Rat

44	54	64	74
乙 Yin Wood	甲 Yang Wood	癸 Yin Water	壬 Yang Water
亥 Pig	戌 Dog	酉 Rooster	申 Monkey

Schmidt's chart contains four earth Stems and Branches, including his own Yang Earth Day Master. There is also a Combination between the Yin Wood and Yang Metal Stems. Schmidt has a Dominant Earth chart. The threat from the Power element wood is removed through the Stem Combination. The Resource element fire is strong as it is seen in the Day and Year Branches. The useful elements for Schmidt are fire and earth, while the negative elements are wood and water.

In 2011 (Yin Metal Rabbit year), Schmidt was in the Yang Wood Luck Cycle at the age of 56. His useful element earth came under attack. On January 20, 2011 (a Yin Wood Pig day), Schmidt stepped down of CEO of Google. Page then replaced Schmidt as CEO on April 4, 2011.

Page entered the Yin Metal Luck Cycle at age 37 in 2010 and his confidence increased. This allowed him to take over as CEO of Google.

Now let us look at the chart of Google, based on the day it was founded. That is the day the entity entered into existence.

Example A6.4 Google (founded September 4, 1998)

Hour	Day	Month	Year
?	甲 Yang Wood	庚 Yang Metal	戊 Yang Earth
?	寅 Tiger	申 Monkey	寅 Tiger

1	11	21	31	41
辛 Yin Metal	壬 Yang Water	癸 Yin Water	甲 Yang Wood	乙 Yin Wood
酉 Rooster	戌 Dog	亥 Pig	子 Rat	丑 Ox

51	61	71	81
丙 Yang Fire	丁 Yin Fire	戊 Yang Earth	己 Yin Earth
寅 Tiger	卯 Rabbit	辰 Dragon	巳 Snake

Google's Day Master is Yang Wood that is born in autumn when metal is strong. There are four earth Stems and Branches within the chart, which represent the Wealth element. The Power element is also strong, as there is a Yang Metal Month Stem. The Yang Wood Day Master has to follow the Wealth element earth. However, as the Day Master sits on top of a Tiger Branch which contains Yang Wood, it qualifies as a False Follow the Wealth chart. False Follow charts are characterized by multiple talents, adaptability, flexibility, charisma and popularity, which describes Google perfectly.

From the age of 1 to 10, Google was in the metal Luck Cycles, which controlled the wood element representing Competitors and the Original self. The fire and earth energy in Schmidt's chart was able to strengthen the positive earth flow within Google's chart. The Horse Day Branch in Schmidt's chart combines with the Tiger Day and Year Branches in Google's chart, forming a Partial Three Harmony Fire Combination. The negative wood element is removed. Google's chart then becomes a True Follow the Wealth (earth) chart whilst Schmidt is CEO.

Google then entered the Yang Water Luck Cycle in 2009 at the age of 11. Schmidt entered the Water Luck Cycle two years later in 2011. The negative water energy for Google revived the original Wood Day Master, thus creating issues for the company. Page's dominant metal energy was then required to control the Competitive wood energy.

In 2013 (Yin Water Snake year), Google turned 15 and entered the Dog Luck Cycle. The Dog combines with the two Tigers present in Google's chart to form a Partial Three Harmony Fire Combination. This is a good Luck Cycle for Google. However, it is a negative element for Page.

On May 15, 2013, Page announced that he has vocal cord paralysis. Can this be explained through the theory of the five elements?

Metal represents the voice. When metal is exhausted, there can be difficulties in speaking. Page's problem is believed to have already been present in 2003 (Yin Water Sheep year) during the Yang Water Luck Cycle. The water Luck Cycle already weakened his Yin Metal Day Master. The Sheep that year combined with the Rabbit in Page's Month Pillar to form a Partial Three Harmony Wood Combination. Wood represents the Wealth element for Page, which drains him even more. The Yin Water that year also strengthened the wood that was formed.

2013 is the year of the Water Snake. The Yin Water Stem of the year once again drains Page's Yin Metal Day Master. He is also approaching the Pig Luck Cycle, which will form a Partial Three Harmony Wood Combination with the Rabbit in his Month Branch. The wood formed will further weaken his Yin Metal Day Master. This does not augur well for Page's health.

Example A7.1 Jeremy Lin 林書豪 (born August 23, 1988)

Hour	Day	Month	Year
?	庚 Yang Metal	庚 Yang Metal	戊 Yang Earth
?	戌 Dog	申 Monkey	辰 Dragon

5	15	25	35	45
辛 Yin Metal	壬 Yang Water	癸 Yin Water	甲 Yang Wood	乙 Yin Wood
酉 Rooster	戌 Dog	亥 Pig	子 Rat	丑 Ox

55	65	75	85
丙 Yang Fire	丁 Yin Fire	戊 Yang Earth	己 Yin Earth
寅 Tiger	卯 Rabbit	辰 Dragon	巳 Snake

Lin has a Commanding Pillars (Kui Gang) chart. Within the Three Pillars, two are Commanding Pillars - Yang Earth Dragon (Year Pillar) and Yang Metal Dog (Day Pillar). As mentioned in Chapter Nine under Teresa Teng's chart (Example 9.4), two Commanding Pillars will give the person much wealth and prosperity. When there are three Commanding Pillars, then the benefits are magnified. It comes as no surprise that in 2012 (Yang Water Dragon year, another Commanding Pillar for him), Lin became a celebrity for his play in the NBA (National Basketball Association. These benefits were brought about by having Three Commanding Pillars.

On January 20, 2011, a Yang Metal Dragon day, Lin once again impressed with his play as a result of the presence of three Commanding Pillars.

So in a Commanding Pillars year, what are the auspicious days? On February 4, 2012, Lin scored a career high 25 points to secure a victory for his team. It was a Yin Wood Sheep day, which is a Wealth day for his Yang Metal Dog Day Master. Yin Wood and Yang Metal combine, which means that the Wealth element comes to the Yang Metal Day Master. It is like someone else lining your pocket with money. On February 14, 2012, a Yin Wood Snake day, Lin scored a winning three-pointer. This once again demonstrates benefits brought about by a Wealth day.

Lin is a very special example as not every Commanding Pillars chart will enjoy such fame and fortune. Others who may share the same day, month and year of birth may differ in terms of genetics, personality and attitude and have different destinies as a result.

As discussed in Chapter Four, the six Commanding Pillars are

1) Yang Earth Dragon 戊辰
2) Yang Earth Dog 戊戌
3) Yang Metal Dragon 庚辰
4) Yang Metal Dog 庚戌
5) Yang Water Dragon 壬辰
6) Yang Water Dog 壬戌

29395561R00157

Printed in Poland
by Amazon Fulfillment
Poland Sp. z o.o., Wrocław